Inside Math
Books 1–4: Whole Numbers

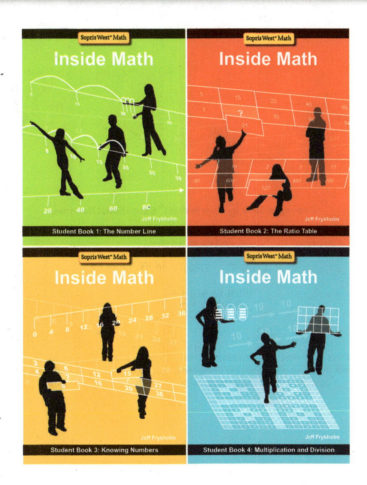

Teacher Edition

Jeff Frykholm, PhD

BOSTON, MA | LONGMONT, CO

Copyright 2009 by Sopris West® Educational Services

All rights reserved.

3 4 5 6 7   FRD   10 11 12 13 14

ISBN 13: 978-1-60218-789-4
ISBN 10: 1-60218-789-4
167732/2-10

No portion of this work may be reproduced or transmitted in any form or by any means, electronic or mechanical, including photocopying or recording, or by any information storage and retrieval system, without the express written permission of the publisher.

Printed in the United States of America
Published and Distributed by

Cambium
LEARNING®
Sopris West®

4093 Specialty Place   Longmont, Colorado 80504
(303) 651-2829   www.sopriswest.com

*With grateful thanks to my parents,
for a lifetime of support and encouragement.*

J.F.

ACKNOWLEDGMENTS

I am greatly indebted to the many talented people who helped move *Inside Math* from a rough idea to an innovative resource for teachers and students.

It was important to me to develop this textbook series based in part on the expertise and knowledge of practicing teachers. Over the course of nearly four years of development, over thirty teachers participated in the project, and the books are certainly stronger by virtue of the feedback they gave me from the initial planning stages through the end of the pilot testing. To mention several individuals in particular, Craig Schneider provided invaluable assistance in reviewing and enhancing earlier drafts of the manuscript and engaged the tedious work of providing the answer key for the entire manuscript. Pilot teacher Schuyler VanZante worked with the team to enhance access for ELL students. Pilot teachers Jennifer Whitten and Julie Soja illuminated our thinking about how beginning teachers engage these sorts of innovative methods and materials. As *Inside Math* neared completion, pilot teachers Paige Larson and Michael Mattassa collaborated with the development team to enrich and refine the content and to examine implementation issues. They improved the program immeasurably. Their enthusiasm in sharing these models with their students provided the necessary momentum for all of us as we turned the final corner toward production. Mary Pittman, Director of Mathematics for Boulder Valley School District in Colorado, provided vital support for this novel approach to mathematics education by sponsoring the pilot implementation.

The editorial, design and production staff, included Jane Brunton, Sherry Hern, Judy Pleau, Geoff Horsfall, Jeff Dieffenbach and Holly Bell. Steve Mitchell, the publisher of *Inside Math*, encouraged and supported our team throughout the project.

As project director, Jack Beers was indispensable. This program would not have been completed without his leadership, vision, insights, and steady hand. Jack made key improvements to the instructional design, helped to underscore important mathematical ideas in the manuscript, and kept the project on course through its final phase. Finally, Christine Willis, as sponsoring director, is the reason this program exists at all. She believed in my first ideas for this textbook series, and her enthusiasm, encouragement, and persistence in the very beginning led to the signing of the project. Chris carefully shepherded the manuscript through its early stages, directed the pilot study and envisioned the *Inside Math* multimedia professional development component of the project. Without both Jack and Chris, this program would never have experienced any wind in the sails, and to both of them, I am both indebted and truly grateful.

J.F.

ABOUT THE AUTHOR

Dr. Jeff Frykholm is an Associate Professor in the School of Education at the University of Colorado at Boulder. A former high school mathematics teacher, Frykholm has spent the last 15 years of his career teaching and researching issues pertinent to the teaching and learning of mathematics. He is widely published in academic journals and recently authored an award-winning integrated mathematics and science curriculum. He was a member of the writing team for the NCTM Navigations series, and continues to be active in promoting mathematics education reform at all levels. Frykholm is recognized nationally and internationally as a top-tier scholar and teacher/educator, recently receiving the highly prestigious National Academy of Education/Spencer Foundation Fellowship, and a Fulbright Fellowship to teach and research in Santiago, Chile, in 2006.

CONTENTS

Book 1: The Number Line

Book One Overview: The Number Line..2
Professional Background...6
Section A: The Number Line and Number Sense...11
Section B: Using the Number Line for Addition and Subtraction 27
Section C: Using the Number Line for Multiplication and Division....................52
End-of-Book Assessment 72

Book 2: The Ratio Table

Book Two Overview: The Ratio Table..78
Professional Background...82
Section A: Ratio Tables, Multiplication, and Division 85
Section B: Applications of the Ratio Table 105
End-of-Book Assessment 124

Book 3: Knowing Numbers

Book Three Overview: Knowing Numbers..134
Professional Background...137
Section A: A Review of the Number Line 142
Section B: The Ratio Table in Review 153
Section C: What's That Number?...167
Section D: Making Change 179
Section E: From Adding to Multiplying..189
End-of-Book Assessment 204

Book 4: Multiplication and Division

Book Four Overview: Multiplication and Division..214
Professional Background...217
Section A: Thinking about Multiplication and Division 222
Section B: The Multiplication Table...230
Section C: Area Models of Multiplication 245
Section D: Ratio Tables and Multiplication 255
Section E: The Lattice Method of Multiplication..269
Section F: The Traditional U.S. Method of Multiplication................................289
Section G: A Model for Division 297
End-of-Book Assessment 307

Corrections to Student Books

Inside Math supports the development of key mathematical concepts through the use of a handful of visual models. Correct models and accurate mathematics are necessary to guide students to an understanding of the mathematical procedures.

In some instances, the mathematics or the models are inaccurate as presented in the first printing of the Student Books. Those inaccuracies that would mislead students and teachers have been corrected in this second printing. The corrected pages appear in the Teacher Edition; student versions of these pages are available for download at www.sopriswest.com/insidemath.

The changes encompass the following pages:

- Student Book 1: Pages 13, 16, and 18
- Student Book 3: Page 17
- Student Book 4: Pages 15 and 30
- Student Book 5: Pages 15 and 22
- Student Book 6: Pages 1, 4, and 21
- Student Book 7: Page 11
- Student Book 8: Page 9

Corrections that affect only the answers in the Teacher Edition are included in this printing.

Book 1:
The Number Line

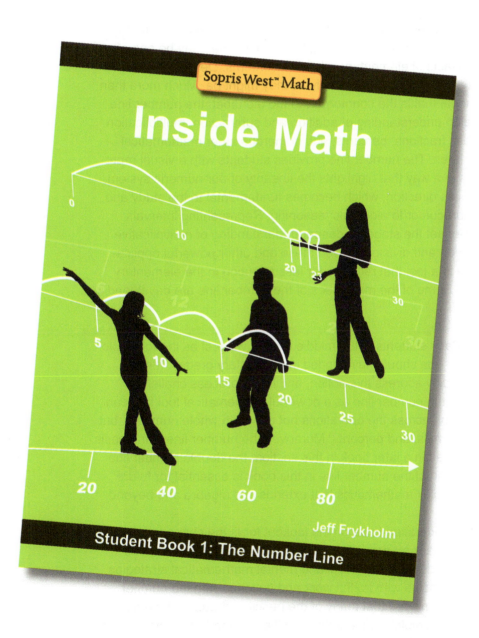

Book One Overview: The Number Line

Introduction

This book is the first in a series of eight units that are geared toward helping middle-grades learners acquire both facility with and understanding of the basic mathematical procedures and concepts that lay the groundwork for more advanced mathematical study. In particular, this series cultivates understanding of a number of mathematical tools that children learn to use with facility in various mathematical and real-world contexts.

Book Focus

Book 1 introduces and develops two number tools that will be used repeatedly throughout the entire curriculum. The first tool, the number line, may be one of the most common artifacts of elementary school classrooms. Despite their prevalence, number lines are not often used as fully as they might be. Much more than simply a counting model that is the counterpart to the alphabet, the number line can be used to develop understanding of addition and subtraction, multiplication and division, decimals, fractions, percents, and numerous other mathematical concepts and procedures. The number line provides students with a visual representation of numbers in a way that highlights the linearity of our numeric system. Linearity, in turn, implies direction, which becomes fundamental to the study and use of integers as a precursor to algebraic reasoning. Representing intervals on the number line can set the stage for deeper understanding of multiplicative reasoning (multiplication and division). Given these and other powerful applications, the number line is a tool that receives far less attention in the elementary grades than it should. Some of the many uses of the number line are developed in this unit.

A word of caution: Many students in the middle grades will feel as though explorations with the number line should have ended in elementary grades. It might be a good idea to explicitly address this notion, and in the process challenge students to think about the number line as a powerful mathematical tool that can be used for computations across the operations not only with whole numbers, but also with fractions, decimals, and percents. Moreover, the number line is the basis for another tool developed in a later book in this section: the double number line. In addition, understanding of the number line in this book is essential for future progress with more complex mathematics that extends into algebra and beyond.

A second important consideration to be on the lookout for is the chance that many students will wish to fall back on previously learned algorithms for the various operations rather than to develop the visual and mental mathematical strategies for computation that can come with fruitful work and patience with the number line. Students might be reminded that many of the pencil-and-paper algorithms they know are difficult to complete without the pencil and paper! The number line gives a visual model that students can use effectively as a mental strategy. Those students who commit to serious study and application of the number line will be rewarded with greater sense of numbers, operations, and strategies for computation.

The second tool introduced in Book 1, the ratio table, is a product of sophisticated work with the number line. The ratio table is a powerful mathematical model that can be used for multiple purposes. Although its use will be restricted to multiplication and division in Book 1, it will be revisited later in the series as a way to help students acquire understanding of decimals, percents, fractions, and ratio and proportion.

Book 1 is separated into three content focus areas. *Section A* explores the number line as a tool for helping develop number sense. The number line helps students to order and compare numbers and to explore number relationships. *Section B* helps learners use the number line as a computational tool. Through the understanding of skip-counting, students begin to navigate the number line in flexible and productive ways. With repeated practice, using comfortable skip intervals, students develop informal strategies for addition and subtraction that resonate with their intuition and build upon their unique number strengths. *Section C* introduces both the double number line and, subsequently, the ratio table. This beginning foray into the use of the ratio table foreshadows the powerful ways in which it can be used to picture number relationships and serve as an efficient computational tool. Students explore a number of contexts that require them to add, subtract, multiply, and divide. Repeated use of the number line and ratio tables as developed in Book 1 will help students become efficient at completing straightforward, mental computations within the four operations.

How to Use this Book

There are two primary sections in every lesson. The lesson starts with a discussion that helps you assess what students already know and a suggestion for how to model the type of mathematical thinking they will be doing on their own. What follows is a resource guide to support the development of concepts and skills as students solve the problems. Throughout the resource guide, you will be provided with insights into the mathematical content of the problems, pedagogical ideas to enhance teaching and learning, samples of anticipated student work, insights about student thinking related to the topics at hand, and ideas about assessment. You will also find a reproduction of the student page that includes answers. This program is meant to be flexible and relies on your craft and knowledge. Toward that end, the resource materials that accompany this text are not intended to be used as a script. Instead, the intention of this program is that you will have a chance to apply your knowledge of students, your own experiences with these mathematical tools, and your intuition about teaching to make this program as effective as possible.

Models of Implementation

This program has been designed to be as flexible as possible. While this series of books may be used as the primary curriculum for the classroom, it was not designed as the full curriculum for any given grade level. Rather, it was crafted to support you as you help students understand the number operations and concepts that precede more advanced work in algebra. You may therefore choose to use this program either as a guide for whole-class explorations or as the text for smaller, pull-out groups of students. In both cases, it is important to note that this program is designed on the principle that students learn mathematics in large measure through interactions with one another. Throughout the books, you will find numerous questions that ask students to explain their thinking. These occasions should not be taken lightly. It is in the sharing and comparing of solution strategies that children begin to build a firm foundation of understanding. The social dynamic of learning mathematics is important to recognize. Participation in mathematical discourse may be the most powerful impetus for learning mathematics available to young learners, and you should take advantage of every opportunity to encourage children to talk about their mathematical thinking and processes. Given a commitment to this principle, this program is likely to be most successful when students are progressing through the problems with their peers.

Addressing Issues of Language

There is no question that one of the greatest challenges facing teachers today is to make instruction relevant and accessible for second language learners. *Inside Math* has been written with this concern in mind. Careful consideration was given to the language that appears in directions, contextually based problems, and other sections of the book where text is necessary. When possible, for example, we have limited new vocabulary to only what is essential to the concepts being presented, and we revisit new vocabulary words and concepts repeatedly throughout the text. To assist teachers in making instruction accessible for English language learners, as well as other students for whom reading presents particular challenges, several supporting features were added to the teacher's edition. First, within the section planner that introduces each new major mathematical concept contained in the book, there is a heading that reads: Language Development. In this section of the overview, new vocabulary words are introduced and defined. Later in the text, when these words and concepts are introduced in a specific lesson, the teacher notes include additional information about pertinent language considerations and vocabulary. These notes appear as Encouraging Language Development under the Concept Development and Continue the Problem Solving headings.

Assessment

At the conclusion of each section, you will find several problems that may be used for formative assessments. These problems review key concepts discussed in the previous section. At the end of each book are additional assessment problems that cover the content of the entire book. These problems may be used as a cumulative assessment of student understanding of the key concepts in the book. The teachers' guide contains insights as to how the assessment problems might best be used and what they are intended to measure.

Assessment rubrics and scoring guides for every assessment may be found in Assessment Teacher Edition. Detailed instructions regarding assessment in general, and the use of the program rubrics in particular, are included in the introduction of Assessment Teacher Edition.

Professional Background

Perhaps one of the most overlooked tools of the elementary and middle school classroom is the number line. The number line is often hanging on the classroom wall, but is rarely used as effectively as it might be. Historically, the number line has been used to help young children memorize and practice counting with ordinal numbers. Additionally, though less often, the number line may have been used like a ruler to illustrate the benchmark fractions of ½ or ¼. Beyond an illustration for these representations of whole numbers and some fractions, however, the number line is underutilized as a mathematical model that could be instrumental in fostering number sense and operational proficiency among students.

Recently, however, there has been a growing body of research to suggest the importance of the number line as a tool for helping children develop greater flexibility in mental arithmetic as they actively construct mathematical meaning, number sense, and an understanding of number relationships. Much of this emphasis has come as a result of rather alarming performance of young learners on arithmetic problems common to the upper elementary grades. For example, a study about a decade ago of elementary children in the Netherlands, a country with a rich mathematics education tradition, revealed that only about half of all students tested were able to solve the problem 64 – 28 correctly, and even fewer students were unable to demonstrate flexibility in using arithmetic strategies. These results, and other research like them, prompted mathematics educators to question existing models used to promote basic number sense and computational fluency.

Surprising to some, these research findings suggested that perhaps the manipulatives and mathematical models typically used for teaching arithmetic relationships and operations may not be as helpful as once thought. Base-10 blocks, for example, were found to provide excellent conceptual understanding, but weak procedural representation of number operations. The hundreds chart was viewed as an improvement on arithmetic blocks, but it too was limited in that it was an overly complicated model for many struggling students to use effectively. On the other hand, the number line is an easy model to understand and has great advantages in helping students understand the relative magnitude and position of numbers, as well as to visualize operations. As a result, Dutch mathematicians in the '90s were among the first in the world to return to the empty number line, giving this time-tested model a new identity as perhaps the most important construct within the realm of number and operation. Since that time, mathematics educators across the world have similarly turned to this excellent model with great results.

The Big Ideas

As noted above, the number line stands in contrast to other manipulatives and mathematical models used within the number realm. Some of the reasons for developing the number line as a foundational tool are illustrated below as key ideas for this text book.

Big Idea #1: The Linear Character of the Number Line The number line is well-suited to support informal thinking strategies of students because of its inherent linearity. In contrast to blocks or counters with a set-representation orientation, the tick marks on a number line are much more natural for young learners to appreciate as they visually represent the mental images that most people have when they learn to count and develop understanding of number relationships. It is extremely important to note the difference between an open number line (shown below) and a ruler with its predetermined markings and scale.

<----|--------------------------------->
     0

The open line allows students to partition, or subdivide, the space as they see fit, and as they may need, given the problem context at hand. In addition, the open number line allows for flexibility in extending counting strategies from counting by ones, for example, to counting by tens or hundreds all on the same size of open number line. This strategy is used repeatedly in this book.

Big Idea #2: Promoting Creative Solution Strategies and Intuitive Reasoning A prevalent view in math education reforms is that students should be given freedom to develop their own solution strategies. But to be clear, this perspective does not mean that it is simply a matter of allowing students to solve a problem however they choose. Rather, the models being promoted by the teacher should themselves refine and push the student toward more elegant, sophisticated, and reliable strategies and procedures. This process of formalizing mathematics by having students recognize, discuss, and internalize their thinking is a key principle in math education reforms, and is one that can be viewed clearly through the use of the number line. It is a tool that can be used to model mathematical contexts and to represent methods, thinking progressions, and solution strategies. As opposed to blocks or number tables that are typically cut off or grouped at ten, the number representation on the open line is clear, ongoing, natural, and intuitive to students. Because of this transparency and intuitive match with existing cognitive structures, the number line is well suited to model subtraction problems, for example, that otherwise would require regrouping strategies common to block and algorithmic procedures.

Big Idea #3: Cognitive Engagement Finally, research studies have shown that students using the empty number line tend to be more cognitively active than when they are using other models, such as blocks, which tend to rely on visualization of stationary groups of objects. The number line, in contrast, allows students to engage more consistently in the problem as they draw jumps on the number line in ways that resonate with their intuitions. While they are jumping on the number line, they are able to better keep track of the steps they are taking, leading to a decrease in the memory load otherwise necessary to solve the problem. For example, a student who is adding 30 + 23 can think of the addition as a series of jumps of ten and a series of jumps of one as follows:

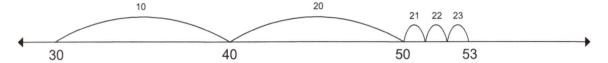

Like any mathematical tool, the more teachers are aware of both the benefits and constraints of the model, the more likely they are to use it effectively with students. Throughout this book, the previous big ideas, though theoretical in nature, are drawn upon repeatedly as students view and subsequently manipulate various open number lines that are used to represent numerous mathematical contexts and operations.

Teaching Ideas

A large portion of this book is devoted to helping students develop a rich sense of numbers and their relationships to one another. The number line is centrally related to this task. As noted above, perhaps the most important teaching point to convey regarding the number line is the notion that, unlike a ruler, it is open and flexible. Given this starting point, students will quickly recognize that they need to create their own actions on the number lines to give the model meaning. In the first section of the book, students are given opportunities to partition a number line as they see fit. The important thing for students to recognize is that one point alone on a number line does not tell us much about the scale or magnitude of numbers being considered. In the number line below, we know very little about this mathematical context other than the fact that it identifies the number 0 on a line.

By putting a second mark on the line, suddenly each number line takes on its own significant meaning, and to work with each of these respective lines would require a different kind of mathematical thinking.

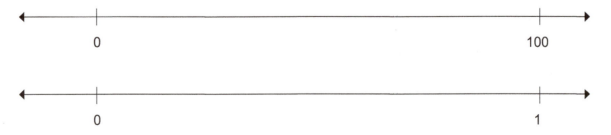

8   The Number Line *Teacher Edition*

In the first case, students will likely begin thinking immediately in terms of tens and twenties, perhaps 50, as they imagine how they might partition a line from 0 to 100. They will, therefore, use doubling and halving strategies, among others, as they mark the number line. In the second, fractional distances between zero and one are likely to come to mind. Once again, students may be using halving strategies if they are finding a number like 1/4, but finding thirds or fifths requires a different type of thinking. Note the radically different outcomes that might be pursued with the two number lines that each shared a rather simple beginning. As noted, students actively create this meaning as they partition the many open number lines presented in the initial sections of the book.

In subsequent sections of the book, the number line is developed as a reliable tool to help students add and subtract. Developed in the book is the idea of a skip-jump, or progression along a number line that is done in specific increments. In this way, the number line becomes a helpful model to mirror how students add and subtract mentally. Students become quite adept at skip-jumping by 10s or 100s, for example, and eventually begin to make mental adjustments to the number sentences at hand in order to take advantage of more sophisticated (or for them, easier) intervals for skip-jumping. Consider the following problem:

The Problem:
Kerri was trying to set her record for juggling a soccer ball. On her first attempt, she juggled the ball a total of 57 times before it hit the ground. On her second attempt, she only got a total of 29 juggles. Combining both her first and second attempts, how many times did she juggle the ball in total?

Using a number line flexibly, students may choose to solve this problem in any number of ways, each of which anchors on fundamental understandings of number. The first solution, for example, shows a student who counts on from 57, first by 10s. After skip-jumping forward by 30 (three jumps of 10), the student realizes that she needs to compensate by hopping back by one to arrive at the correct answer to 57 + 29.

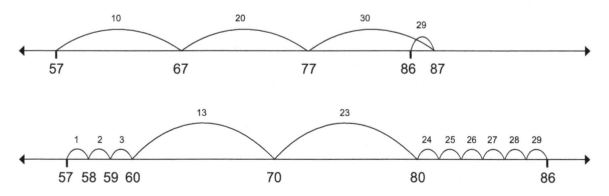

What are the thinking strategies of the other two students? Take a moment to consider how the number line can be used to mirror the actual thoughts contributing to the solution strategies of these two children. In the second, add 3 to get to an even decade number of 60. Now it becomes rather trivial to add 26 to 60. In the third example, take one away (57 − 1 = 56), and now we add 30 (instead of 29) to 56 to arrive at a total of 86.

An Important Consideration

This book contains numerous examples for students to practice to develop proficiency and sophisticated strategies with the number line. You will soon see the benefit of having students work many slightly different problems, but be prepared initially for some resistance from students. Students may feel as though they are doing the same things repeatedly, without recognizing the ways that subtle changes in the parameters of the problems elicit a different kind of thinking, or perhaps even a new strategy. An additional by-product of this intensive practice manipulating the number line is that there are far fewer real-world problem contexts in this book than the others in this series. While the importance of context as a tool for teaching and learning is vital, in the case of number lines students must practice in order to develop confidence in the number line. Please keep in mind the unique challenge of providing students with enough support and enough practice opportunities. Also be flexible in your expectations of student progress. As you see your students gaining facility with the number line, you may wish to add additional real-world examples in your teaching of this book. You may also choose to skip various problems in the book to move students along. If you decide to skip problems, be careful to check that the problems you are skipping do not include new or vital concepts.

You may wonder why the emphasis in this book is specifically on the number line, rather than on number concepts, addition, and subtraction. The emphasis on the number line is because of the degree to which the number line models the natural ways in which we think about all number relationships and number operations. The premise underlying this book, and the series as a whole, is that a curriculum best serves students when it provides powerful mathematical tools and understandings that can be used in numerous mathematical contexts and with different types of numbers. Specifically, the tools that students learn to employ in this book can be used with larger whole numbers, integers, fractions, and decimals. It is for that reason that this book has been placed first as a foundation for the rest of the books in this series. The intent is that, perhaps without fully recognizing, students will gain rich intuitions about numbers and operations in this book that will serve them well in years to come.

Section A: The Number Line and Number Sense

SECTION A PLANNER

THE MATHEMATICS CONTENT AND GOALS

GOALS

Students will:
- Be able to identify, place, and locate points on a number line with reasonable accuracy (into the thousands).
- Use estimation, halving, and other strategies to partition a number line.
- Order and compare numbers.
- Accurately extend a number line based on an existing pattern.
- Develop understanding of the number line in order to facilitate mental computation.

LANGUAGE DEVELOPMENT

Mathematical language in this section includes:

Number Line: A number line is a mathematical model that is used to represent points (or coordinates) that are placed correctly, according to a uniform scale, along a continuum. In this book, the open-ended number line, a line that has not been labeled in any preconceived way, is used repeatedly to help students develop understanding of numbers and their relationship to one another. A simpler definition for students might be: A line with numbers placed in their correct position.

Graph: In this book, graph is used to refer to instances in which students are asked to locate a point on a number line (e.g., graph the number 10 on the number line), or labeling a point on a number line that already exists (e.g., what is the number value of Point A on the number line?). Several synonyms for graph might also have been used appropriately (e.g., mark, label, place), but for simplicity, graph is used in each of these various contexts. A simpler definition for students might be to put a number on a number line in the right place.

Multiple: In this book, a multiple is used to refer to a fixed increment that students use to partition a number line. For example, students might be asked to graph points on a line in multiples of 10: 10, 20, 30, etc. Or they may be asked to identify how many multiples of 5 exist on a given number line. A common synonym for multiple that some students might use is increment. Another mathematical definition of multiple is the product of the given number and another number.

Explain your thinking: In this section, students are invited to explain their thinking. You might want to help students recognize that this process is not one they are likely to be familiar with, but that it is an extremely important skill to develop. They may need practice learning how to find the salient features of their thinking strategies, and time to develop the confidence to articulate those thoughts in a public discussion.

PACING

The projected pacing for this section is 2–4 class periods (based on a 45 minute period).

PROBLEM SETS: OVERVIEW

As stated previously, the number line is a tool that can help students develop number sense and facilitate mental computations. In this section, students will develop the foundation for intuitive strategies that will let them add and subtract 1-, 2-, and 3-digit numbers mentally and with reasonable accuracy. As students indicate readiness they should be encouraged to use these models mentally as much as possible.

Set 1 (pp. 1–2; problems 1–10)
With these problems, students learn to label numbers on a number line and identify those numbers that are already highlighted. It is important for students to develop an intuitive understanding of the relative scale of a number line, as addressed in problem 1. Watch for students to demonstrate an ability to reasonably partition a number line based on a particular scale.

Set 2 (p. 3; problems 1–6)
These problems introduce the important concept of an increment on the number line: an increase in number or size based on a multiple of a number. For simplicity regarding language learners, the word multiple is highlighted in this section where other words like increment might have otherwise been used. In order to do these problems well, students will need to be able to visualize, for example, half of a particular distance on the number line in order to label the point between 0 and 20 that corresponds with 10. Check that students are labeling points and extending number lines uniformly based on the scale and increments in use. Problem 6 especially lends itself to monitoring satisfactory performance in this regard.

It is important to recognize that the primary intent of the exercises throughout this book, and certainly in this section, is to help students estimate the relative size, magnitude, and position of numbers in relation to each other on a number line. So resist students' inclination to want to measure the number line with a ruler, and subsequently label points on the line. That would significantly undermine the attempt in this book to help students develop an intuitive understanding of the number line as a flexible mathematical model.

CONCEPT DEVELOPMENT (Pages 1–2)

INTRODUCE THE CONCEPT

ASSESS STUDENTS' PRIOR KNOWLEDGE
Draw a number line from 0 to 10 on the board and draw reference marks for 0 and 10.

Ask:
What do I know that can tell me about where the number 8 would fall on this number line?

Listen for: (Language that describes proximity)
- 8 is closer to 10 than to 0.
- 8 is between 5 and 10.
- 8 is a little closer to 10 than to 5.

MODEL MATHEMATICAL THINKING
Then model the thinking for another example by asking, How do I find where 14 is on the number line?

Talk Through the Thinking:
Let's see. I know that 14 is greater than 10, so I'll need to extend the number line. The number 20 is twice as much as 10, so I can double the length of the number line and label the end as 20.
I think the number 15 will be halfway between 10 and 20. I know that 15 is 5 more than 10 and 5 less than 20. So it must be halfway between 10 and 20. Yes, that's right. The number 14 will be just less than 15, so that's where I'll put the point for 14.

Ask:
What if the number had been 24 instead of 14? What would have been different?

Listen for:
- I would need to add on another 10 beyond 20.
- The next 10 would have to be the same length as the other 2 tens.

LAUNCH THE PROBLEM SOLVING

Have students work individually to solve the problems on page 1. As they work, circulate and monitor their work. As they finish each problem, have them compare and discuss their answers with a partner. Then have each pair share their answers in a class discussion of the problem. Refer to the **Teacher Notes: Student Page 1** for more specific ideas about the problems on this page.

As students work and report their conclusions, focus on these issues:

Look for Misconceptions – Students may draw number lines that are not proportional.

Facilitate Students' Thinking – If students use a halving strategy or a doubling strategy to locate numbers, encourage them to build on it.

Validate Representations – When several students make different drawings, have them think about whether they are all correct.

Encourage Language Development – Define graph as an act of placing a number on a number line in the right place. The right place will depend on other numbers already on the number line that give a point of reference and an idea of scale.

Allow Waiting Time – When students struggle to explain their thinking, be sure to allow them at least 20 seconds to organize their thoughts (this may feel like a long time).

Student Page 1: Problems and Potential Answers

Section A: Number Line and Number Sense Set 1

1. Graph these numbers on the two number lines below:

   a) 5   b) 15   c) 18 | *Can you do these too?* d) 3   e) 12   f) 9

2. What is the number value of each letter shown on the number line below?

   A = __10__   B = __25__   C = __40__   D = __55__   E = __75__   F = __90__   G = __98__

3. Graph five points on the number line in addition to those that are already there. **Graph the number 50** as one of your five points. (Answers will vary.)

4. Draw a number line that **starts with the number 20,** and **ends with the number 80.** Graph the numbers 30 and 50 on your number line, and 2 other points. (Answers will vary.)

(number line showing 20, 30, 40, 50, 70, 80)

Book 1: *The Number Line*   1

TEACHER NOTES: STUDENT PAGE 1

Problem 1: Problem 1 asks students to place the same set of numbers on two different number lines, each with a different scale. For many students, this is a difficult task, despite the fact that they may think it is somewhat beneath them. Be sure to avoid taking it for granted that your students will be able to do this with certainty. *Watch for:* Many students will hesitate at the second number line, not sure how to reconcile why the same set of numbers would appear to be in different locations on two number lines of the same length. On the first number line, three points appear to the right of the midpoint. On the second number line, none of the points appear to the right of the midpoint. *Teaching Strategy:* Pause at this problem to remind students of the notion of scale. Although the two number lines are the same length on paper, they have very different meanings as soon as a scale is used to label them. To help clarify this concept, ask students which they would prefer, half of ten dollars or all of three dollars. They should recognize that half of ten dollars is more than all of three dollars. This idea can be used to help students understand that the scale of one number line may be different than the scale of another.

Watch for: Many students will intuitively begin to decipher relative positions of numbers on a number line by using a halving strategy. *Teaching Strategy:* Build on this intuitive strategy. For example, students are asked to place the number 15 on each line. On the second number line, they may use a halving strategy, thinking, "I know that 10 is halfway between 0 and 20." They will mark 10 on the line, then find 15. "I also know that 15 is halfway between 10 and 20." They mark the midpoint of 10 and 20, labeling this value 15. Students can use this point to estimate the positions of other points nearby; for example, 18. This strategy of visualizing half of a segment with known endpoints is extremely valuable and will be used by students to complete many mental computations.

Problem 2: This problem is similar to problem 1, only now it asks students to identify a point that is already on the line. *Watch for:* Expect students to be accurate to within roughly +/- 1 of the intended value.

Problem 3: Problem 3 asks students to duplicate an interval and to use a scale that has been established to extend a number line. *Watch for:* Students should find an informal way to measure the original span between 0 and 10. They may do this with a small piece of paper, blocks, pennies, or measuring a pencil from its tip. *Teaching Strategy:* Encourage the use of such informal, non-standard units of measurement, as this will help students recognize that number lines are relative in scale.

Problem 4: Students are asked to use an interval (likely an interval of 10) to complete the problem. This time, however, they are responsible for creating the actual scale. *Watch for:* This is a good problem for students to use to compare number lines. Students will inevitably choose different lengths to represent the common interval length of 10. *Teaching Strategy:* It is critical to pause at this problem to ensure that students recognize that a length of 10 will be different depending on the scale of the number line. The best way to illustrate this is to show students a ruler in metric units and one in customary units to illustrate that 10 centimeters is a much smaller length than 10 inches.

On the Lookout for Misconceptions

Watch for students to use a "sliding scale" on their number lines. That is, they may not use the same length on the line to designate the same numeric interval, for example:

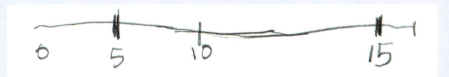

In such cases, students should be encouraged to measure the corresponding intervals with non-standard units of measurement, such as blocks, beans, or beads.

CONTINUE THE PROBLEM SOLVING

Have students work individually to solve the problems on page 2. As they work, you may want to circulate and monitor their work. As students finish each problem, have them compare and discuss their answers with a partner. Then have each pair share their answers in a class discussion of the problem. Refer to the **Teacher Notes: Student Page 2** for more specific ideas about the problems on this page.

As students work and report their conclusions, focus on these issues:

Look for Misconceptions – Students may partition an interval into subintervals using too many reference marks.

Facilitate Students' Thinking – If students use a halving strategy to partition an interval (such as with fourths) encourage them to use it or modify it for other intervals (such as fifths).

Validate Alternate Solutions – When several students use different multiples to extend a number line, have them discuss whether they are all correct.

Help Make Connections – If students are successful using a halving or doubling strategy with small numbers, remind them that the same strategy will work with greater numbers.

Encourage Language Development – There are many terms students can use in describing their thinking as they work on these problems. To the extent that it is appropriate for your students, help them develop their mathematical vocabulary by introducing explicit use of terms such as, half, double, multiple, interval, increment, and about. These ideas will surface throughout the remainder of the book as students use number lines and ratio tables.

Student Page 2: Problems and Potential Answers

Section A: Number Line and Number Sense   Set 1

5. Graph all of the multiples of 10 up to 100 (for example, 10, 20, 30…). How many 10's are in 100? __10__

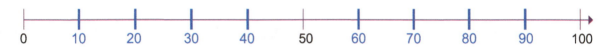

6. Graph all of the multiples of 5 up to 40 (for example, 5, 10, 15…). How many 5's are in 40? __8__

7. Graph all of the multiples of 4 up to 40 (for example, 4, 8, 12…). How many 4's are in 40? __10__ How many 4's are there in 20? __5__

8. Graph all of the multiples of 6 up to 60 (for example, 6, 12, 18 …). How many 6's are in 60? __10__ How many 6's are there in 30? __5__

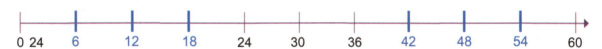

9. Graph all of the multiples of 1 up to 10 (for example, 1, 2, 3 …). How many 1's are in 10? __10__

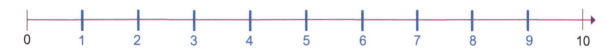

10. Graph where the number 200 would be on this line. (Answers will vary.)

TEACHER NOTES: STUDENT PAGE 2

Problems 5–10 ask students to partition each number line in equal intervals. *Watch for:* Students should use their prior knowledge of number relationships, such as there are ten 10s in 100, to determine ahead of time how many intervals they will need to mark on the number line.

Problem 5: Problem 5 introduces the notion of multiples of a given number. Pause to ask students to share their own definitions of what a multiple might be. To facilitate the discussion, you might ask what it means to have multiple friends or to score multiple goals in a soccer game. Connect the notion of a multiple to the idea of repeated and equal intervals on a number line. This idea will be further developed when the strategy of skip-counting is presented in Section B. *Teaching Strategy:* Be sure to stress the fact that there are 10 intervals of equal length in 100. Then connect the visual representation of this relationship on the number line to the numeric relationship $10 \times 10 = 100$, which students have probably seen before.

Problems 6-8: These problems are similar to Problem 5, but here students are working with different multiples, using increments of 5, 6, and 4 respectively, and are given slightly different arrangements of anchor points on the number line. Students are also asked to use their sense of number relationships to determine how many multiples might be contained in an interval of twice the given distance (e.g., how many 5s in 20? In 40?). *Watch for:* By the end of problem 8, look for students to answer this question without having to consult the number line. They might suggest, for example:

I know there are five 6s in 30. Since 30 + 30 = 60, then I know there must be another five 6s between 30 and 60. So there are ten 6s in 60.

Teaching Strategy: Capitalize on this kind of response to connect the visual representation to the numeric relationship $10 \times 6 = 60$.

Problem 9: *Watch for:* Students should return to halving strategies to divide the number line into equal intervals. *Teaching Strategy:* Remind students that the scale of a number line is always relative. That is, the same line might be used to illustrate a range of 0–100 or, as in this case, 0–10.

Problem 10: This problem is different from the previous problems in that students cannot use a halving strategy (without some further work on their own) because only the first two marks on the line are visible. *Watch for:* Students should use a sliding scale as they mark subsequent intervals, and look for them to use manipulatives as non-standard measuring tools to ensure accuracy.

> ### On the Lookout for Misconceptions
>
> A common representational misconception is likely to emerge in these problems, and problem 9 is a particularly good candidate. For example, the student needs to mark the number line from 0–10 based on an interval of 1. The student might think: "I know there are 10 ones in ten, so I need to make 10 marks on my number line." Indeed, there are 10 intervals. However, given that the beginning and ending marks are already placed on the line, the student only needs to add 9 marks on the line to represent the intervals. Pause at this misconception if it emerges to again connect the numeric ($1 \times 10 = 10$) and visual (9 ticks on the number line between 0 and 10) representations.

CONCEPT DEVELOPMENT (PAGE 3)

INTRODUCE THE CONCEPT

ASSESS STUDENTS' PRIOR KNOWLEDGE
Discuss number patterns with single-digit numbers and their products when multiplied by 10, 100, and 1,000. Write the following on the board:

7
70
700
7,000

Ask:
What patterns do you see in this set of numbers? How are all four numbers alike? How are they different? How much greater is each number than the one above it?

Listen for:
(Place-value language)
- The first digit (the digit on the left) is the same.
- In 7, the 7 is in the ones place. There are zeros in the ones place in 70, in the ones and tens places in 700, and in the ones, tens, and hundreds places in 7,000.
- 70 is 10 times greater than 7. The number 700 is 10 times greater than 70 and 100 times greater than 7. The number 7,000 is 10 times greater than 700, 100 times greater than 70, and 1,000 times greater than 7.

MODEL MATHEMATICAL THINKING
Then model the thinking for another example. Draw the number lines below on the board, and ask: *How many 5s are in 25? How can that help me to know how many 50s are in 250?*

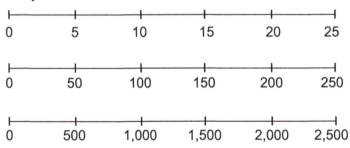

Talk Through the Thinking:
I can skip-count by 5 from 0 to 25 to find how many 5s in 25: 5, 10, 15, 20, 25. That's 5 skips, so there are five 5s in 25. To find how many 50s there are in 250, I need to skip-count from 0 to 50: 50, 100, 150, 200, 250. That's 5 skips, so there are five 50s in 250. I think I see a pattern. If I cross off the zero in the ones place on the second number line, the numbers that are left match the numbers on the first number line. So if there are five 5s in 25, then there must be five 50s in 250.

Ask:
How can you use the pattern to find how many 500s there are in 2,500? How many 500s are there in 2,500?

Listen for:
- If I cross off the zeros in the ones and tens places in the numbers on the third number line, the numbers that are left match those on the first number line. If I cross off the zeros in the ones in the numbers on the third number line, the numbers that are left match those on the second number line.
- There are five 500s in 2,500.

LAUNCH THE PROBLEM SOLVING

Have students work individually to solve the problems on page 3. As they work, you may want to circulate and monitor their work. As students finish each problem, have them compare and discuss their answers with a partner. Then have each pair share their answers in a class discussion of the problem. Refer to the **Teacher Notes: Student Page 3** for more specific ideas about the problems on this page.

As students work and report their conclusions, focus on these issues:

Allow Waiting Time – When students struggle to explain their thinking, be sure to allow them at least 20 seconds to organize their thoughts (this may feel like a long time).

Facilitate Students' Thinking – If students are successful using a strategy to find one number, encourage them to build upon that success, using the same strategy to find other numbers.

Encourage Language Development – Words that might have new mathematical meaning for students in this section include: extend, between, and strategy. You may wish to pause at these words to ensure understanding.

Validate Alternate Solutions – When several students use different multiples on a number line, have them discuss whether they are all correct.

Help Make Connections – Encourage students to look for similarities between smaller and greater numbers, such as 20 and 200. Remind them that what works for a smaller number can be applied to the larger, similar number.

Student Page 3: Problems and Potential Answers

Section A: Number Line and Number Sense Set 2

1. Graph the following numbers on the number line.

   a) 300   b) 150   c) 25   d) 375   e) 180   f) 90   g) 240

2. Based on where you see the number 15, graph 5 more points on the line. **Include the number 150.** (Answers will vary.)

3. Graph the following numbers on the number line. You can graph other numbers also if it helps.

   a) 300   b) 450   c) 650   d) 100   e) 1450   f) 1200   g) 900

4. Graph the number line in multiples of 300. How many 300's are in 2400? __8__ How many 300's are in 1200? __4__ How many 150's are in 1200? __8__ How many 600's in 2400? __4__

5. Graph the number line in multiples of 10 beginning at 200. How many 10's are there between 200 and 300? __10__

6. Draw a number line. **Start with zero. Make the next number 300,** and then extend the number line **to 3000.** (Answers will vary.)

Book 1: *The Number Line*   3

The Number Line Teacher Edition   21

TEACHER NOTES: STUDENT PAGE 3

Problem 1: *Watch for:* Students should use informal strategies, such as using a halving strategy to identify 100 and 250, to find other values. *Teaching Strategy:* Encourage students to think about number relationships as they try to place the given values on the number line (e.g., *If I know how many 25s there are in 400, I can cut the line up in the right number of intervals.*). Students should also be encouraged to use information repeatedly. That is, what might be used to find one number could be used again for a related number later on; for example, intervals of 25 can be used to find 150.

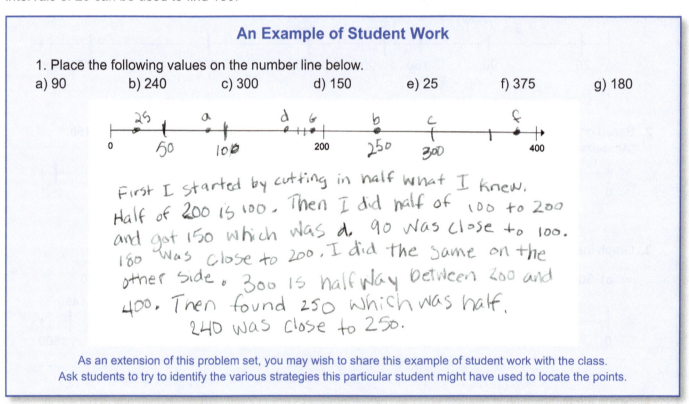

As an extension of this problem set, you may wish to share this example of student work with the class. Ask students to try to identify the various strategies this particular student might have used to locate the points.

Problem 2: *Watch for:* Students may find it difficult to think in multiples of 15. *Teaching Strategy:* If so, encourage them to decompose the number 15 into two parts: 15 = 10 + 5. Adding by 10s, then 5s will be easier for them.

Problem 3: While students will likely use strategies they have found successful in the past, this problem will identify students who have already developed good number sense with larger numbers.

Problems 4-6: These problems again emphasize the magnitude of numbers. *Teaching Strategy:* To help students see connections across representations and number relationships, you may wish to pause and ask:

What is similar between these two statements?
- How many 3s are in 24?
- How many 300s are in 2400?

To build on this idea, you might also display two number lines as shown below to illustrate the parallels between these two number relationships.

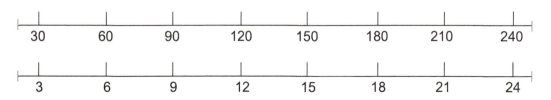

22 The Number Line *Teacher Edition*

SECTION A ASSESSMENT (PAGE 4)

LAUNCH THE ASSESSMENT

Have students turn to the Section A Assessment, page 4. An additional copy is found on page 2 of the Assessment Book. Have students work individually to solve the problems and write their explanations. As they work, circulate to be sure students understand what they need to do for each problem. Be sure that students are completing each part of the problem. For example, in problem 1 students need to explain the strategy used and complete the problem. You may find it helpful to read the directions for all the problems before students begin, discussing the types of responses they will need to make for each problem.

Encourage students to use whatever space they need to explain their thinking. If the space on the page is inadequate they should use an additional sheet of paper or use the back of the page.

Refer to the **Teacher Notes: Student Page 4** for more specific ideas about the problems on this page.

Evaluate Student Responses
Use the Assessment Rubric on page 1 of the Assessment Book (pictured on page 26 of the Teacher Edition) to evaluate student responses. The Assessment Book has some general suggestions for using the rubric that may be helpful to you.

Student Page 4: Problems and Potential Answers

Section A: Problems for Assessment

1. Here's how a student began his number line. He was trying to get to 300. Explain the strategy he was using. What can he do next to reach 300?

   Explain:
   Explanations will vary, but students should note that he was using a doubling strategy. He can add 60 to 240 to get 300.

2. A student wanted to challenge herself to get to 200 by graphing only 4 more numbers on the number line. Show how she can do it. Explain your steps.

   Explain:
   Explanations will vary. Doubling strategies are common.

3. Start at zero. Pick any starting number and place it in the **Start** box. Choose a **target number** to **end your number line**. Where on the line does your target number go? Graph numbers to help you find where your target number belongs on the line. Pick a new start and target number for Trial 2.

   (Responses will vary.)

   Trial 1: My Target Number _____

   Trial 2: My Target Number _____

4. Describe how a number line can be used to work with numbers.

   Explain: (Responses will vary.) _____
   _____
   _____

4   Book 1: *The Number Line*

TEACHER NOTES: ASSESSMENT PROBLEMS FOR SECTION A, STUDENT PAGE 4

Problem 1: Problem 1 assesses students' recognition and understanding of strategies that can be applied to the use of number lines. In particular, this problem illustrates perhaps the most powerful strategy to which children gravitate, doubling intervals. *Watch for:* Students should recognize the doubling strategy employed in this problem: 30 doubled is 60; 60 doubled is 120; 120 doubled is 240. Once at 240, the student must then add another 60 to reach the desired goal of 300. Since the interval of 60 is already highlighted on the number line, students should recognize that 300 can be found rather easily by adding on from 240. For this problem be sure students realize that the doubling relationship must hold in the numeric representation (60 → 120) as well as the graphical representation. As an example, the length of the line segment from 0–60 should be exactly half as long as the segment from 0–120. On these kinds of problems, be attentive to the starting points that students select, and whether those initial intervals are reasonable given the various constraints of the problem context.

Problem 2: Problem 2 limits the number of marks students can place on the number line as they extend it to 200. *Watch for:* Hold students to this requirement as it will force them to be more sophisticated in the strategies they use. For example, rather than simply duplicating the length of the segment from 0–20 ten times, students should be encouraged to use more sophisticated and efficient methods, such as doubling 20 to get 40, doubling 40 again to get 80, adding 20 to get 100, and then doubling to get 200. Students may have used these intuitive strategies throughout the previous problems.

Problem 3: Be sure students understand the directions for this problem before they begin. The intent is for students to establish their own scale for the number lines by choosing their own starting intervals and their ultimate destination down the line. This problem will illuminate students' understanding of scale. *Watch for:* Students should have a mismatch between the scale they choose (their start box) and their intended target number. See an example of this potential problem in the box above.

> **On the Lookout for Misconceptions**
>
> Here is an example of a problem students might experience in determining a relevant scale for a number line. Given the space available, students will not be able to illustrate successfully an accurate visual representation of the number relationship they desire.
>
> Target number: 100
>
> In this case, the number line would have to be extended much longer in order to allow for an accurate placement of the target number of 100. Students will need to adjust their starting number.

Problem 4: Problem 4 is open-ended. *Watch for:* Students should mention strategies for placing numbers on a line based on the intervals they already know (e.g., by doubling or halving) as well as how the number line can be used to compare numbers.

SCORING GUIDE BOOK 1: THE NUMBER LINE

Section A Assessment
For Use With: Student Book Page 4

PROBLEM DESCRIPTION	SCORING: WHAT TO LOOK FOR	SCORE AND COMMENTS
Problem 1 Extend a number line to 300 based on a given doubling strategy. Level 2: Tool Use Level 4: Evaluation	Do students: • Place 300 on the number line in an accurate scale? • Recognize the doubling strategy? • Adequately describe the use of the strategy?	Points:_____ of 3
Problem 2 Starting with zero and twenty, use 4 marks to reach 200. Level 2: Tool Use Level 4: Evaluation	Do students: • Place 200 on the number line in an accurate scale? • Use the starting value of 20 in the problem? • Use the doubling strategy? • Adequately describe the process?	Points:_____ of 3
Problem 3 Starting with a beginning point, find two ways to get to a target number. Level 1: Knowledge Level 2: Tool Use	Do students: • Accurately use scale on the number line? • Demonstrate two strategies to get to the target? • Feel comfortable using many strategies?	Points:_____ of 2 Points:_____ of 2
Problem 4 Describe utility of number line. Level 3: Connection and Application	Do students: • Understand the value of representing numbers on the number line? • Articulate ways to place numbers on number line?	Points:_____ of 2

TOTAL POINTS:_____ OF 12

Section B: Using the Number Line for Addition and Subtraction

SECTION B PLANNER

THE MATHEMATICS CONTENT AND GOALS

GOALS

Students will:
- Visualize addition and subtraction using the number line as a model.
- Develop understanding and facility with adding on along the number line.
- Apply number-line strategies for addition and subtraction in various problems and contexts.
- Compare different solution strategies for addition and subtraction.
- Develop efficiency in calculating addition and subtraction problems (2- and 3-digit) mentally.

LANGUAGE DEVELOPMENT

Mathematical language in this section includes:

Skip-counting: Skip-counting, or skip-jumping is a student-friendly term used to describe the action of adding on from a given point, using a specified multiple. For example, to add 43 and 39, I might start at 43, and then skip-count along the number in increments of 10: 53, 63, 73, etc. In any given problem, students may use skip-counts of different sizes, moving by 5, by 10, by 100, or often times, by 1.

Number Sentence: In this section students are asked to provide number sentences to accompany the work they do expressing their strategies for addition and subtraction on the number line. A number sentence is simply a symbolic statement (e.g., 24 + 48 = 70) that matches a given problem context. Many times the number sentences in this book contain an open element, such as, for example: 24 + ___ = 48. In these cases students must reason about which values may or may not make the statement true.

Point: In this section, a point is used to refer to a specific location on the number line. Students may need to find a point, or they may need to give a numeric value for a specified point on a line.

Distance: Here we use distance to mean the relative difference between two points. Students may not yet have made the connection that subtracting the numeric value of two points is the same as determining the distance between those two points.

PACING

The projected pacing for this unit is 3–6 class periods (based on a 45 minute period).

PROBLEM SETS: OVERVIEW

Set 1 (pp. 5–6; problems 1–6)
These problems develop the technique of skip-counting. This technique helps students navigate along the number line by taking advantage of familiar number relationships, such as adding on 10s. Problems 1–3 encourage students to practice skipping by 10. Problems 3b–3d hint at strategies that will be developed later, using skip-counting and estimation to arrive at reasonable conclusions about number sentences. Problems 4-6 encourage students to skip with convenient numbers other than 10.

Set 2 (pp. 7–8; problems 1–8)
Problems 1–8 reinforce earlier work and introduce the idea that multiple strategies may be used to complete the same operation. Be sure to adequately engage students in a discussion of problem 10 in particular, as it encourages students to explore two quite different ways of looking at the same number sentence. This problem is important because it suggests not only that addition and subtraction are inverse operations, but also that individual problems can always be visualized in more than one way, and that multiple solution strategies can be common to the same problem.

Set 3 (p. 9; problems 1–7)
This stand-alone activity could be used as a formative assessment partway through this unit. In this activity, students are asked to think about the most efficient (i.e., least number of steps) mental strategies to use to arrive at the answer for various addition and subtraction problems. Encourage students to compare solution strategies with each other, or engage the class in conversation about the various ways to use the number line. Students could extend this activity by trading their own problem solutions with each other.

Set 4 (pp. 10–11; problems 1–6)
These problems will extend students' thinking and also serve as helpful assessment items for teachers as they ask students to decipher the thinking of others. Several problems challenge students to compare solution strategies and in the process, continue to refine their number sense, understanding of additive and subtractive relationships, and their use of the number line as a tool for mental computation. For problem 3, make sure students have ample time to evaluate each solution strategy. Before answering the question in the box at the end of the problem, you may wish to have students provide written explanations of each of the solutions, as each example illustrates a unique strategy for skip-jumping on the number line.

CONCEPT DEVELOPMENT (Pages 5–6)

INTRODUCE THE CONCEPT

ASSESS STUDENTS' PRIOR KNOWLEDGE

On the board, draw a number line from 0 to 100, marking 0 and 100. Draw a point at 0.

Ask:
How can I get from 0 to 60 on this number line using only 6 equal intervals?

Listen for:
- There are ten 6s in 60.
- I can skip-count by 10s: 10, 20, 30, 40, 50, 60.

MODEL MATHEMATICAL THINKING

Mark the increments of 10 on the number line. Then model the thinking for another example by asking, How can I use 10s and one other interval to get from 5 to 40?

Talk Through the Thinking:
First I have to locate 5 on the number line. Five is halfway between 0 and 10. If I count on 10 from 5, I get to 15. Then another 10 and I get to 25. Another 10 brings me to 35. From 35 to 40 is less than 10. It is 5. So when I get to 35 I can count on 5 to get to 40.

Ask:
What if I want to go from 20 to 45 using 10s and 5s. What would be the same? What would be different?

Listen for:
- Same: you would use only one 5.
- Different: you would use two 10s.
- Different: you are counting on from a ten (or multiple of 10).

LAUNCH THE PROBLEM SOLVING

Have students work individually to solve the problems on page 5. As they work, you may want to circulate and monitor their work. As they finish each problem, have them compare and discuss their answers with a partner. Then have each pair share their answers in a class discussion of the problem. Refer to the **Teacher Notes: Student Page 5** for more specific ideas about the problems on this page.

As students work and report their conclusions, focus on these issues:

Allow Waiting Time — When students struggle to explain their thinking, be sure to allow them at least 20 seconds to organize their thoughts.

Look for Misconceptions — Students may assume they should always use 10s and then 5 to get to a target number.

Encourage Language Development — Be sure to emphasize key vocabulary for this section including skip-count, point, and distance.

TEACHER NOTES: STUDENT PAGE 5

Skip-counting is one of the key strategies developed in this book. If students are given a good opportunity to learn how to skip-count effectively, it will become a valuable tool for them to use in mental computations. Although they may be tempted to do so, students should not rush through the beginning problems of Section B. These problems lay the foundation for what will follow as skip-counting gets developed in more sophisticated ways with the ratio table.

Problem 1: Although some students may be able to complete this problem mentally, encourage them to draw the skips of ten and five on the number line with a pencil. *Teaching Strategy:* Encourage students to place their pencil tips on 25 and draw loops of ten on the top of the number line without lifting their pencils. As their use of skip-counting becomes more sophisticated with the introduction of more complicated numbers and contexts, this strategy of marking the skips with a pencil will become helpful. In time, you should encourage students to see these jumps mentally as they compute without pencil and paper. In order for students to imagine these manipulations on the number line, they will first need to see many real examples on paper.

Problem 2: This problem is similar to the problem 1. Using skips of ten is particularly helpful and valuable for students. *Watch for:* Be sure they recognize the value and ease of skipping by tens. Later, the use of 10 as a convenient skip number will be used as an anchor for skipping with other values.

Student Page 5: Problems and Potential Answers

Section B: Using the Number Line for Addition and Subtraction Set 1

By using **skip counting** and **counting on**, the number line can help you add and subtract large numbers quickly. Choosing easy numbers to "skip" (like 5 or 10 or 100) along the number line is the key! Look at the following example:

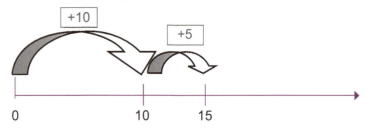

We can skip by 5's and 10's to help us arrive at the sum of two numbers, for example:

13 + 25…

13 + 25 → 13 + (10 + 10 + 5) = 38

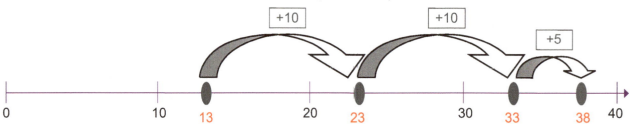

The following problems will help you learn the skill of skip counting.

1. Beginning with 25, skip count by 10's until you **get to 75**. Show each "skip" of ten with a small arrow, and graph each number with a point on the number line. How many "skips" to 75? __5__

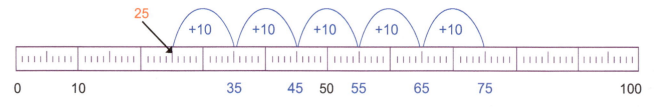

2. Beginning with 38, skip count by 10's until you **get to 68**. Show each "skip" of ten with a small arrow, and graph each corresponding number with a point on the number line. How many "skips" to 68? __3__

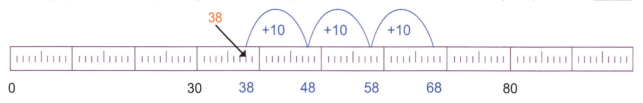

Book 1: *The Number Line*

CONTINUE THE PROBLEM SOLVING

Have students work individually to solve the problems on page 6. As they work, you may want to circulate and monitor their work. As they finish each problem, have them compare and discuss their answers with a partner. Then have each pair share their answers in a class discussion of the problem. Refer to the **Teacher Notes: Student Page 6** for more specific ideas about the problems on this page.

As students work and report their conclusions, focus on these issues:

Facilitate Students' Thinking – Help students understand that in problem 3b, because 77 is 1 less than 78, the total distance from 18 to 77 will be 1 less than the distance from 18 to 78. This relational thinking becomes a very helpful mental strategy for addition and subtraction.

Validate Alternate Solutions – When students begin their skip-counting at different starting points, have them discuss whether they are all correct.

Help Make Connections – In the number sentences students complete or write, have them discuss how each number in the number sentence relates to the skips on the number line.

Student Page 6: Problems and Potential Answers

| Section B: Using the Number Line for Addition and Subtraction | Set 1 |

3. a) How far is it from 18 to 78? __60__ Show this below by graphing points and using skip-count arrows. Complete this **number sentence** that corresponds with your skip counting: 18 + __60__ = 78

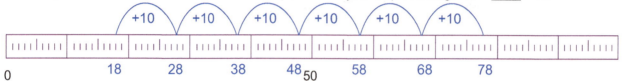

Use what you know from above …

b) How far is it from 18 to 77? __59__

c) How far is it from 18 to 80? __62__

d) How far is it from 17 to 78? __61__

4. Beginning with the number 45, **add 55** using multiples of 10 and 5. Show this with arrows. Label each skip number, including your final number.

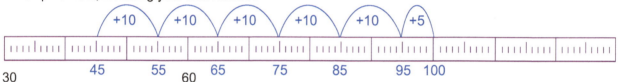

5. Use the number line and skip counting to show the distance from 17 to 77. Write a number sentence that corresponds with your number line.

Number sentence: __17 + 60 = 77__

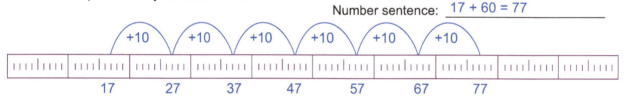

6. Use the number line below to find the distance from 26 to 66. Write the distance in the box.

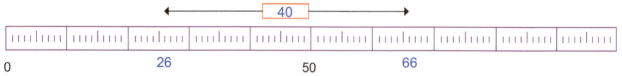

a) Write a number sentence: __26 + 40 = 66__

b) How far is it from 26 to 64? __38__

c) How far is it from 26 to 68? __42__

6   Book 1: *The Number Line*

TEACHER NOTES: STUDENT PAGE 6

Problem 3a: Rather than being told how many times to skip by 10 as in problems 1 and 2, problem 3 asks students to count how many skips are necessary to reach a desired target on the number line. While some students may recognize that there is a gap of 60 between 18 and 78, others will not be able to compute that difference quickly and with certainty. Yet they can learn to skip along the number line quite efficiently. *Watch for:* Be sure students find the correct starting point for the problem, 18, and then count accurately as they draw their skip intervals. *Teaching Strategy:* It is important to emphasize the number sentence at the end of this problem. It is imperative that students see the connection between their physical manipulation of the number line, making six skips of 10, and the symbolic representation of their action in the number sentence 18 + 60 = 78.

Problem 3b–3d: These extension problems are important. *Watch for:* You do not want to see students creating a new number line for each of these problems. Instead, students should be encouraged to see the close connection between these problems and problem 3a. They should understand that the distance from 18 to 78 is very close to the distance from 18 to 77. *Teaching Strategy:* Encourage students to think critically about these problems before starting them. Students should be able to adjust their previous answer of 60 slightly based on the nuances in these extension problems.

Problem 4: This problem introduces the notion of skip-counting by an interval in addition to 10.

Problem 5: There is no scale or starting point indicated on this number line. *Watch for:* Students may choose their own starting point. As most students will assume that the number line shown starts at 0 at the far left, you may take this opportunity to present a counterexample.

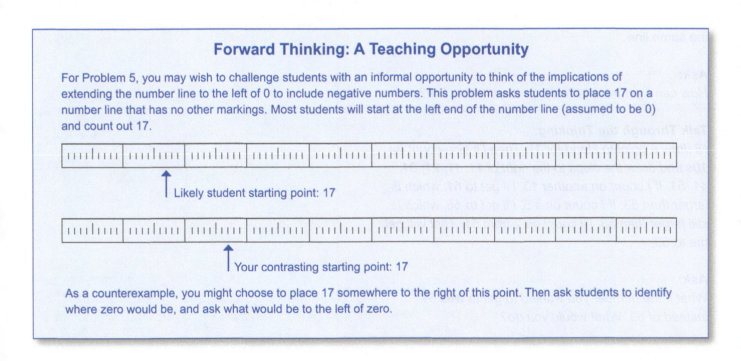

Forward Thinking: A Teaching Opportunity

For Problem 5, you may wish to challenge students with an informal opportunity to think of the implications of extending the number line to the left of 0 to include negative numbers. This problem asks students to place 17 on a number line that has no other markings. Most students will start at the left end of the number line (assumed to be 0) and count out 17.

↑ Likely student starting point: 17

↑ Your contrasting starting point: 17

As a counterexample, you might choose to place 17 somewhere to the right of this point. Then ask students to identify where zero would be, and ask what would be to the left of zero.

Problem 6: Students should first use skip-counting techniques to determine the distance between 26 and 66. Using that information, they should be able to make subtle adjustments for their answers in 6b and 6c.

CONCEPT DEVELOPMENT (Page 7)

INTRODUCE THE CONCEPT

ASSESS STUDENTS' PRIOR KNOWLEDGE
Draw a horizontal line on the board. Do not label it with any reference numbers.

Ask:
I want to use this line to skip-count from 11 to 41. How can I know where to start? How can I know where to end?

Listen for:
(Indications of students' understanding that the beginning number can be placed anywhere on the line)
- You can draw a point for 11 on the line.
- You can make 1 skip of 10 from 11 to the right. Then you can draw a point and label it. Then make as many skips of 10 as you need until you get to 41.
- You can draw a point at the end of the skips.

MODEL MATHEMATICAL THINKING
Then model the thinking for another example, using the same line.

Ask:
How can I get from 11 to 53 on the number line?

Talk Through the Thinking:
I'll draw a point to stand for 11. Then I'll skip-count by 10s and draw the skips to the right of 11: 11, 21, 31, 41, 51. If I count on another 10, I'll get to 61, which is larger than 53. If I count on a 5, I'll get to 56, which is still larger than 53. I'll count on 2 from 51. That will get me to 53.

Ask:
What if the number you wanted to get to was 64 instead of 53. What would you do?

Listen for:
- I would need to skip another 10 after getting to 51. That would get me to 61.
- I would need to count on a 3 from 61 to get to 64.

LAUNCH THE PROBLEM SOLVING

Have students work individually to solve the problems on page 7. As they work, you may want to circulate and monitor their work. As they finish each problem, have them compare and discuss their answers with a partner. Then have each pair share their answers in a class discussion of the problem. Refer to the **Teacher Notes: Student Page 7** for more specific ideas about the problems on this page.

As students work and report their conclusions, focus on these issues:

Help Make Connections – If students have been successful skip-counting by 10s on previous pages, suggest that they begin each problem by using the same increment.

Allow Waiting Time – When students struggle to explain their thinking, allow them ample time to organize their thoughts. This is particularly important when students explain the difference in problem 4. Students may assume they should always use 10s and then 5 to get to a target number.

Student Page 7: Problems and Potential Answers

Section B: Using the Number Line for Addition and Subtraction Set 2

1. Use skip counting to extend the following number line to 57. For each "skip" of 10, extend the line, add a point, and graph the number.

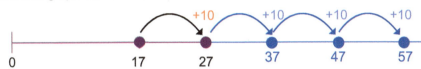

2. Starting with the number 23, add 70 by skip counting. For each multiple of 10 (or whatever "skip" you choose to use), extend the number line, add a point, and write the number. Complete the number sentence that expresses your number line.

   Number sentence: 23 + 70 = __93__

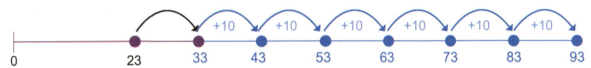

3. Starting with the number 121, add 40 using multiples of 10. Extend your number line by graphing each point and number.

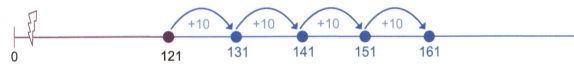

   a) What is the sum if you start with 121 and add 40? __161__

   b) What is the sum if you start with 121 and added 42? __163__

   c) What is the sum if you start with 121 and add 38? __159__

4. In October, the average high temperature in Chicago is 67 degrees. At night, the average low temperature is 42 degrees. How much warmer is it in the day than at the night? __25__ Both of the number lines below illustrate this problem.

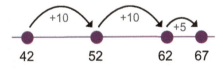 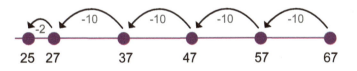

Explain how the number lines are different: _____

_____

Book 1: *The Number Line*   7

The Number Line Teacher Edition   35

TEACHER NOTES: STUDENT PAGE 7

Problem 1: *Watch for:* As students are skipping by 10s, be sure that their visual representations on the number line are close to equal in length.

Problem 2: For Problem 2, the starting point of 23 is highlighted. Students are asked to increase that amount by 70. The intent of the problem is to invite students to determine and use any increment that is meaningful and understandable to them in the process of adding 23 + 70. Students may skip-count by 10 (to 23, 33, 43, etc.). *Watch for:* Students should skip by a combination of increments such as 10, 10, and 50, (resulting in positions on the number line corresponding to 33, 43, and 93). *Teaching Strategy:* Encourage efficient strategies that allow students to solve the problem with fewer steps, although it is important never to minimize the solution strategy of a student who took more steps.

Problem 3: For this problem students determine the scale of the number line as they make their first skip of 10. Questions 3a-3c are important because they encourage students to make subtle mental manipulations of the kind that occur frequently both in and out of a classroom context. *Teaching Strategy:* Students who are comfortable skipping 40 from 121 to 161 should be encouraged to use that knowledge to make a slight change, adding 41 instead of 40. These problems are excellent for eliciting student thinking about the strategies they are using. Confident students with a good understanding of number relationships will recognize a series of steps that will ultimately lead to the desired outcome. These students will be able to break down the addition or subtraction process into a series of simpler steps that they can complete mentally. See, for example, the sample of such thinking by a 5th grader below.

Problem 4: Problem 4 requires students to apply skip-counting techniques in a real-world context. Students can solve this problem in several ways once they are certain of the task required. The two number lines illustrate different ways of thinking about the problem. The first number line reflects an additive approach: begin with the low number, then skip-count by convenient intervals and then count on by 5 until reaching 67. The second number line reflects a subtractive approach: begin with the large number, then skip-count backwards and then count back by 2 until reaching 25. *Teaching Strategy:* Pause at this question to allow students time to discuss these two ways of solving the problem as well as methods they may have developed on their own.

An Example of Student Work

3a) What is the total when you start with 121 and add 40? _____
3b) What would your total be if you started with 121 and added 42? _____
3c) What if you start with 121 and add 38? _____

> If you know that the first problem is 161, then the rest are easy because 42 is just 2 more than 40, so add 2 to equal 163. Then do the opposite because 38 is 2 less than 40, so subtract 2 from 161 to get 159.

CONCEPT DEVELOPMENT (Page 8)

INTRODUCE THE CONCEPT

ASSESS STUDENTS' PRIOR KNOWLEDGE
Draw a horizontal number line on the board with no reference marks or numbers.

Ask:
There are 18 crayons in one box and 24 crayons in another box. How can I use a number line to find how many crayons are in both boxes?

Listen for:
- Draw a point for 18 on the number line.
- You can make 2 skips of 10 from 18 to the right of 18. That will add 20 to 18 to get you to 38.
- Then you can make a skip of 4 because 20 + 4 = 24. That will get you to 52.

MODEL MATHEMATICAL THINKING
Then model the thinking for another example. Ask, *Suppose I have 52 crayons and I give away 18 of them. How can I use a number line to find how many crayons I have left?*

Talk Through the Thinking:
I had 52 crayons, so I'll draw a point at 52. Since I gave away 18 crayons, I'll wind up with fewer crayons than when I started. So the number I have left will be less than 52, and when I skip-jump, I have to skip to the left to get a smaller number. Let's try it: 10 less than 52 is 42. I can't count back another ten because that would be a total of 20. So I'll try 5 and then 3, for a count of 8; 5 less than 42 is 37 and 3 less than 37 is 34. So if I give away 18 crayons, I'll have 34 left.

Ask:
Suppose I gave away 24 crayons instead of 18. How many would I have left? How do you know?

Listen for:
(An intuitive understanding that if $a + b = c$, then $c - a = b$ and $c - b = a$)
- You would have 18 crayons left.
- If two numbers have a total of 52, then if you subtract one of the numbers from 52 the answer is the other number.

LAUNCH THE PROBLEM SOLVING

Have students work individually to solve the problems on page 8. As they work, you may want to circulate and monitor their work. As they finish each problem, have them compare and discuss their answers with a partner. Then have each pair share their answers in a class discussion of the problem. Refer to the **Teacher Notes: Student Page 8** for more specific ideas about the problems on this page.

As students work and report their conclusions, focus on these issues:

Help Make Connections – If students have been successful completing number sentences for their number-line manipulations in previous problems, help them understand that the number sentences on this page take the same form.

Validate Alternate Representations – If students use different representations to solve problems 2 and 3, have them discuss whether and why each representation is correct.

Allow Waiting Time – When students struggle to explain their thinking, allow them ample time to organize their thoughts. This is particularly important when students discuss problem 4.

The Number Line *Teacher Edition*

Student Page 8: Problems and Potential Answers

Section B: Using the Number Line for Addition and Subtraction Set 2

Create number lines and skip patterns to solve the following problems.

5. There are 38 species of beetles that live in Colorado. There are another 15 species of beetles that live in Kansas. How many different species of beetles live in both states? Write a number sentence for this problem: 38 + 15 = 53

6. There were 86 packs of gum in the school store on Monday morning. On Friday, there were 44 left. How many were sold during the week? Write a number sentence: 86 - 42 = 44

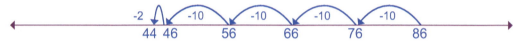

7. Kelli bought 68 red bricks for her sidewalk and another 43 grey bricks for her garden. How many **more red bricks** does she have than grey bricks? Write a number sentence: 43 + 25 = 68

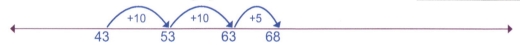

8. Solve the following problem in **three ways**. Use a different skip counting pattern for each method, and draw each method on a number line.

   East middle school had 18 students from 8th grade on the track team, and 75 students from 7th grade on the team. How many 8th and 7th grade students in all are on the track team?

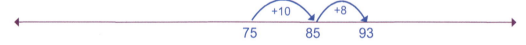

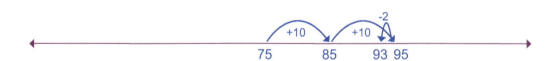

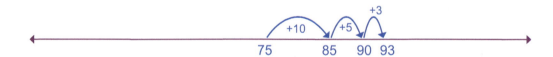

8 Book 1: *The Number Line*

TEACHER NOTES: STUDENT PAGE 8

Page 8 provides students with several chances to practice informal strategies for addition and subtraction that utilize counting on and skip-counting on the number line. The problems are presented in contexts that will elicit different thinking strategies. For problem 5, students will likely read the problem as a straightforward addition problem with the result unknown. Problem 6 may cause students to think subtraction, given that the total is known (86 packs of gum) but the change is unknown. In problem 7, students are asked to compare two quantities. The point is to make sure that students recognize that simple addition and subtraction problems come in different forms and can be solved using different strategies. Not every addition problem needs to be in the form 21 + 13 = ? Problems in the real world rarely present themselves in such a simple format. As teachers, we must recognize this fact and make sure we help students learn to read problem contexts carefully both in and out of class and apply appropriate solution strategies. *Teaching Strategy:* Lastly, you need to emphasize the inverse relationship between addition and subtraction and teach the concepts simultaneously. This is the power of the number line as a computational tool. When students are skipping in both directions along the number line, it is not important that they think about what operation they are performing. It is important that they are reasoning wisely as they explore relationships between numbers. Be sure students give thought to the number sentences that accompany each problem. These number sentences help students understand the underlying number relationships and structures in addition and subtraction problems.

Problem 5: This is a combining problem with the result unknown. *Watch for:* Students will likely start with 38, then skip-count by 10s, and then count on an additional 5 to reach an answer of 53.

Problem 6: Problem 6 is part-part-whole with the change unknown. This problem may feel like a subtraction problem to students, and can be solved by subtraction, but it can also be solved by addition by starting at 44 and then skip-counting and counting on until reaching a target of 86. *Teaching Strategy:* Be sure to allow students to share their solution strategies with each other.

Problem 7: This problem is a comparison problem and can be solved in different ways: by adding on from 43 or subtracting from 68.

Problem 8: Problem 8 asks students to think about an addition problem in at least three different ways. This is a great problem to elicit the thinking strategies of students. Encourage dialogue about these various strategies. *Watch for:* Students should add on from both the smaller starting number (18) and the larger number (75). It is hoped that with repeated experiences, students will begin to recognize that using the larger number as a starting point is a good strategy to consider. For many students, the cognitive challenge of adding 18, especially when computing mentally, will be perceived to be significantly less than adding on 75. This is particularly true if students are already comfortable adding 18 by adding 20 and then subtracting 2. *Teaching Strategy:* After students finish problem 8, it would be a good time to pause and consider the differences between the mental, skip-counting computations, and strategies emphasized in the exercises with the more traditional, algorithmic approach to problems of this kind. Problem 8, if solved traditionally, would look something like this:

$$\begin{array}{r} \overset{1}{1}8 \\ + 75 \\ \hline 93 \end{array}$$

Solving the problem in the traditional manner requires a regrouping process that many students do not fully understand. *Teaching Strategy:* It would be an excellent extension of this problem to try to illustrate and model the traditional addition algorithm for it on the number line. In this way you might be able to help your students understand what it means to regroup when they add. This is not an immediately transparent process.

CONCEPT DEVELOPMENT (Pages 9–10)

INTRODUCE THE CONCEPT

ASSESS STUDENTS' PRIOR KNOWLEDGE
Draw a number line on the board with no reference marks or numbers.

Ask:
How can I use skip-counting to get from 30 to 141 on the number line?

Listen for:
(Students to suggest that you can begin skipping in increments greater than 10)
- First, draw a point for 30 on the number line.
- You can then skip by 10 to 140 and then skip 1 to get to 141.
- You can then skip by 100 and one 10s and then 1.

MODEL MATHEMATICAL THINKING
Then model the thinking for another example by asking, How can I get from 20 to 99 using skip-jumps of 1, 10, and 100 only and using as few jumps as possible?

Talk Through the Thinking:
I can start with increments of 10 and then use 1s: 20, 30, 40, 50, 60, 70, 80, 90, 91, 92, 93, 94, 95, 96, 97, 98, 99. That's 16 skip-jumps in all. What would happen if I start with a skip-jump of 100? Let's try it: 20, 120. Now I can work backwards: 120, 110, 100. Now I can count back 1 to get to 99. That's only 4 skip-jumps.

Ask:
Suppose the starting number were 80 instead of 20 and the ending number were 95 instead of 99. Would I use more or fewer skip-jumps by starting with an increment of 100 or of 10? Explain.

Listen for:
- If you start with 10, you would use 1 skip of 10 and 5 skips of 1 for a total of 7 skip-jumps.
- If you start with 100, you would use 1 skip of 100 and then 9 skips of 10 to get back to 100. Then you would use 5 skips of 1 to get back to 95 for a total of 16 skip-jumps.

LAUNCH THE PROBLEM SOLVING

Have students work individually to solve the problems on page 9. As they work, you may want to circulate and monitor their work. As they finish each problem, have them compare and discuss their answers with a partner. Then have each pair share their answers in a class discussion of the problem. Refer to the **Teacher Notes: Student Page 9** for more specific ideas about the problems on this page.

As students work and report their conclusions, focus on these issues:

Facilitate Students' Thinking – When students approach a new problem, suggest that they think about the size of the beginning and ending numbers before beginning their skip trip.

Allow Trial-and-Error – Some students may need to try more than once to find the fewest possible skip-jumps on the number line.

Allow Waiting Time – When students struggle to explain their thinking, allow them ample time to organize their thoughts.

Encourage Language Development – The beginning of this lesson would be a good time to revisit key vocabulary for this set of problems including: Point, multiple, and skip-count.

Student Page 9: Problems and Potential Answers

Section B: Using the Number Line for Addition and Subtraction — Set 3

SKIP JUMPS

Try to get to the target number with as few skip jumps as you can. You may only make skip jumps of 1, 10, or 100. Illustrate your strategies on the number lines. It may take you two tries!

1. **EXAMPLE:** Go from 0 to 23 in the fewest skip jumps possible.

   How many skips?

   5

2. Go from 0 to 53 in the fewest skip jumps possible.

   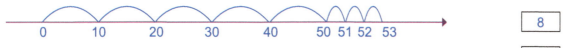

   8

3. Go from 35 to 77 in the fewest skip jumps possible.

   6

4. Go from 108 to 240 in the fewest skip jumps possible.

   6

5. Go from 46 to 163 in the fewest skip jumps possible.

   6

6. Go from 986 to 1200 in the fewest skip jumps possible.

   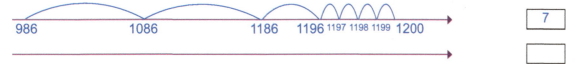

   7

7. Go from 5 to 93 in the fewest skip jumps possible.

   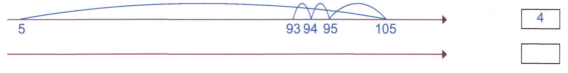

   4

Book 1: *The Number Line* 9

TEACHER NOTES: STUDENT PAGE 9

Students typically enjoy skip-jumping. After they understand the process, they may be encouraged to create their own skip-jump parameters and share them with peers. As students try to formulate problems with solutions that their peers might overlook, they will be enhancing their own number sense and developing continued expertise and confidence with the number line.

For these problems, be sure that students understand the intent of the activity. *Watch for:* Students are to begin at the starting point and use skips of 1, 10, and/or 100 to arrive at the target in as few skips as possible. Do not over-prepare students for these problems. Students will learn the most from the problems as they discuss their strategies and compare them with those of their peers. For example, without peer discussion some students will not immediately consider that it could be more efficient to skip beyond the target and then backtrack. This is exemplified in problem 7. *Teaching Strategy:* When students complete these problems, encourage them to formulate new problems to be solved by their peers.

CONTINUE THE PROBLEM SOLVING

Have students work individually to solve the problems on page 10. As they work, you may want to circulate and monitor their work. After students complete the page, have them compare and discuss their answers with a partner. Then have each pair share their answers in a class discussion of the problem. Refer to the **Teacher Notes: Student Page 10** for more specific ideas about the problems on this page.

As students work and report their conclusions, focus on these issues:

Validate Representations – When several students use different skip patterns to mark the number lines in problems 1 and 2, have them share and discuss their solutions to determine whether all are correct.

Allow Waiting Time – When students struggle to explain their thinking, be sure to allow them at least 20 seconds to organize their thoughts (this may feel like a long time).

Help Make Connections – Remind students of the strategies they have used before to represent a real-world problem on a number line. This may help them understand how to represent these problems.

TEACHER NOTES: STUDENT PAGE 10

Problems 1–2: These problems give students more practice with the concept of change unknown, this time using larger numbers. *Teaching Strategy:* Emphasize the multiple routes students might take to find to the solution.

Problem 3: This problem contains a powerful teaching strategy: asking students to first understand and then compare and explain the thinking of others.

Student Page 10: Problems and Potential Answers

Section B: Using the Number Line for Addition and Subtraction Set 4

Create number lines and skip counting patterns to solve the following problems.

1. Joel is reading a book with 246 pages. He has already read 127. How many more pages does he need to read to finish the book? **119 pages**

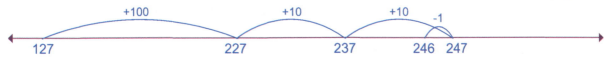

2. Jon had **$396**. He spent **$99** on a new bicycle. How much money does he have left? **$297 left**

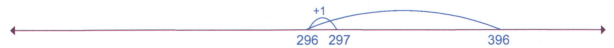

3. The following 3 number lines were drawn by students as they tried to figure out the problem below. Study each number line. Be prepared to explain the process used for each solution strategy. Each strategy starts skipping from the number 57.

   The Problem: Kerri was trying to break her record for juggling a soccer ball. On her first attempt, she juggled the ball 57 times before it hit the ground. On her second attempt, she only got 29 juggles. Combining both her first and second attempts, how many times did she juggle the ball?

Solution #1
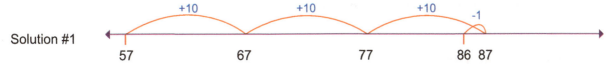

Solution #2
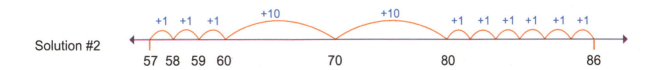

Solution #3
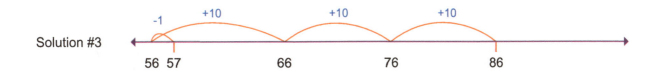

Question: Which of these methods would you choose if you had to do this problem mentally? Explain.
(Responses will vary.)

10 Book 1: *The Number Line*

CONCEPT DEVELOPMENT (Page 11)

INTRODUCE THE CONCEPT

ASSESS STUDENTS' PRIOR KNOWLEDGE

Draw a number line on the board with no reference marks or numbers. Remind students that they have already learned how to represent word problems on a number line.

Ask:
Silas started his stamp collection with 32 stamps. Then he was given 55 more stamps. How can I use a number line to find how many stamps he has now? What number sentence can I write to show how many stamps Silas has now?

Listen for:
(Indications that students understand this is an addition problem)
- First, draw a point for 32 on the number line.
- Adding 55 is five skips of 10 and one skip of 5. So starting with 32 and moving to the right, make those skips on the number line.
- You will end up at 87; 32 + 55 = 87. Silas has 87 stamps now.

MODEL MATHEMATICAL THINKING

Then model the thinking for another example by posing this problem and drawing the solutions below on the board. *Janine has already read 157 pages of a chapter book that is 215 pages long. How many more pages does Janine have to read to finish the book?*

Talk Through the Thinking:
For the first number line, I started at 157, the number of pages Janine has already read. Then skipped 50 to get to 207 because 157 + 50 = 207. Next I skipped 5 to get to 212. Finally I skipped by 1s three times to get to 215, the total number of pages in the book. The skips are 50 + 5 + 1 + 1 + 1, or 58. Janine has to read 58 more pages to finish the book.

Ask:
The second number line also represents the problem. How would you explain what I did on this number line and how it answers the same question?

Listen for:
- You started at 157. Then you skipped back by 2 to 155.
- From 155, you skipped 50 to get to 205. Then you skipped 10 to get to 215.
- The skips to the right can be written as 50 + 10 = 60. The skip to the left stands for -2. So 60 − 2 = 58.

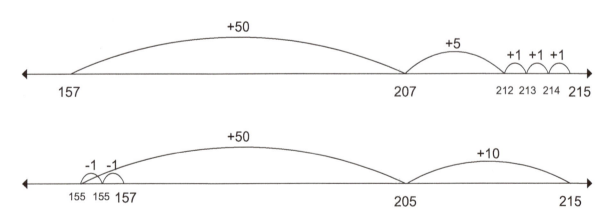

44 The Number Line *Teacher Edition*

LAUNCH THE PROBLEM SOLVING

Have students work individually to solve the problems on page 11. As they work, you may want to circulate and monitor their work. As they finish each problem, have them compare and discuss their answers with a partner. Then have each pair share their answers in a class discussion of the problem. Refer to the **Teacher Notes: Student Page 11** for more specific ideas about the problems on this page.

As students work and report their conclusions, focus on these issues:

Encourage Language Development – Encourage students to use directional terms, e.g., forward or backward on the number line, as well as mathematical terms when analyzing student solutions #1 and #2. Listening to the verbal explanations of students' thinking on these problems can be an excellent opportunity for formative assessment within this section of problems.

Facilitate Students' Thinking – Remind students that they can break apart larger numbers by place value. For example, 123 can be broken apart as 100 + 20 + 3.

Student Page 11: Problems and Potential Answers

Section B: Using the Number Line for Addition and Subtraction Set 4

The Problem

In two days, Thursday and Friday, the student council sold a total of $506 in raffle tickets for a fundraiser. On Thursday they sold $270 in raffle tickets. How much did they sell on Friday?

4. **a)** Use a number line to help you solve this problem.

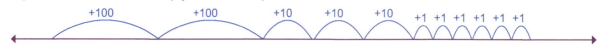

   b) Write a number sentence for this problem.   270 + 236 = 506

5. **Explain** how the number-line diagrams below were used by two students to solve this problem:

   Jon needed $175 to buy a new tool for his workshop. He had $85 in the bank, and he earned another $90 mowing lawns all summer. Does he have enough money to buy the new tool?

Student Solution #1

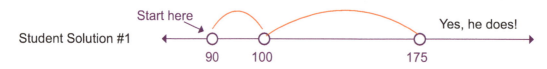

Explain this student's thinking: Starting at 90, the first skip is +10 and the next skip is +75. These two skips total + 85, which is how much Jon had in the bank. 90 + 85 = 175

Example #2

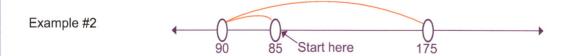

Explain this student's thinking: Starting at 85, the first skip is -10 and the next skip is +100. These two skips total + 90, which is how much Jon earned mowing lawns. 85 + 90 = 175

6. **Explain** how the skip-diagrams below were used to solve the following problem: 428 + 571 = ?

a) 428 ... 928 ... 998 ... 999   Breakdown 428 and 571 into parts

b) 400 ... 900 ... 920 ... 990 ... 998 ... 999   Breakdown 428 and 571 into parts

TEACHER NOTES: STUDENT PAGE 11

Problem 4: This problem provides another example of a change unknown problem. Students may solve this in various ways. *Watch for:* Check to see whether students' number sentences match their visual representational strategies on the number line.

Problem 5: Problem 5 asks students to analyze and decipher the work of others. Most students over the years have been conditioned to work math problems as they read, from left to right. Hence, while Example #1 illustrates the strategy students will be most comfortable explaining and using, Example #2 shows a new kind of thinking for some students. It requires students to recognize that a skip-jump of 90 is close to a skip-jump of 100. So by first jumping back on the number line by a distance of 10, the student is then able to jump forward by an easily recognized interval of 100. *Teaching Strategy:* Be sure to have students discuss the differences in these two strategies for the same problem.

Problem 6: Problem 6 requires students to think about the decomposition of numbers. When adding 571 to a known quantity, for example, one could decompose 571 into three numbers that are more easily manipulated: 500, 70, and 1. In the first solution, a decomposed 571 is added (in parts) to the existing quantity of 428. In the second solution, both 428 and 571 have been decomposed. Once broken into their respective smaller parts, the two numbers are added in pieces: first the hundreds, then the tens, and finally the ones. *Teaching Strategy:* This problem is an excellent candidate for using base-10 block manipulatives because it is a rather typical problem for their use. What makes problem 6 unique in this context is the way in which students might connect the use of base-10 blocks to the number line.

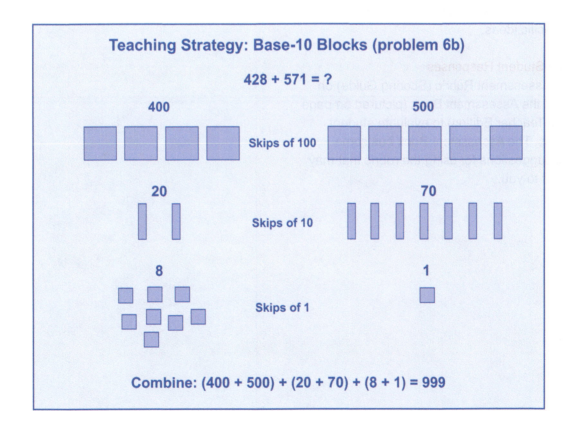

SECTION B ASSESSMENT (PAGE 12)

LAUNCH THE ASSESSMENT

Have students turn to the Section B Assessment, page 12. An additional copy is found on page 4 of the Assessment Book. Have students work individually to solve the problems and write their explanations. As they work, circulate to be sure students understand what they need for each problem. Be sure that students are completing each part of the problem. For example, in each part of problem 1, students need to choose a multiple (or multiples) by which to skip-count, explain their thinking, and complete a number sentence. You may find it helpful to read the directions for all the problems before students begin, discussing the types of responses they need to make for each problem.

Encourage students to use whatever space they need to explain their thinking. If the space on the page is inadequate, they should use an additional sheet of paper or use the back of the page.

Refer to the **Teacher Notes: Student Page 12** for more specific ideas.

Evaluate Student Responses

Use the Assessment Rubric (Scoring Guide) on page 3 of the Assessment Book (pictured on page 51 of the Teacher Edition) to evaluate student responses. The Assessment Book has some general suggestions for using the rubric that may be helpful to you.

Student Page 12: Problems and Potential Answers

Section B: Problems for Assessment

1. Use the number line and skip counting to fill in the box to make the following number sentences true.

   a) 48 + 93 = 141

   Explain your thinking: _Responses will vary._ _____

   _____

   b) 84 - 57 = 27

   Explain your thinking: _Responses will vary._ _____

   _____

   c) 78 + 158 = 236

   Explain your thinking: _Responses will vary._ _____

   _____

   d) 112 - 73 = 39

   Explain your thinking: _Responses will vary._ _____

   _____

2. Joel went hiking to the top of a large mountain. He started climbing at an elevation of 9000 feet above sea level. He climbed for two miles to the top of a ridge, which was at 11,500 feet of elevation. The trail then went downhill for 1 mile to the bottom of a valley at 11,000 feet of elevation. The trail then went up steeply again for the last 4 miles to the top of the mountain at 14,000 feet! How many **total feet of elevation** did Joel have to climb during the hike to the top? Use a number line and skip jumps to help find your answer.

   + 2500   + 3000

   Joel's Hike

   11,500 ft.

   11,000 ft.

   Start: 9000 ft.

   Explain your thinking: _2500 + 3000 = 5500 feet of elevation_ _____

   _____

12 Book 1: *The Number Line*

TEACHER NOTES: ASSESSMENT PROBLEMS SECTION B

Problem 1: The four problems on this page are structured to elicit different strategies and thinking. *Watch for:* By this point in the unit, you should be seeing students use a variety of strategies and be comfortable with the number line. The important thing to assess in these problems is the explanations that students give. Students who have developed a rich understanding of numbers and the use of the number line will evidence these strengths by using different strategies for each problem. Also students should be gravitating toward more efficient and elegant strategies. For example, see the following three responses to an addition problem:

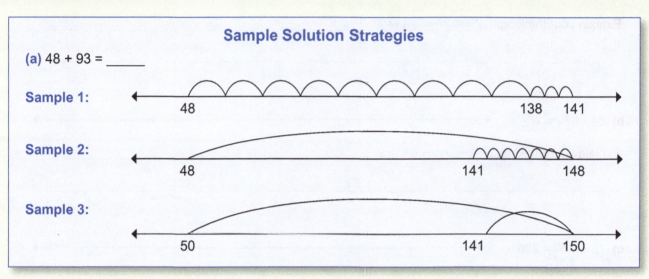

These three solution strategies illustrate growing sophistication. Sample 1 skipped by 10, nine times and then skipped by 1 three more times. This left-to-right strategy certainly works, but is less efficient (and indicates a more fragile number sense) than the third solution. In the third solution, the student would recognize that 48 is close to 50 (subtract 2 later) and 93 is close to 100 (subtract 7 later). By adding 50 and 100, the student needs only to subtract 7 from the total. *Watch for:* As you assess students on these problems, look for these kinds of variations in the strategies students may be using.

Problem 2: This problem is sure to cause hesitation for many students. In addition to being challenging conceptually, there is a large amount of text in the problem that teachers may wish to preview with students. One of the questions at the heart of problem 2 is the notion of elevation gain. On the one hand, students might interpret this problem to mean that they should subtract the starting elevation (9000 feet) from the ending elevation (14,000 feet), for a total net gain of 5000 feet. For students who may have gone hiking, however, it may mean something entirely different. Certainly in the course of a 6-mile hike, one would likely have to regain elevation that may have been lost while hiking down hill. In that sense, one would have to climb more than a total of 5000 feet over the course of the hike. In this problem, the hiker loses 500 feet of elevation and will need to make up the lost feet on the way to the top, resulting in a total of 5500 feet that must be climbed. This tension should be left unresolved at the beginning of the problem, although it is vitally important that you help students become familiar with the context, sometimes you walk uphill, sometimes downhill, and this problem is concerned with how many feet of uphill are required on this trail. Some students will recognize that a different interpretation of elevation gain will result in a different final answer. Also be aware that some students may confuse miles traveled with elevation gain. Problem 2 will therefore spark good discussion if students are allowed to argue from their own perspectives. It is important to foster debate because, in participating, students will necessarily be juggling the different totals as they try to reconcile their mental calculations of the elevation gain with its various other interpretations.

SCORING GUIDE BOOK 1: THE NUMBER LINE

Section B Assessment
For Use With: Student Book Page 12

PROBLEM DESCRIPTION	SCORING: WHAT TO LOOK FOR	SCORE AND COMMENTS
Problem 1 (a-d) Use a number line to represent addition and subtraction problems. Level 2: Tool Use	Do students: • Find the correct addition/subtraction facts? • Understand the use of skip-counting? • Demonstrate facility skipping in various intervals? • Correctly represent skip-counting on the number line?	Suggested 2 points per problem Points:_____ of 8
Problem 2 Use a number line to represent a real-world context (elevation gain). Level 3: Connection and Application	Do students: • Have an understanding of the context? • Appropriately apply the number line? • Explain the representation of the context on the number line?	 Points:_____ of 4

TOTAL POINTS:_____ OF 12

The Number Line *Teacher Edition*

Section C: Using the Number Line for Multiplication and Division

SECTION C PLANNER

THE MATHEMATICS CONTENT AND GOALS

GOALS
Students will:
- Develop the double number line as a strategy for comparing sets of objects.
- Use the double number line to develop the ratio table.
- Use the ratio table to think multiplicatively.
- Use the ratio table to solve multiplication and division problems.

LANGUAGE DEVELOPMENT
Mathematical language in this section includes:

Ratio Table: The ratio table is a very powerful tool, an idea that students should realize. Simply put, a ratio table contains columns that might be thought of as equivalent fractions. That is, each column might be thought of as a ratio between the top row and the bottom row, and every column maintains the same ratio between the top and bottom rows. Specifically, a table in which the ratio between the numbers in one column is the same for every column.

Ratio: In order to understand ratio tables, it is essential to understand the idea of a ratio. Simply put, a ratio is a fraction. Many young students will think of a fraction as a quantity, such as 2/3 of the pizza, or 1/2 of a dollar. With ratios, however, we are concerned with a slightly nuanced understanding in which we compare the number of elements in the numerator with the number of elements in the denominator. As a fraction 2/3 might mean a large slice of pizza for one person, but when using 2/3 in terms of a ratio, we are concerned that, for every 2 parts in the numerator, there are 3 parts in the denominator. So a ratio is used to identify a preserved relationship between two quantities. We might say, "For every one of these, we have two of these." It is this proportional reasoning that is important for students to comprehend.

Multiple: As noted in earlier sections, a multiple is a fixed increment that students may use to partition a number line, or move along a number line in equal steps. Another definition of multiple is the product of the given number and another number.

Double Number Line: In this section students are introduced to an important concept that will become central in other books in this series. The Double Number Line is a number line that has two scales that are set opposite one another to compare two different measures (or scales) of one variable. For example, 75 pennies might be thought of as 75 cents, 75%, or ¾ of a dollar. We can use a double number line to represent these various conceptions of 75 cents, perhaps as a fraction (3/4) on the top of a number line, and as a decimal (0.75) on the bottom of the number line.

PACING

The projected pacing for this unit is 4–7 class periods (based on a 45 minute period).

52   The Number Line *Teacher Edition*

PROBLEM SETS: OVERVIEW

The ratio table is a flexible tool that students can use to solve a variety of problems. Throughout this section, students will build on the additive strategies they learned in Sections A and B as they organize ratios in a table. Intuitive strategies such as skip-counting, doubling, and halving will be helpful in this section. The development of the ratio table in this unit is important in that it will be revisited in subsequent chapters and used for more complex work with ratios, fractions, percents, and decimals.

Set 1 (p. 13; problems 1–5)
These problems develop the notion of a double number line, a number line that has two scales. Examples that will populate this section are introduced here in which particular items are bundled or grouped. Help students make the transition in the graphical representations between problems 1 and 2. While problem 1 uses the familiar number line, problem 2 transitions to the use of the ratio table. Problem 4 is also an important linking context between the two models. Problem 5 points to the kind of thinking the students will do by the end of this unit: using the ratio table (and ratios themselves) to multiply and divide.

Set 2 (p. 14; problems 1–2)
These problems aid students in understanding the nature of multiples and common multiples. Help students make the connection between the skip-counting strategies used earlier and the use of multiples in this context. Problems 1d and 2c are particularly important because they introduce the idea of common multiples. Sometimes common multiples are referred to as number families. In any event, it is important to help children recognize these number patterns and how they can be modeled on the number line.

Set 3 (p. 15; problems 1–2)
The problems on page 15 build on the concepts developed in the previous two sets of problems. Connecting back to Set 1, students are making use of a double number line (precursor to the ratio table) to partition a number of objects into a given number of groups. As well, students are doing so based on their explorations of multiples from the problems in Set 2. The double number lines are used, therefore, to illustrate the ratios that are preserved when partitioning a given number of objects by one of its factors (e.g., divide 24 objects into a=8 groups: 8 is a factor of 24 → 8 × 3 = 24).

Set 4 (pp. 16–17; problems 1–5)
This set of problems extends the thinking of students in important ways. In this set, students use ratio tables to solve several problems in different problem contexts, which include various representations of multiplication and division, an important consideration. Students should not only be able to use models to compute, but also recognize when a given operation is needed. Again, it is most important for the teacher to pause along the way to stress the many ways in which ratio tables can be used to help students make sense of problem contexts. As students examine the thinking and ratio tables of their peers, they will be developing their own intuitions about numbers and number operations. Through these exercises, students should start being aware that ratio tables can be used flexibly. That is, different students might use different combinations in a ratio table that are unique to them and yet result in the same final answer. The problems in Set 4 build on previous work with multiples, skip-counting, and halving, and at the same time encourage students to use the ratio tables as efficiently as possible, but not to the sacrifice of accuracy. Students should be reminded to do as much of this work mentally as possible. Problem 5 is different from the others in that it asks students to work backwards. Instead of being given the starting ratio, students must infer that information from the data in the table. This problem asks students once again to compare solution strategies. Pause long enough here for students to appreciate the thinking of their peers.

Set 5 (p. 18; problem 1)
What should be emerging in the thinking of students at this point is that with the use of ratio tables, there are always several paths to the solution of any given problem. The primary intent of this section is to reinforce that idea. It cannot be stated strongly enough that in this section students must be allowed to discuss these varied approaches, appreciating the mathematical steps and thinking that make one strategy distinct from another. Students may wish to identify particular strategies by name. For example, Will's method uses

a doubling strategy; Catherine's method includes multiplication by 10 and proportional addition. Students might wish to recognize and identify other common strategies such as halving, and multiplying by 5. If given time to do so, students will engage in a good discussion of problem 1d as they defend their own strategies when compared to those of their peers.

CONCEPT DEVELOPMENT (Page 13)

INTRODUCE THE CONCEPT

ASSESS STUDENTS' PRIOR KNOWLEDGE
Draw this table on the board:

1	2	3	4	5
2	4	6	8	10

Ask:
What patterns can you see in the table? How is each number in the bottom row related to the number just above it?

Listen for:
(Any and all patterns students may see)
- The numbers in the top row are the counting numbers from 1 to 5.
- The numbers in the bottom row are all the even numbers in order from 2 to 10.
- Each number in the bottom row is double the number above it.

MODEL MATHEMATICAL THINKING
Draw this double number line on the board:

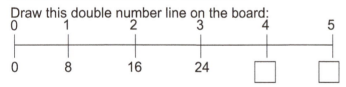

Explain: This is a double number line. A double number line is a number line that has two scales. The top scale stands for the number of crayon boxes. The bottom scale stands for the number of crayons. Ask: How many crayons would there be in 4 boxes? 5 boxes?

Talk Through the Thinking
If I look at the numbers 1 and 2 on top scale and then directly below it, I see that there are 8 crayons in one box and 16 crayons in 2 boxes. If I multiply 1 × 8, the answer is 8, and if I multiply 2 × 8 the answer is 16. Let's check with 3: 3 × 8 = 24. That's the same number on the bottom scale. So I'll multiply 4 × 8 to find there are 32 crayons in 4 boxes. Then I'll multiply 5 × 8 to find there are 40 crayons in 5 boxes.

Explain that you can show the same information in a table called a ratio table. Then draw this ratio table on the board:

Boxes	0	1	2	3	4	5	6
Crayons	0	8	16	24	32	40	

Ask:
How many crayons would there be in 6 boxes? How do you know?

Listen for:
- There would be 48 crayons in 6 boxes.
- 6 times 8 equals 48.

LAUNCH THE PROBLEM SOLVING

Have students work individually to solve the problems on page 13. You may wish to circulate and monitor their work and recorded answers. As they finish each problem, have students compare and discuss their answers with a partner. Then have each pair share their conclusions in a class discussion of the problem. Refer to the **Teacher Notes: Student Page 13** for more specific ideas about the problems on this page.

As students work and report their conclusions, focus on these issues:

Help Make Connections – If students have difficulty thinking of the multiplication, remind them that they can skip-count by the given intervals in both the double number line and the ratio table.

Allow Waiting Time – When students struggle to explain their thoughts, be sure to allow ample time for them to organize their thoughts.

Encourage Language Development – Be sure check for students' understanding of the definition of a double number line.

Student Page 13: Problems and Potential Answers

Section C: Using the Number Line for Multiplication and Division — Set 1

1. There are 4 baseball cards in every pack of bubble gum. Use the double number line below to list the number of cards you will receive if you buy 2 packs of gum, 3 packs of gum, 4 packs of gum, etc. Complete your double number line up to 10 packs of gum.

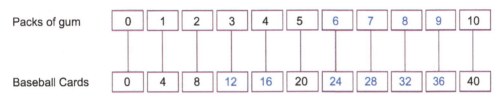

2. The number line can be changed into a math tool called the *ratio table*. Use the ratio table below to illustrate how many baseball cards are in various packs of bubble gum. Fill in the empty boxes.

Packs of gum	0	1	2	3	4	5	6	7	8	9	10	11	12	13
Baseball cards	0	4	8	12	16	20	24	28	32	36	40	44	48	52

3. There are 24 tennis balls in 4 containers. Use the ratio table below to determine how many balls are in 1 container, 2 containers, and so on.

Containers	0	1	2	3	4	5	6	7	8	9	10
Tennis balls	0	6	12	18	24	30	36	42	48	54	60

4. Each pizza has 8 slices. Use the double number line below to determine the number of slices in 2, 4, 8 and 12 pizzas.

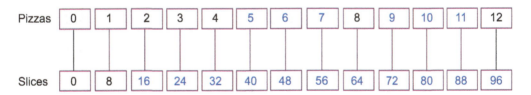

5. Eggs are usually sold in cartons that hold 1 dozen eggs. Use the table below to list the number of eggs that can be found in different numbers of cartons.

Containers	0	1	2	3	4	5	10
Eggs	0	12	24	36	48	60	120

Question: Once you know how many eggs are in 5 cartons, is it easy to determine how many eggs will be in 10 cartons without extending the number line (ratio table) all the way to 10? Please explain.

Explain your strategy: Double the number of eggs in 5 cartons to get the number of eggs in 10 cartons.

TEACHER NOTES: STUDENT PAGE 13

Problems 1–4: The first four problems introduce the double number line and the representation of the same information in a ratio table. The double number line is one line upon which two different scales are placed. In problem 1, the numbers below the line represent the total number of baseball cards. The numbers above the line represent the total number of packs of gum. At any point on the line, one could answer one of two questions: How many packs? How many cards? This use of two scales with one number line is an extremely powerful learning tool, one that will be revisited throughout this textbook series. One can imagine placing decimals on the bottom and fractional representations of the same quantity on top of the same line.

The ratio table is a tool that helps students organize these relationships in a meaningful way. As the problems in this section become more complicated, students will learn to manipulate the ratio table quickly and effectively. *Teaching Strategy:* For these first four problems, however, it is all right for students to simply expand the respective sides of the number line by using the provided intervals.

Problem 5: This is an important problem. It hints at the strategies students will use in subsequent problems. Students are asked to use proportional reasoning to extend the ratio table to a desired endpoint without filling in each step along the way as in the previous problems. That is, there is a gap in the ratio table between 5 and 10. This gap is where the ratio table diverges from the number line. With a ratio table, we are not bound to the physical intervals that are required for the number line. Rather, we can use the ratio table flexibly to make mental calculations based on already known ratios. In this case, if students know that there are 60 eggs in 5 cartons of one dozen each, then they can deduce that doubling the number of cartons from 5 to 10 will result in a doubling of the number of eggs from 60 to 120. See the example of student thinking below that illustrates this use of proportional reasoning. Encourage similar thinking among your students.

An Example of Student Thinking

If you would have to add 12 every time to get to 10 cartons, that would be a pain because adding by 12 isn't always easy. But if you do it this way it is easy. Once you get to half cartons, then you just times the eggs by 2. So 120 eggs.

CONCEPT DEVELOPMENT (Pages 14–15)

INTRODUCE THE CONCEPT

ASSESS STUDENTS' PRIOR KNOWLEDGE
Draw a number line from 0 to 24 on the board, and mark and label it in increments of 3. Explain that a multiple of a number is the product of that number and another number, including itself.

Ask:
What are the multiples of 3 on this number line? If you extend the number line, what would be the next two multiples of 3?

Listen for:
- 0, 3, 6, 9, 12, 15, 18, 21, 24
- 27, 30

MODEL MATHEMATICAL THINKING
Then draw another number line below the first, and mark and label it in increments of 4. Ask: *What are the multiples of 4 on this number line? Besides zero, what multiples do 3 and 4 have in common?*

Talk Through the Thinking
When we talked about multiples of 3, I noticed that they are all the numbers I could find by skip-counting by 3s, starting with zero. So let's try starting with zero and skip-counting by 4s to 24: 0, 4, 8, 12, 16, 20, 24. Which of these numbers is also a multiple of 3? I won't count the zero. The numbers 4 and 8 are not multiples of 3. The number 12 is, but not 16 or 20. The number 24 is also a multiple of 3 and 4. So the multiples on these number lines that 3 and 4 have in common, or common multiples, are 12 and 24.

Ask:
What if we drew a number line from zero to 24 and skip-counted by 2s. What would be the multiples of 2? Besides zero, what would be the common multiples of 2 and 3? 2 and 4? 2, 3, and 4?

Listen for:
- Some multiples of 2 are 0, 2, 4, 6, 8, 10, 12, 14, 16, 18, 20, 22, and 24.
- Some common multiples of 2 and 3 are 6, 12, 18, and 24.
- Some common multiples of 2 and 4 are 4, 8, 12, 16, 20, and 24.
- Some common multiples of 2, 3, and 4 are 12 and 24.

LAUNCH THE PROBLEM SOLVING

Have students work individually to solve the problems on page 14. You may wish to circulate and monitor their work and recorded answers. As they finish each problem, have students compare and discuss their answers with a partner. Then have each pair share their conclusions in a class discussion of the problem. Refer to the **Teacher Notes: Student Page 14** for more specific ideas about the problems on this page.

As students work and report their conclusions, focus on these issues:

Help Make Connections – Remind students that one way to find the multiples of a number is to skip-count by that number.

Look for Misconceptions – When students notice that, for example, all the multiples of 6 are also multiples of 3, caution them that the reverse is not true; all the multiples of 3 are not multiples of 6. Have students discuss why this is so.

The Number Line Teacher Edition

Student Page 14: Problems and Potential Answers

Section C: Using the Number Line for Multiplication and Division   Set 2

Skip counting with the number line can help us recognize multiples of numbers. On the following number line, we can see what happens when we skip count by 3's. These numbers are called **multiples of 3**.

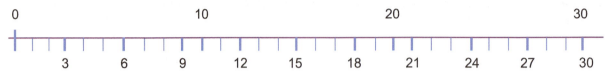

1. a) Graph the **multiples of 2** on the number line below.

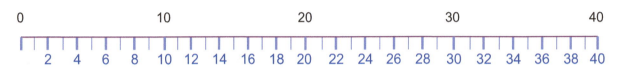

b) Graph the **multiples of 4** on the number line below.

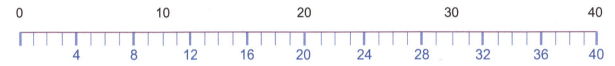

c) Graph the **multiples of 8** on the number line below.

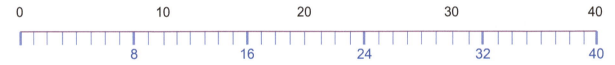

d) Graph all of the numbers between 0 and 40 that are **multiples of 2, 4, *and* 8**.

8, 16, 24, 32, 40

2. a) Graph the **multiples of 6** on the number line below.

b) Graph the **multiples of 9** on the number line below.

c) List all the multiples between 0 and 30 that are multiples of **3, 6, *and* 9**.

18

TEACHER NOTES: STUDENT PAGE 14

In order to work flexibly with ratio tables, students must possess a relatively good intuitive understanding of ratio and proportion. Central to this pursuit is an understanding of multiples. This set of problems highlights the notion of **multiples,** emphasizing in particular the idea of common multiples. This understanding will be important in later, context-based problems that may ask students to share, for example, a certain number of items among friends. Depending on the number of items and friends, it may not be possible to share equally. Recognizing common multiples and their role in making such decisions is an important skill that is introduced in these problems. When possible, connect this idea of a multiple to the skip-counting practiced earlier.

Problem 1: *Teaching Strategy:* Explain that numbers that are multiples of two or more numbers are called common multiples. Make sure to pause at 1d to explore what it means to be a common multiple. Students should notice that 2 and 4 both go into 8. Therefore, because 4 is twice 2, and 8 is twice 4, any multiple of 4 will be a multiple of 2. Likewise, any multiple of 8 will also be a multiple of 4. *Watch for:* Students must be careful not to assume that these relationships necessarily lead to others. See the box below on potential misconceptions.

Problem 2: As you did with problem 1, help students recognize different common multiples of 3, 6, and 9. *Teaching Strategy:* You might also ask students to think about common multiples across these two problems, for example, what might be a common multiple of 4 and 9. This will elicit good discussion and will quite likely bring up the notion of odd and even numbers.

> ### On the Lookout for Misconceptions
>
> Once students find a relationship between numbers as in problem 1 above, it is easy for them to assume that all numbers will work in a similar way. For example, any multiple of 8 (8, 16, 24, 32, etc.) will also be a multiple of 4 (8, 12, 16, 20, 24, 28, 32 etc.). But the reverse is not true. Multiples are not necessarily reciprocal. Just because all multiples of 8 are also multiples of 4 does not mean that all multiples of 4 are multiples of 8. Be sure to explore this idea with students when appropriate throughout these problems.

CONTINUE THE PROBLEM SOLVING

Have students work individually to solve the problems on page 15. You may wish to circulate and monitor their work and recorded answers. As they finish each problem, have students compare and discuss their answers with a partner. Then have each pair share their conclusions in a class discussion of the problem. Refer to the Teacher Notes: Student Page 15 for more specific ideas about the problems on this page.

As students work and report their conclusions, focus on these issues:
Look for Misconceptions – Remind students that equal sharing means that each friend gets the same number of objects and that there are no objects left over.
Allow Waiting Time – When students struggle to explain their thinking, as in problem 1, allow them at least 20 seconds to organize their thoughts.

TEACHER NOTES: STUDENT PAGE 15

The problems on this page require students to think about common multiples in the context of real-world problems. These problems return to the idea of the ratio table. As such, students might be encouraged to think in terms of sets and double number lines. You might remind them of the baseball cards/packs of gum problem.

Problem 1: The number 24 is sometimes called a friendly number because it is a multiple of 2, 4, 6, 8, and 12. Hence, sharing 24 objects among various numbers of groups will be more easily done here than with other numbers. *Teaching Strategy:* You might ask students to think of some unfriendly numbers in this regard. They will almost certainly come up with odd numbers and, perhaps, prime numbers. Encourage students to pursue this conversation.

Problem 2: The number 36 is also relatively friendly. *Teaching Strategy:* You might ask students to think of other numbers that would also divide evenly into 36 (3, 9, 12, 18, 36).

Problem 2c: *Teaching Strategy:* Pause at this problem to discuss what it means to share equally. Undoubtedly, a student will raise the question of whether the pieces of candy can be cut in half. If so, they can be shared equally among the 8 friends. However, what students should recognize is that they have really changed the unit under examination. Although 8 does not divide 36, it does divide 72. So 4 1/2 candy bars, for example, is really the same amount as 9 half-pieces of the same sized candy bar. As these topics surface, be sure to allow students ample time to discuss and broaden their understanding of ratios and proportions.

Student Page 15: Problems and Potential Answers

Section C: Using the Number Line for Multiplication and Division — Set 3

1. Three friends combine their money and buy 24 pencils from the school store. Sharing equally, each friend gets 8 pencils, as shown below.

   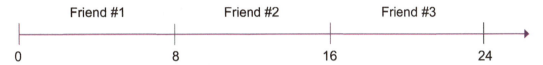

   a) Use the number line to show how **4 friends** can equally share 24 pencils.

   b) Use the number line to show how **6 friends** can equally share 24 pencils.

   c) Use the number line to show how **8 friends** can equally share 24 pencils.

   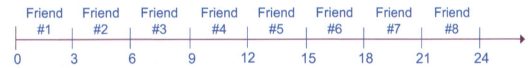

2. a) Draw a number line to illustrate how **6 friends** can equally share **36 pieces of candy**.

   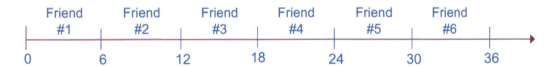

   b) Draw a number line to illustrate how **4 friends** can equally share **36 pieces of candy**.

   c) Can **8 friends** share the 36 pieces of candy equally?

   Explain. No, because each friend would get four and a half pieces, unless the candy can be broken in half.

Book 1: *The Number Line* 15

CONCEPT DEVELOPMENT (Pages 16–18)

INTRODUCE THE CONCEPT

ASSESS STUDENTS' PRIOR KNOWLEDGE
Draw this table on the board:

Packages	1	2	3	4	5	6
Pens	5	10	15	20		

Ask:
What strategies can I use to find how many pens there are in 5 packages? In 6 packages?

Listen for:
(Relevant strategies students can justify)
- I can skip-count by 5 to find there are 25 pens in 5 packages and 30 pens in 6 packages.
- I know that 6 is double 3, so the number of pens in 6 packages is double 15, the number of pens in 3 packages. The number of pens in 5 packages would be 5 less than the number in 6 packages.

MODEL MATHEMATICAL THINKING
Explain that a toy company ships toy trucks in boxes, with 9 trucks in each box. Draw this table on the board:

Boxes	1	2	10	12
Toy Trucks	9			

Ask:
How can I use this table to find how many toy trucks are in 12 boxes?

Talk Through the Thinking:
I know that there are 9 trucks in one box. If I double 1, it is 2 so the number in 2 boxes must be double 9. There are 18 trucks in 2 boxes, and I can write 18 under 2 in the table. To find how many trucks there are in 10 boxes, I can multiply 9 by 10. That's 90. So I can write 90 under 10 in the table. Now I can find the number of toy trucks in 12 boxes. Because I know 10 + 2 = 12, I can add the number of trucks in 2 boxes to the number of trucks in 10 boxes: 18 + 90 = 108. There are 108 trucks in 12 boxes.

Ask:
How can I find how many toy trucks are in 23 boxes?

Listen for:
- I can double 90 to find how many trucks there are in 20 boxes, 180. I know there are 9 trucks in 1 box and 18 trucks in 2 boxes. That's 3 more boxes. So I can add 180 + 9 + 18 for a total of 207 trucks.
- There are 108 trucks in 12 boxes. I can double 108 to get 216, the number of trucks in 24 boxes. Then I subtract 9 to find how many in 23 boxes. 216 − 9 = 207.

LAUNCH THE PROBLEM SOLVING

Have students work individually to solve the problems on page 16. As they finish each problem, have students compare and discuss their answers with a partner. Then have each pair share their conclusions in a class discussion of the problem. Refer to the **Teacher Notes: Student Page 16** for more specific ideas about the problems on this page.

As students work and report their conclusions, focus on these issues:

Validate Alternate Strategies – When students use different strategies to solve a problem, have them discuss their strategies to determine if they all lead to the same correct solution.

Help Make Connections – Remind students of the strategies they have already learned, such as doubling and halving, to help solve these problems.

Student Page 16: Problems and Potential Answers

Section C: Using the Number Line for Multiplication and Division Set 4

1. Markers come in boxes of 6, 12, or 24. There are 54 children in second grade. Use the ratio tables below to determine how many boxes of each size it would take to make sure that every child has one marker.

Boxes	1	2	3	6	9			
Markers	6	12	18	36	54			

How many boxes of 6 are needed?
9

Boxes	1	2	4	5				
Markers	12	24	48	60				

How many boxes of 12 are needed?
5 with some left over

Boxes	1	2	3					
Markers	24	48	72					

How many boxes of 24 are needed?
3 with some left over

2. For a fundraiser, the West High band is selling boxes of oranges. There are 8 oranges in each box. Without using the shaded boxes, can you complete the ratio table to find how many oranges are in 4 boxes, 6 boxes, and 9 boxes?

Boxes	0	1			4	5	6			9	10
Oranges	0	8			32	40	48			72	80

a) Use the table below to show how many oranges are in 12 boxes.

Boxes	1	2	10	12
Oranges	8	16	80	96

Explain your strategy: _____
Step 1: Double the oranges in 1 box to get the oranges in 2 boxes
Step 2: Multiply the oranges in 1 box by 10 to get the oranges in 10 boxes
Step 3: Add the oranges in 2 boxes and 10 boxes to get the oranges in 12 boxes

b) Use the table below to show how many oranges are in 22 boxes.

Boxes	1	10	20	2	22
Oranges	8	80	160	16	176

Explain your strategy: _____
Step 1: Multiply the oranges in 1 box by 10 to get the oranges in 10 boxes
Step 2: Double the oranges in 10 boxes to get the oranges in 20 boxes
Step 3: Double the oranges in 1 box to get the oranges in 2 boxes
Step 4: Add the oranges in 2 boxes and 20 boxes to get the oranges in 22 boxes

c) Use the table below to show how many oranges are in 29 boxes.

Boxes	1	10	20	30	29
Oranges	8	80	160	240	232

Explain your strategy: _____
Step 1: Multiply the oranges in 1 box by 10 to get the oranges in 10 boxes
Step 2: Double the oranges in 10 boxes to get the oranges in 20 boxes
Step 3: Add the oranges in 10 boxes and 20 boxes to get the oranges in 30 boxes
Step 4: Subtract the oranges in 1 box from those in 29 boxes to get the oranges in 29 boxes

Book 1: *The Number Line*

TEACHER NOTES: STUDENT PAGE 16

Problem 1: Students are likely simply to increase in equal increments across the table, which is fine. As the problem contexts get progressively more complicated, students will begin to gravitate toward more sophisticated solutions, using their growing number sense and confidence with ratio tables. While it is all right at this time for them simply to count across the table by 6s, 12s, etc., they should shortly move away from this initial strategy with additional practice and varied problems. While 54 is a multiple of 6, it is not a multiple of 12 and 24. *Watch for:* Students should inquire about the leftovers when they must go beyond the target number of 54 when counting by boxes of 12 and 24.

Problem 2: Students will use various strategies to solve these problems. *Teaching Strategy:* Be sure to highlight, compare, and contrast their thinking on problems 2b-2c.

Teaching Strategy: Becoming Comfortable with Ratio Tables

One of the hardest things for students to adjust to in using ratio tables is the abandonment of the left-to-right habit of thinking and practice developed over years of socialization in math classrooms. Students develop perceptions of the appropriate order in which manipulations must be done. With ratio tables, however, there is no prescribed order for operations. Because we are essentially working with ratios and proportions in a ratio table, operations can be done at any time.

For example, on problem 2b, it might feel strange for students to be multiplying by 10 at first (the first two columns in the table), and then abandon that strategy to determine how many oranges are in 2 boxes. Students will have the preconception that whatever they did last must be used next in any following computation. This is not the case with ratio tables. Often information that gets generated in a ratio table doesn't end up being used in the end. Examples of this will abound as you review the ratio tables your students will use in the coming problems.

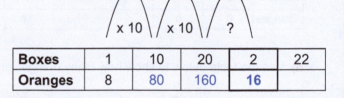

The third step will often throw students for a loop because it does not directly appear to use what they just computed in the previous column. Yet determining how many oranges are in 2 boxes is an important part of the process of going from 1 box to 22 boxes. Of course, upon closer inspection, there is a relationship between column three and column four; dividing the top (20) and the bottom (160) by 10 preserves the ratio. They could also go from one box to two boxes simply by doubling 8. Ask students to think about these relationships

64 The Number Line *Teacher Edition*

CONTINUE THE PROBLEM SOLVING

Have students work individually to solve the problems on page 17. You may wish to circulate and monitor their work and recorded answers. As they finish each problem, have students compare and discuss their answers with a partner. Then have each pair share their conclusions in a class discussion of the problem. Refer to the **Teacher Notes: Student Page 17** for more specific ideas about the problems on this page.

As students work and report their conclusions, focus on these issues:

Validate Alternate Strategies – When students use different strategies to solve a problem, have them discuss their strategies to determine if they all lead to the same correct solution.

Help Make Connections – Remind students of the various strategies they have already learned, such as doubling and halving to help them solve these problems.

TEACHER NOTES: STUDENT PAGE 17

Problem 3: Students should be allowed to pursue this problem in whatever way they see fit. *Watch for:* Students may wonder whether they have to fill in all the columns in the ratio table (They do not.). *Teaching Strategy:* Students should be encouraged to solve the problem in any way they can using various ratios.

Problem 4: Problem 4 contains more practice problems with ratio tables. *Teaching Strategy:* Be sure to encourage your students' explanations for each problem.

Problem 5: Students will have to work backwards to solve this problem. Students can do this in several ways. *Watch for:* The most likely strategies include subtracting 75 from 90, consecutive entries in the ratio table, to find the difference between the total number of boxes in 5 and 6 packs; or to divide 150 boxes by 10 packs. In both cases, they should arrive at an answer of 15.

Student Page 17: Problems and Potential Answers

Section C: Using the Number Line for Multiplication and Division — Set 4

3. There are 6 juice boxes in 1 pack. 90 students are going on a field trip, and the teacher wants to make sure that each student gets one juice box. How many packs of juice boxes must she buy? Use the ratio table below to illustrate your thinking.   **15 packs**

Packs	1	10	5	15					
Juice Boxes	6	60	30	90					

4. Another brand of juice contains 12 juice boxes in 1 pack. Use the following ratio tables to find out how many boxes there are in different numbers of packs.

a) 8 packs

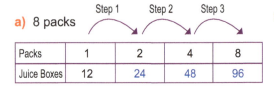

Packs	1	2	4	8
Juice Boxes	12	24	48	96

Explain what you did as you completed each step of the ratio tables:

Step 1: Double the juice boxes in 1 pack to get the juice boxes in 2 packs
Step 2: Double the juice boxes in 2 packs to get the juice boxes in 4 packs
Step 3: Double the juice boxes in 4 packs to get the juice boxes in 8 packs

b) 6 packs

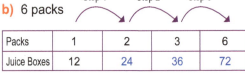

Packs	1	2	3	6
Juice Boxes	12	24	36	72

Step 1: Double the juice boxes in 1 pack to get the juice boxes in 2 packs
Step 2: Add the juice boxes in 1 and 2 packs to get the boxes in 3 packs
Step 3: Double the juice boxes in 3 packs to get the juice boxes in 6 packs

c) 5 packs

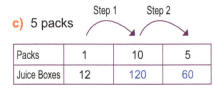

Packs	1	10	5
Juice Boxes	12	120	60

Step 1: Multiply the juice boxes in 1 pack by 10 to get the juice boxes in 10 packs
Step 2: Divide the juice boxes in 10 packs by 2 to get the juice boxes in 5 packs

d) 9 packs

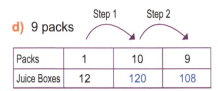

Packs	1	10	9
Juice Boxes	12	120	108

Step 1: Multiply the juice boxes in 1 pack by 10 to get the juice boxes in 10 packs
Step 2: Subtract the juice boxes in 1 pack from those in 10 packs to get the juice boxes in 9 packs

5. A third company sells its juice boxes in yet another, different size package. Use the ratio table below to determine how many juice boxes are contained in one package of this brand.

Packs	1	2	3	4	5	6	7	8	9	10
Juice Boxes	15	30	45	60	75	90	105	120	135	150

There are many ways to solve this problem. **Explain** the way **you** solved it: _____   *Responses will vary.*

Book 1: *The Number Line*

CONTINUE THE PROBLEM SOLVING

Have students work individually to solve the problems on page 18. You may wish to circulate and monitor their work and recorded answers. As they finish each problem, have students compare and discuss their answers with a partner. Then have each pair share their conclusions in a class discussion of the problem. Refer to the **Teacher Notes: Student Page 18** for more specific ideas about the problems on this page.

As students work and report their conclusions, focus on these issues:

Allow Waiting Time – When students struggle to explain their thinking, allow them ample time to organize their thoughts.

TEACHER NOTES: STUDENT PAGE 18

Problem 1: Student responses will vary widely for this problem. This would be an excellent opportunity to structure students into small groups to discuss the relative merits of each of the solution strategies presented. Be sure to allow them time to record their own strategies after they have discussed the three used in the problem. *Teaching Strategy:* Do not rush through this problem. Each sample ratio table illustrates important informal strategies for working with ratio tables (doubling, multiplying by a factor, adding incrementally, etc.).

Student Page 18: Problems and Potential Answers

Section C: Using the Number Line for Multiplication and Division   Set 5

1. The manager for a grocery store needs to order more peaches. One box contains 30 peaches. He wants to order 16 boxes. Three of his workers use ratio tables to figure out how many peaches this will be. Each used a different method.

   a) Sandy's method:

Boxes	1	2	3	4	5	6	7	8	16
Peaches	30	60	90	120	150	180	210	240	480

   Explain Sandy's strategy:
   She went in order adding 30 peaches to the previous number of peaches until she got to 8 boxes. Then she doubled the number of peaches in 8 boxes to get the number of peaches in 16 boxes.

   b) Will's method:

Boxes	1	2	4	16
Peaches	30	60	120	480

   Explain Will's strategy:
   He doubled the number of peaches in each box until he got to the number of peaches in 4 boxes. Then he multiplied by 4 to get the number of peaches in 16 boxes.

   c) Catherine's method:

Boxes	1	10	2	6	16
Peaches	30	300	60	180	480

   Explain Catherine's strategy:
   She multiplied the number of peaches in 1 box by 10 to get the number of peaches in 10 boxes. Then she doubled the number of peaches in 1 box to get the number of peaches in 2 boxes. She then tripled the number of peaches in 2 boxes to find how many peaches were in 6 boxes. Finally, she added the number of peaches in 10 boxes to the number in 6 boxes to get the total number of peaches in 16 boxes.

   d) Which strategy or strategies do you prefer? Do you have a better one of your own? **Explain.**

   Responses will vary.

SECTION C ASSESSMENT (PAGE 19)

LAUNCH THE ASSESSMENT

Have students turn to the Section C Assessment, page 19. An additional copy is found on page 6 of the Assessment Book. Have students work individually to solve the problems and write their explanations. As they work, circulate to be sure students understand what they need for each problem. Be sure that students are completing each part of the problem. For example, in problem 1, students need to complete a ratio table and explain their solution strategy. You may find it helpful to read the directions for both problems before students begin, discussing the types of responses they will need to make for each problem.

Encourage students to use whatever space they need to explain their thinking. If the space on the page is inadequate they should use an additional sheet of paper or use the back of the page.

Refer to the **Teacher Notes: Student Page 19** for more specific ideas about the problems on this page.

Evaluate Student Responses

Use the Assessment Rubric on page 5 of the Assessment Book (pictured on page 71 of the Teacher Edition) to evaluate student responses. The Assessment Book has some general suggestions for using the rubric that may be helpful to you.

TEACHER NOTES: ASSESSMENT PROBLEMS FOR SECTION C

Problem 1: Problem 1 requires students to expand the ratio table from 1 ride to 12 rides. There are several ways to do so. It is intentional that there is not enough space in the ratio table to simply add incrementally until arriving at the final answer of 48. *Watch for:* Students should use strategies they have developed previously. Some students will immediately jump to multiply 12 × 4. That is fine as long as they can also make connections between their strategy and the use of a ratio table.

Problem 2: This problem gives students plenty of practice with ratio tables within the context of one problem. Students may choose to use different strategies for each of the ingredients. Many students will recognize immediately that if one cup of sugar is necessary for a serving of 10, then 5 cups are necessary for a serving of 50. Other ingredients (salt, for example) may elicit different strategies.

The Number Line Teacher Edition

Student Page 19: Problems and Potential Answers

Section C: Problems for Assessment

1. You want to go to the fair. Each ride at the fair costs 4 tickets. You are interested in riding all 12 rides at the fair. Use a ratio table to figure out how many tickets you will need to go on all the rides.

Rides	1	2	4	8	12				
Tickets	4	8	16	32	48				

Explain your solution strategy: _____

Double the number of tickets for 1 ride to get the number of tickets for 2 rides.
Double the number of tickets for 2 rides to get the number of tickets for 4 rides.
Double the number of tickets for 4 rides to get the number of tickets for 8 rides.
Add the number of tickets for 4 rides to the number for 8 rides. That will give the number of tickets for 12 rides

2. Your school is hosting a pancake breakfast. Your job is to make up the ingredients list so that others can go to the store and buy all that is needed. The recipe you have says that it serves 10 people. You are expecting to serve **50 people**. Use the ratio table below to find how much of each item you need to make pancakes to serve all 50 people. You know how much you will need to serve 10.

Ingredients	Serves 10	Serves 20	Serves 40	Serves 50			
Eggs	8	16	32	40			
Flour	6 Cups	12 cups	24 cups	30 cups			
Baking Soda	4 Tablespoons	8 Tbsp.	16 Tbsp.	20 Tbsp.			
Butter	1 Stick	2 Sticks	4 Sticks	5 Sticks			
Sugar	1 Cup	2 cups	4 cups	5 cups			
Salt	3 Tablespoons	6 Tbsp.	12 Tbsp.	15 Tbsp.			
Syrup	2 Jars	4 jars	8 jars	10 jars			

Explain your solution strategy: _____

Double the amount of each ingredient to get 20 servings, then 40 servings. Then add the ingredients from 10 servings to those from the 40 servings to get the ingredients for 50 servings.

Book 1: *The Number Line*

SCORING GUIDE BOOK 1: THE NUMBER LINE

Section C Assessment
For Use With: Student Book Page 19

PROBLEM DESCRIPTION	SCORING: WHAT TO LOOK FOR	SCORE AND COMMENTS
Problem 1 This section introduced the ratio table as an algebraic extension of the (visual) number line. It utilizes ratios and proportions to formalize the skip-counting procedures developed earlier. In this problem, students must use a ratio table to determine how many tickets are needed for 12 rides at the county fair. Level 3: Connection and Application	Do students: • Have a correct interpretation and understanding of the problem? • Have the ability to translate from linear thinking (skip-counting on the number line) to proportional reasoning (using the ratio table)? • Accurately multiply and add within the ratio table? • Have the ability to articulate reasoning and strategy use on the ratio table? NOTE: There are many appropriate solution strategies for this problem.	Suggested: 2 points for ratio table; 2 points for explanation Points:_____ of 4
Problem 2 This problem provides practice with ratio tables. The context asks students to think about the ingredients for a recipe that serves 10. How much more of each ingredient would you need to serve 50 people? This problem provides an opportunity for students to get a great deal of practice with proportional thinking and the use of ratio tables as an extension of number lines. Level 3: Connection and Application	Do students: • Understand the problem context? • Appropriately use ratio tables and proportional thinking? • Vary their use of strategies (doubling, halving, etc.) depending on starting point?	Suggested: 2 points for each ingredient Points:_____ of 14

TOTAL POINTS:_____ OF 18

End-of-Book Assessment (Pages 20–21)

LAUNCH THE ASSESSMENT

Have students turn to the End-of-Book Assessment, pages 20–21. An additional copy is found on page 8 of the Assessment Book. Have students work individually to solve the problems and write their explanations. As they work, circulate to be sure students understand what they need for each problem. Be sure that students are completing each part of the problem. For example, in problem 1, students need to place given numbers accurately on the number line and then explain their thinking. You may find it helpful to read the directions for all the problems before students begin, discussing the types of responses they need to make for each problem.

Encourage students to use whatever space they need to explain their thinking. If the space on the page is inadequate, they should use an additional sheet of paper or use the back of the page.

Refer to the **Teacher Notes: End-of-Book Assessment, Student Pages 20–21**, for more specific ideas about the problems on this page.

Evaluate Student Responses

Use the Assessment Rubric on page 7 of the Assessment Book (pictured on page 75 of the Teacher Edition) to evaluate student responses. The Assessment Book has some general suggestions for using the rubric that may be helpful to you.

TEACHER NOTES: END-OF-BOOK ASSSESSMENT, STUDENT PAGES 20–21

This collection of problems is intended to give teachers a quick glimpse of students' understanding of the major concepts of this book. See the answers for anticipated strategies that students may use for these problems. In general, look for students to be able to make the seamless transition across concepts: placing numbers (that are not necessarily in numerical order) on the number line given a particular scale (Problem 1), using a number line to add and subtract, choosing which number to begin with in a given operation (Problem 2), and developing a double number line for more complex computations. As with any good assessment, the problems should challenge all students along the learning continuum. Problem 3 in particular is a great example of one such problem. Students may need some prompting to understand that multiplying 4 groups of 5 simply means adding 5 to itself three additional times. You should have a good idea whether your students are ready for the problems on this assessment. You may wish to extend the assessment by asking students to write about or discuss the connections between the number line and ratio tables.

Student Page 20: Problems and Potential Answers

End-of-Book Assessment

1. Graph the following numbers on the number line.

   a) 50   b) 150   c) 25   d) 175   e) 10   f) 40   g) 180

   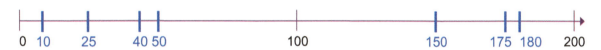

   0 10 25 40 50   100   150 175 180 200

   Explain how you knew where to place each value on the number line. *Responses will vary.*

   a) _____
   b) _____
   c) _____
   d) _____
   e) _____
   f) _____
   g) _____

2. Use a number line, skip counting, and counting on to solve the following problems. Show your steps on the number lines.

   a) 23 + 49 =72

   b) 36 + 101 =137

   c) 38 − 17 =21

   d) 89 − 35 =54

20   Book 1: *The Number Line*

Student Page 21: Problems and Potential Answers

End-of-Book Assessment

3. Illustrate and explain how you can use a number line to multiply 4 groups of 5.

Explain:
Responses will vary.

4. There are 51 kids at Camp Timberline. They want to take boats out onto the lake to go fishing. Four campers can fit into each boat. How many boats do they need for all 51 campers fishing? Use a ratio table to help solve this problem.   13 boats

Boats	1	2	4	8	12	13			
Campers	4	8	16	32	48	52			

Explain your strategy:
Double the number of campers in 1 boat to get the campers in 2 boats. Double those campers to get the number in 4 boats. Double those campers to get the number in 8 boats. Add the campers in 4 boats and 8 boats to get the campers in 12 boats. Add the campers in 1 boat and 12 boats to get the campers in 13 boats.

SCORING GUIDE BOOK 1: THE NUMBER LINE

End-of-Book Assessment
For Use With: Student Book Pages 20–21

PROBLEM DESCRIPTION	SCORING: WHAT TO LOOK FOR	SCORE AND COMMENTS
Problem 1a–g Place numbers on a number line given three reference points. Level 1: Knowledge	Do students: • Appropriately place values given reference points and scale of number line? • Appropriately explain placements?	Points:_____ of 14
Problem 2a–d Use a number line and skip-counting to complete addition and subtraction problems. Level 2: Tool Use	Do students: • Find correct answers to addition/subtraction problems? • Appropriately use skip-counting? • Appropriately represent skip-counting on the number line?	Points:_____ of 4
Problem 3 Apply the use of number lines to a different mathematical concept: Multiplication. This introduces the idea of multiplication as repeated addition. Level 2: Tool Use Level 3: Connections and Application	Do students: • Find the correct answer to the problem: 4 groups of 5? • Correctly represent numbers on the number line (likely the use of skip-counting by 5)? • Proportionally represent numbers on the number line? • Adequately explain their use of skip-counting to represent multiplication?	Points:_____ of 4
Problem 4 Use a ratio table to solve a real-world problem: How many small boats are needed to accommodate 51 campers? Level 2: Tool Use Level 3: Connection and Application Level 4: Synthesis and Evaluation	Do students: • Have an appropriate understanding of the context? • Appropriately use the ratio table to represent and solve the problem? • Find the appropriate starting point in a ratio table? • Use various strategies with the ratio table? • Have an understanding of the leftover campers and the need for an additional boat? (51 is not divisible by 4, therefore there will be one boat that is partially filled.)	Points: ___ of 6

TOTAL POINTS:_____ OF 28

Book 2:
The Ratio Table

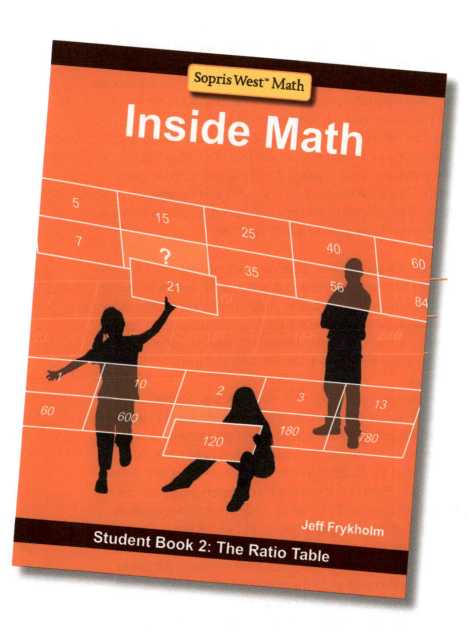

Book Two Overview: The Ratio Table

Introduction

This book is the second in a series of eight units that are geared toward helping middle-grades learners acquire both facility with, and understanding of, the basic mathematical procedures and concepts that lay the groundwork for more advanced mathematical study. In particular, this text series cultivates understanding of a number of mathematical tools that children learn to use with facility in various mathematics and real-world contexts.

Book Focus

This book develops the use of ratio tables that were introduced in *Book 1: The Number Line*. The ratio table is a powerful mathematical model that can be used for multiple purposes. In Book 1, the ratio table was used as an extension of the number line, primarily for the purpose of repeated addition. In this book, students will multiply and divide using ratio tables and use the structure of the tables to help them work fluently with ratios that are commonplace in everyday life. *How much money should be left as a tip on a bill of $24.75? If my car gets roughly 26 miles per gallon of gas, how much gas will I need to drive from Chicago to Denver? If the average cost of gas is $2.15 per gallon, how much should I expect to spend?* These are the kinds of problems that confront us in our daily lives. The ratio table, if developed thoroughly, will furnish students with the tools and processes to engage these problems with confidence.

The ratio table is exactly what it sounds like, a series of equivalent ratios that are recorded in a table. Students use the table to develop a sequence of ratios that, ultimately, lead to the solution of a particular problem. The ratio table allows great flexibility because students can include the intermediate steps that may be intuitively obvious to them. Students become familiar with the idea of equivalent ratios such as those represented by the fractions 3/4, 6/8, and even 75/100.

Book 2 is divided into two components. Section A: Ratio Tables, Multiplication, and Division builds on the previous experiences learners may have had with ratio tables. It uses ratio tables primarily for the purpose of multiplication and division, utilizing students' intuition about strategies such as doubling or halving. The exercises provide opportunities for students to think of multiplication and division as inverse operations, leading them to understand that division problems can often be solved using multiplication, and vice versa. In Section B: Applications of the Ratio Table, students learn to apply ratio tables in various ways. Students work a number of real-world problems in which ratio tables are helpful and use ratio tables to both understand and manipulate equivalent fractions. Although not explicitly stated, this section impels students to develop their proportional reasoning as they apply ratio tables to a wide variety of problem contexts. The goal of this book is to give students enough experience with ratio tables so that they begin to look to them as a primary strategy for completing operations and comparisons with numbers. It is highly recommended that students who begin this book be encouraged to finish it. It does take students a short while to become committed and comfortable with the use of ratio tables. Once they do, however, they will have found one of the most powerful mental computational tools available. Encourage students to use ratio tables.

How To Use This Book

There are two primary sections to this book. On the left-hand page are student work problems with solutions. On the right-hand page is an accompanying teacher resource guide. Throughout the resource guide, teachers will be provided with insights into the mathematical content of each section of the book, pedagogical ideas to enhance teaching and learning, samples of anticipated student work, insights about student thinking related to the topics at hand, and ideas about assessment. This program is meant to be flexible, and certainly relies on the craft and knowledge of the teachers who will use it. The resource materials that accompany this text are not intended to be used as a script. Instead it is the intention of this program that teachers will apply their knowledge of students, their own experiences with some of these mathematical tools, and their intuition about teaching to make this program as effective as possible.

Models Of Implementation

This program has been designed to be as flexible as possible. While this series of books may be used as the primary curriculum for the classroom, it was not designed as the full curriculum for any given grade level. Rather it was crafted to support teachers as they help students understand the number operations and concepts that precede more advanced work in algebra. Teachers may therefore choose to use this program as a guide for whole-class explorations or as the text for smaller pull-out groups of students. In both cases, it is important to note that the program is designed on the principle that students learn mathematics in large measure through interactions with one another. Throughout the books, you will find numerous questions that ask students to explain their thinking. These occasions should not be taken lightly. It is in the sharing and comparing of solution strategies that children begin to build a firm foundation of understanding. The social dynamic of learning mathematics is important to recognize. Participation in mathematical discourse may be the most powerful impetus for learning mathematics available to young learners, and teachers should take advantage of every opportunity to encourage children to talk about their mathematical thinking and processes. Given a commitment to this principle, this program is likely to be most successful when students are progressing through the problems with their peers.

Addressing Issues of Language

There is no question that one of the greatest challenges facing teachers today is to make instruction relevant and accessible for second language learners. *Inside Math* has been written with this concern in mind. Careful consideration was given to the language that appears in directions, contextually based problems, and other sections of the book where text is necessary. When possible, for example, we have limited new vocabulary to only what is essential to the concepts being presented, and we revisit new vocabulary words and concepts repeatedly throughout the text. To assist teachers in making instruction accessible for English language learners, as well as other students for whom reading presents particular challenges, several supporting features were added to the teacher's edition. First within the section planner that introduces each new major mathematical concept contained in the book, there is a heading that reads: Language Development. In this section of the overview, new vocabulary words are introduced and defined. Later in the text, when these words and concepts are introduced in a specific lesson, the teacher notes include additional information about pertinent language considerations and vocabulary. These notes appear as Encouraging Language Development under the Concept Development and Continue the Problem Solving headings.

Explaining Thinking

Throughout this series, and specifically in this book, students will be instructed to explain their thinking. The ability to articulate mathematical ideas and solution strategies is a feature of mathematics education that continues to grow in importance. We see numerous examples in state, national and international achievement tests in which answers alone are not enough; students must also be able to express their thought processes, give rationales for answers, and articulate steps for any given strategy. In this book there are numerous opportunities for students to do so.

Because this is a new and challenging task for students, it is important for teachers to be able to model the process of making thinking explicit. At the beginning of each section in the book, there are suggestions for ways to introduce the content at hand, many of which are suitable for teachers to illustrate what it means to explain thinking in an intelligible way. Be aware of both the importance of this feature of the program and the challenge it provides students as they practice this skill for what might be the first time.

Assessment

At the conclusion of each section, you will find several problems that may be used for formative assessments. These problems review key concepts discussed in the section. At the end of the book you will find additional assessment problems that cover the content of the entire book. These problems may be used as a cumulative assessment of student understanding of the key concepts in the book. The teachers' guide contains insights as to how the assessment problems might best be used and what they are intended to measure.

Assessment rubrics and scoring guides for every assessment may be found in Assessment Teacher Edition. Detailed instructions regarding assessment in general, and the use of the program rubrics in particular, are included in the introduction of Assessment Teacher Edition.

Professional Background

This book is devoted to developing understanding of, and facility with, one of the most powerful number tools available to learners of all ages. A growing number of researchers in mathematics education are pointing to the ratio table as possibly the most important tool we can give young learners as we prepare them for success in algebra. One of the reasons for this assertion is the degree to which the ratio table is a visual representation, or a structural model, that embodies numerous mathematical concepts and relationships. The ratio table promotes proportional reasoning, makes use of equivalent fractions, can be a model for percents, functions as a double number line, and can be a sophisticated computational tool in contexts that require both multiplication and division.

The mathematics education community still suffers at times from unnecessary debates about the difference between teaching for algorithmic proficiency and teaching for conceptual understanding. We need both. The growing popularity of the ratio table may be attributed to the fact that it serves as a conduit between these two schools of thought. On one hand, it is an excellent computational tool that, when understood well by students, can be used quickly, efficiently, and accurately to multiply and divide, calculate percentages, etc. On the other hand, the structure of the model itself promotes conceptual understanding and understanding of mathematical connections. These connections are not apparent in standard algorithms, which are followed by students with little understanding of why they work.

The ratio table is an extremely powerful tool. As you and your students use this book, you'll be able to provide many opportunities for your students to embrace ratio tables not only as a tool for calculations, but also as a way of thinking about mathematical relationships.

What is a ratio table? Why should we use it?

Imagine the following problem:

Wilson Middle School has an annual school ski trip, and 149 students signed up. If each van can hold 12 students, how many vans need to be reserved for the trip?

At first glance, this appears to be a division problem. The most common solution strategy for students trained in a traditional mathematics classroom would be to use the long division algorithm to divide 149 by 12. Doing so results in an answer of 12, with a remainder of 5. One of the problems students have when encountering these kinds of contexts is that although they can compute an answer with a remainder, they do not understand what the remainder in the problem means. So given this problem context, we can expect to see three common incorrect solutions offered by students who either do not have conceptual understanding of division or do not know how to apply the division algorithm appropriately. Here's how three of our students might struggle with this problem:

The first likely incorrect solution is, "12 vans are needed to transport the skiers." In this solution, our first student ignored the remainder in the problem, in this case, five students needing a ride to the ski area. Our second struggling student might respond with the answer, "12 R5 vans are needed for the trip." Our third student computes the decimal equivalent of the remainder, in this case, an answer of "12.42 vans." Although these solutions that contain the notion of a partial bus are nonsensical, they occur all too often because students do not fundamentally understand what division means or because they have been drilled in the algorithm without ever being asked to pause and consider whether their answers are reasonable.

In contrast to these methods, a ratio table can be used to solve the same problem with a greater likelihood that the student will not fall into one of the common misconceptions described in the previous paragraph. One powerful element of the ratio table is that it more clearly illustrates the close relationship between multiplication and division: two methods that are equally suited to solve this problem. Certainly using a ratio table makes it less likely that the student would end up with a solution that contained partial vans. A ratio table can be used to solve the problem.

Foundational ratios provide a starting point for student thinking.
One van holds 12 students. This beginning point is the foundation for the rest of the informal calculations that students will make as they use the ratio table as a computational strategy.

Vans	1	2	10	12	**13**	
Students	12	24	120	144	**156**	

In this solution, the student uses mental math to calculate combinations that are based on common numeric relationships. For example, if one van holds 12 students, then two vans hold 24. Similarly, 10 vans would hold 120 students (10 × 12). Adding the totals for 10 and 2 vans leads to 144 students. This solution is close, but there are not quite enough vans for all the students. So one more van is necessary.

The beauty of ratio tables is that students may choose to follow their own paths (based on strengths in their own number sense) to complete the computation. For example, a second method for finding the same solution might have been the following ratio table:

Vans	1	2	3	10	**13**
Students	12	24	36	120	**156**

In this example, the student may have first computed the total number of students that could ride in 3 vans, then found the total for 10 vans, then added the results to determine that 13 vans would be needed to transport all 144 students. It is easy to see in this example why students would be much less prone to make the mistake of calling for 12.42 vans to transport all the students.

Notice that in both of these solutions each column is a fraction (e.g., 1/12, 2/24), and each fraction is simply an equivalent representation of the same ratio. That is, 1/12 = 2/24 = 10/120, and so on. Also notice that although students will be using addition and subtraction as they complete the tables, they will do so with an understanding that this addition or subtraction must be done proportionately. So in the table above, the final step is to add 3 vans to 10 vans to get a total of 13 vans. Correspondingly, students add 36 students (the number that can fit in 3 vans) to 120 students (the number that fit into 10 vans) to find the total number of students in 13 vans. A common temptation for many students is to fail to add proportionally. That is, a student who adds 10 vans in the top row (to 3 vans) of the ratio table might make the mistake of adding 10 students on the bottom row. Once students recognize the problems with this kind of faulty thinking, they rarely make the same mistake again.

In this book you will lead your students down a path that leads to deep understanding of the ratio table. Students will become familiar with the table itself, its design, structure, and ability to serve as a model for multiplication and division problems. Students will also develop mental mathematical strategies to use the table efficiently (doubling, halving, multiplying by ten, etc.). By the end of the book, students should be comfortable enough with the ratio table to apply it to widely varying mathematical contexts, each with different objectives, with great success.

Section A: Ratio Tables, Multiplication, and Division

SECTION A PLANNER

THE MATHEMATICS CONTENT AND GOALS

GOALS
Students will:
- Intuitively build on the notion of a double number line to develop the ratio table.
- Use the ratio table to think multiplicatively.
- Use the ratio table to solve multiplication and division problems.

LANGUAGE DEVELOPMENT
Mathematical language in this section includes:

Ratio: A proportional relationship between two different numbers or quantities.

Ratio table: A collection of equivalent ratios organized in a table.

Multiples: A number that is the product of a specific number and another number. Students encountered multiples in Book 1, thinking of them as equal increments that can be represented visually on the number line.

Row: The ratio table has two rows. In a ratio table, the top row is used for counting the number of groups in a given column. The bottom row is used for counting the total number of objects in all the groups noted in the top row. The ratio between the numbers in the top row and the corresponding values in the bottom row remains constant throughout a ratio table.

Column: Each ratio is expressed in a given column. The ratio across columns is constant.

Ratio Table Strategies: In order to use ratio tables effectively, it is crucial that students have a basic understanding of commonly used computational strategies such as multiplying by ten or doubling. Each of these strategies is discussed below. If students are unaware of these ideas, reinforce them prior to beginning this book. Students will become comfortable with these ideas as they use them frequently throughout the text.

- ◆ **Multiplying:** It is crucial that students understand multiplication as groups of a given number. For example, 12 × 13 might be thought of as 12 groups of 13. When students understand this fundamental notion of multiplication as repeated addition, they are ready to use ratio tables.

- ◆ **Multiplying by 10:** A very common strategy used with ratio tables is multiplying by 10. Again, the groups of idea is important. For example, 4 × 10 might be thought of as, 4 groups of 10: 10, 20, 30, 40. Larger numbers work the same way: 14 × 10 can be thought of as 14 groups of ten: 10, 20, 30, …130, 140. Once students understand the idea of repeatedly adding ten, they will quickly begin to use a shortcut, simply annexing a zero to whatever number is being multiplied by ten. For example, 13 × 10 = 130.

- ◆ **Doubling:** Doubling is also an important strategy in using ratio tables. For example, if 2 cases of juice contain 14 bottles, then 4 cases (double the amount) contain 2 × 14, or 28 bottles. Help students with informal methods for doubling. For example, 14 might be thought of as 10 + 4. Therefore, doubling 14 might be thought of as doubling (10 + 4), meaning that we can double the 10 (20) and then double the 4 (8), which is 20 + 8 = 28.

- ◆ **Halving:** Halving a given amount is also a valuable strategy. For example, if 10 boxes of apples contain 180 apples, then 5 boxes would contain 90 apples. The breaking apart method discussed above may be used to help students divide a given quantity in half; 180 might be thought of as (100 + 80). Half of 100 is 50, and half of 80 is 40. Hence, half of 180 is 50 + 40 = 90.

- ◆ **Adding:** Adding across the columns in a ratio table is another important strategy. For example, if 4 cartons contain 40 crayons, and 2 cartons contain 20 crayons, then taken together, the 6 cartons would contain 40 + 20 = 60 crayons.

- ◆ **Subtracting:** The same can be said for subtraction. If one carton holds 12 eggs, and 4 cartons hold 48 eggs, then three cartons would hold, 48 – 12 = 36 eggs.

PACING

The projected pacing for this section is 4–5 class periods (based on a 45 minute period).

PROBLEM SETS: OVERVIEW

The ratio table is a flexible tool that students can use to solve a variety of problems. Throughout this section, students will build on the additive strategies they learned about in Book 1 as they organize ratios in a table. Intuitive strategies such as skip-counting, doubling, halving, adding, multiplying by 10, and so forth that were developed in Book 1 will be helpful in this section. The further development of the ratio table in this unit is important in that it will be revisited and used for more complex work with ratios, fractions, percents, and decimals.

Set 1 (pp. 1–2; problems 1–9)

The problems in Set 1 reintroduce the ratio table. Although the introductory problem illustrates two strategies that will be developed later, the bulk of the problems in this section can be solved using simple addition to illustrate the progression of ratio tables. Important in this section are occasions for students to compare various strategies. In comparing strategies, they begin to recognize the mathematical principles inherent in the problems.

Set 2 (pp. 3–4; problems 1–4)

Strategies for using ratio tables effectively are introduced in this section. Specifically, students are introduced to doubling, multiplying, and halving strategies as well as the additive strategies utilized in Set 1. Set 2 focuses primarily on multiplicative contexts.

Set 3 (pp. 5–6; problems 1–5)

Division is introduced explicitly in this section. Students find that ratio tables can be adapted for creative use in many problem contexts. Instead of problems that elicit a repeated addition mindset (e.g., Each box contains 8 bottles; how many bottles in 5 boxes?), the problems in Set 3 often involve separation (How many 16s in 256?).

CONCEPT DEVELOPMENT (Pages 1–2)

INTRODUCE THE CONCEPT

ASSESS STUDENTS' PRIOR KNOWLEDGE

Write the following on the board:
Parking Lot: $1.00 for every 30 minutes

Ask:
How long could I park in the lot if I had $4?
What if I had $5?

Listen for:
(The strategies students use to solve the two problems, and in particular if they are using proportional and/or multiplicative reasoning.)
- If $1 gets me 30 minutes, then $2 would be a full hour, and $4 would be two hours.
- I multiplied $1 by 4 to get 4 dollars, and then I multiplied 30 minutes by 4 to get 2 hours.

MODEL MATHEMATICAL THINKING

Model the thinking for a related problem by asking:
Suppose I needed to park for 2 hours and 45 minutes. How much money would I need to pay?
Allow students to think about this problem for 30-45 seconds.

Talk Through the Thinking:
This is a good problem to model the practice of explaining thinking. Indicate to students that the following dialogue is an example of what it means to express the thinking that leads to a solution strategy. Of course, we would not expect students to write all of this for a given response. But, this sort of thought process is important to make explicit. Students need practice as they learn how to express their mathematical thoughts, and modeling in this fashion is a helpful beginning.

What do we know so far? We know that $1 gets us 30 minutes of parking. Or thinking of it in the other direction, 30 minutes of parking requires $1. So to park for one hour, it would require $2. We want to park for two hours and 45 minutes. Let's start with the two hours. If the first hour requires $2, the second hour would require $2 also. So two hours requires $4. Now we have to figure out how much we need to pay for the last 45 minutes. We know 30 minutes requires $1 more. Now we have accounted for 2 hours and 30 minutes. We need to pay for the final 15 minutes. If 30 minutes requires $1, then 15 minutes (half of 30) requires 50 cents (half of $1). Let's summarize what we have paid. Draw this (or similar) diagram on the board.

Hour/minutes	2	30 min	15 min	total
Will cost me:	$4	$1	$0.50	$5.50

Invite students to examine this table to look for any patterns they might find. For example, they might see a doubling pattern, or a halving pattern that occurs twice.

Ask:
How is this problem different from the first two problems?

Listen for:
- This time we have to go in the other direction.
- We know how long we want to park.
- We need to figure out how much money it will cost.

LAUNCH THE PROBLEM SOLVING

Initially, have students work individually to come up with two strategies for solving problem 1. As they work, circulate throughout the room noting the different strategies students might be using. As students finish each problem, have them compare and discuss their answers with a partner. When you move into a full class discussion of the first problem, be sure to talk through the variety of strategies used by the students. Refer to the **Teacher Notes: Student Page 1** for more specific ideas for each problem in this section.

As students work and report their conclusions, focus on these issues:

Facilitate Students' Thinking – Initially, many students will solve ratio problems by repeated addition. Encourage them to use more sophisticated strategies such as doubling and halving.

Allow Processing Time – It is imperative that students work slowly enough on these problems so they can develop confidence and facility with ratio tables.

Encourage Language Development – Focus on terms that have explicit mathematical meanings, such as doubling, halving, and times ten.

Validate Students' Thinking – When several students use different strategies to solve a problem, have them discuss whether all their strategies resulted in a correct answer.

Student Page 1: Problems and Potential Answers

Section A: Ratio Tables, Multiplication, and Division — Set 1

1. Mr. Palmer runs a soccer camp each summer. He says that the player-coach ratio is 8 to 1. That means for every 8 players, Mr. Palmer has to hire another coach. This year, 118 students are at the camp. How many coaches does Mr. Palmer need to hire? Show two different strategies to solve the problem.

STRATEGY #1	STRATEGY #2
Count by 8's until you reach or exceed 118. You counted 14 eights with 6 players left over. So 15 coaches are needed.	118 divided by 8 equals 14 remainder 6, 15 coaches are needed.

2. Mr. Palmer used the strategy below to solve the problem.

Coaches	1	10	5	15
Players	8	80	40	120

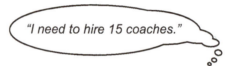

"I need to hire 15 coaches."

Explain his strategy. He multiplied the number of players for 1 coach by 10 to get the number of players for 10 coaches. Then he halved the number of players for 10 coaches to get the number of players for 5 coaches. Finally, he added the number of players for 10 coaches to the number of players for 5 coaches to get 120 players. He then knew that 15 coaches would be enough.

3. Mr. Palmer used the *ratio table* above to solve this problem. Compare his strategy to the strategies you used for problem 1. _Responses will vary_

4. Which strategy do you like best? Why? _Responses will vary_

5. Mr. Palmer needs to order a bottle of *PowerJuice* sports drink for each player in camp. A case of *Power Juice* contains 20 bottles, and costs $25 per case. Use the ratio table below to help you.

Cases	1	2	3	4	5	6	7	8
Bottles	20	40	60	80	100	120		

6. How many cases does Mr. Palmer need to order for his 118 campers?

Explain. Explanations may vary. He needs 6 cases. I doubled the number of bottles in 1 case to get the number of bottles in 2 cases. I doubled the number in 2 cases to get the number of bottles in 4 cases. I then added the number of bottles in 2 cases to the number of bottles in 4 cases to get the number of bottles in 6 cases. I only needed 118 bottles, so 6 cases is enough.

Book 2: *The Ratio Table*

TEACHER NOTES: STUDENT PAGE 1

Problem 1: Some students will know how to use the traditional division algorithm, $8\overline{)118}$. *Watch for:* Be careful to watch what students do with the remainder. Other likely strategies will include repeated addition. *Teaching Strategy:* You may wish to encourage students to draw a diagram.

Problem 2: This problem introduces the use of the ratio table as a strategy for multiplication and division. Inherent in this particular table are three important strategies often used with ratio tables: multiplying by 10, halving, and addition. *Watch for:* Some students will naturally see these strategies. Others will not have the same kinds of mathematical intuition and number sense. *Teaching Strategy:* While students will have ample opportunities later to experiment with these strategies, you may wish to note them now as a precursor to future problems.

Problems 3–4: It is important early in this book to help students embrace the use of ratio tables as a viable computational tool. Therefore, do not rush through the discussions of problems 3 and 4. It is critical to help students recognize that the ratio table is made up of a number of smaller steps based on common facts and strategies that students will be able to complete rather efficiently. *Teaching Strategy:* When possible, as in the case of repeated addition, try to find similarities between various steps in the ratio table and students' own solutions.

Problem 5: *Watch for:* This problem illustrates the use of repeated addition to solve the problem. Most students will likely continue to add 20 to each successive cell in the table (e.g., 20 + 20 = 40; 40 + 20 = 60; etc.). Some students will be able to recognize and apply other successful strategies (like doubling 40 to get 80). *Teaching strategy:* Do not feel the need to rush students to these more sophisticated strategies as they will be developed later. That being said, you certainly can emphasize them as students discover these advancements in strategy use.

Problem 6: Watch for students' understanding of remainders, and how that remainder is interpreted in a meaningful way.

CONTINUE THE PROBLEM SOLVING

The intent of the problems on page 2 is to encourage students to move away from single-step, repeated addition as a strategy. When faced with the cumbersome process of single-step addition cell after cell, students will be eager to skip steps. Capitalize on students' eagerness to skip steps, and encourage them to complete the ratio tables more efficiently. Refer to the **Teacher Notes: Student Page 2** for more specific ideas about the problems on this page.

As students work and report their conclusions, continue to focus on these issues:

Help Make Connections – Remind students that sometimes the steps taken in completing a ratio table may not be absolutely necessary to solve the problem. Extra steps should not be discouraged, as they represent important proportional reasoning. As students become more comfortable with ratio tables, they will develop great facility in using the tables.

Allow Waiting Time – When students struggle to explain their thinking, allow them at least 20 seconds to organize their thoughts in order to develop confidence and facility with ratio tables.

Encourage Language Development – Focus on terms that have explicit mathematical meanings (e.g., doubling, halving, times 10, etc.). Reinforce the notion of a ratio as a fixed relationship between two different numbers or quantities.

TEACHER NOTES: STUDENT PAGE 2

Problems 7-9: *Watch for:* At this point, some students will begin incorporating shortcuts into their strategy use. Although the top rows of the tables have been labeled incrementally, students might decide that they do not need to use the fifth column, and rather find a different strategy to determine the cost of six cases. For example, students might realize that the cost of 6 cases will simply be double the cost of 3 cases. *Teaching strategy:* Remind students of the strategies they developed while using the number line as a computational tool. Those strategies (doubling, halving, multiplying by 10, etc.) are fundamental to achieving long-term success and confidence with ratio tables.

Student Page 2: Problems and Potential Answers

Section A: Ratio Tables, Multiplication, and Division Set 1

7. Use a ratio table to determine how much it will cost to order enough cases of *PowerJuice*.

Cases	1	2	3	4	5	6	7	8
Cost	$25	$50	$75	$100		$150		

How much will it cost? Explain.
Explanations may vary. 6 cases cost $150. I doubled the cost of 1 case to get the cost of 2 cases. I doubled the cost of 2 cases to get the cost of 4 cases. I then added the cost of 2 cases to the cost of 4 cases to get the cost of 6 cases

8. Mr. Palmer thinks about ordering *Sunshine Lemonade* instead of *PowerJuice*. He thinks it might be cheaper. *Sunshine Lemonade* comes in cases of 15 bottles and costs $18 per case.

How many cases of *Sunshine Lemonade* would Mr. Palmer need to order? _____

Cases	1	2	3	4	5	6	7	8	9	10
Bottles	15	30		60				120		

Explain. Explanations may vary. 8 cases. I doubled the number of bottles in 1 case to get the number of bottles in 2 cases. I doubled the number in 2 cases to get the number of bottles in 4 cases. I then doubled the number in 4 cases to get the number of bottles in 8 cases.

9. How much would it cost for enough *Sunshine Lemonade* for all 118 players? _____

Cases	1	2	3	4	5	6	7	8
Cost	$18	$36		$72				$144

Explain. Explanations may vary. 8 cases cost $144. I doubled the cost of 1 case to get the cost of 2 cases. I doubled the cost of 2 cases to get the cost of 4 cases. I doubled the cost of 4 cases to get the cost of 8 cases.

CONCEPT DEVELOPMENT (PAGES 3–6)

INTRODUCE THE CONCEPT

The purpose of Student Book pages 3–6 is to formalize the ratio table as a computational tool. Students will explore contexts that are inherently multiplicative in nature. Students will learn to use the ratio table as a tool for both multiplication and division. These exercises will also formalize computational strategies such as doubling, halving, and multiplying by 10.

ASSESS STUDENTS' PRIOR KNOWLEDGE

Ask:
Four friends went to a movie. Together, it cost them $10 to buy all 4 tickets. Next in line was a group of 20 students on a field trip. If the ticket price was the same as for the 4 friends, how much did it cost the 20 students to get in? Work with 2 or 3 friends to solve this problem. See whether you can solve it in more than one way. Draw a diagram or picture that matches your strategy and solution.

Listen for:
The different patterns of thinking that students may exhibit. There are many ways that students might solve this problem. Look for connections between their drawings and the mathematical strategies they used.

MODEL MATHEMATICAL THINKING

Repeat the problem above. Allow students to think about this problem for 4 to 5 minutes.

Talk Through the Thinking:
We know that tickets for the 4 friends cost $10. So one way to think about this problem is to imagine paying for the large group of students 4 at a time. If the 4 friends paid $10, then two groups of 4 students, or 8 students, would have to pay $20. The next 4 students would pay another $10, for a total of $30. Now we have accounted for 12 students at a cost of $30. We could keep going, adding 4 students and $10 each time until we get to 20 students. So 16 students cost $40, and 20 students cost $50. That works just fine. But, I wouldn't want to do 4 at a time if it had been a group of 200 students. Did any of you solve the problem a different way that used fewer steps?

Allow processing time. If no students suggest a more efficient strategy, continue.
Is there a shortcut to solving this problem? Because admission for 4 students costs $10, then 40 students would cost $100. Half of 40 is 20, the number of students in the group, so half of $100 is $50.

Draw the diagram below on the board, and allow for student discussion and elaboration in their groups. Ask students to complete the last step of the diagram, going from 40 to 20 students.

Students	4	(4 x 10) = 40 students
Tickets cost	$10	($10 x $10) = $100

Ask:
How many different ways are there to solve the problem about the movie tickets?

Listen for:
Distinct strategies that might include doubling, multiplying by 5, and multiplying by 10.

Depending on the understanding of your students, you may choose to demonstrate one more strategy. For example, if tickets for 4 students cost $10, then tickets for 4 × 5 = 20 students would cost $10 × 5 = $50.

Explaining thinking:
At the conclusion of this part of the problem discussion, pause and ask students how they would explain their thinking for one of the final ratio table solution strategies explored in class. Ask them to do so in two or three sentences. An example of articulation of thinking might be: *I know that tickets for 4 students cost 10 dollars. I need to know how much it will cost for 40 students. Because 4 x 10 = 40, I can find the cost of the tickets by multiplying $10 by 10 as well, which is $100.*

LAUNCH THE PROBLEM SOLVING

Have students begin the problems on page 3. As they work, circulate throughout the room listening to conversations. Encourage students to think efficiently about shortcut strategies that will help them compute their answers. Look for students with strong number sense who are able to use different strategies to think through these problems. Refer to the **Teacher Notes: Student Page 3** for more specific ideas about the problems on this page.

As students work and share their conclusions, focus on these issues:

Look for Misconceptions – Watch for instances in which students fail to maintain equivalent fractions (ratios) across columns in ratio tables. See On the Lookout for Misconceptions in the Teacher Notes: Student Page 3.

Facilitate Students' Thinking – Help students anchor on comfortable manipulations of fractions, such as doubling both the numerator and denominator, and multiplying both numerator and denominator by 10.

Allow Processing Time – Students must be given time as they go through the awkward stage of learning this new model. They will be tempted to abandon the method, but an investment of time and focus here will pay great dividends in years to come.

Encourage Language Development – Students are asked to explain their thinking in these problems. Support students in expressing their mathematical thoughts in words.

TEACHER NOTES: STUDENT PAGE 3

Problem 1: This is a key problem. Students are presented with four different strategies that solve the same problem. It is important for students to recognize the steps that distinguish each of these strategies. For example, in the first table, the familiar strategy of repeated addition is used. The second table is constructed using a doubling strategy. The third table multiplies by 10, halves, and then adds. The fourth table utilizes both a doubling strategy and an additive strategy. *Watch for:* Be sure that students can identify these various strategies because they will be used frequently in subsequent problems. *Teaching Strategy:* You might ask students to go back to the previous problems they have worked to seek instances in which some of these strategies might have been used rather than the repeated addition method that was used in problem 1 on Student Page 1.

Problem 2: Although the responses will vary, be sure to emphasize that each of these strategies might be particularly useful (or not useful) depending on the context of the problem and the numbers inherent in the context. For example, halving strategies with odd numbers are not often desirable strategies.

> ### On the Lookout for Misconceptions
> A common mistake is when students add the same number to the top and bottom rows in a particular column rather than preserving the ratio. For example, to return to the previous context, if tickets for 4 students cost $10 at the movie theater, some students may make the mistake of thinking if they add 4 more students, they need to add 4 more dollars, 8 students = $14. Help students recognize the need to maintain an equivalent fraction. Adding 4 students is actually doubling the numerator, which requires that they double the denominator as well. The primary confusion here stems from the fact one may actually add across columns in a ratio table. If 4 students cost $10, and 8 students cost $20, then 4 + 8 students will cost 10 + 20 dollars. In this case, the ratio is maintained, whereas in the previous example, it is not. This is the primary misconception, leading to faulty use of the ratio table, that students are prone to exhibit.

Student Page 3: Problems and Potential Answers

Section A: Ratio Tables, Multiplication, and Division Set 2

In order to get good at using ratio tables, you need to practice using smart strategies. One problem has been solved 4 different ways below. Look at each strategy and try to explain it.

1. The problem: Luke is in charge of ordering corn seeds for the school garden. The seeds are packaged in small envelopes that are then shipped out in boxes. Each box of corn seeds contains 14 small envelopes. How many envelopes of seeds will he get if he orders 6 boxes?

   STRATEGY A

Boxes	1	2	3	4	5	6
Envelopes	14	28	42	56	70	84

   Explain: The number of envelopes in each box increases by multiples of 14. Or you add 14 envelopes to the previous number of envelopes.

   STRATEGY B

Boxes	1	2	3	6
Envelopes	14	28	42	84

   Explain: Add the first three multiples of 14 to get the number of envelopes in 6 boxes.

   STRATEGY C

Boxes	1	10	5	6
Envelopes	14	140	70	84

   Explain: Multiply the number of envelopes in 1 box by 10. Then halve that number to get the number of envelopes in 5 boxes. Add the number of envelopes in 5 boxes to those in 1 box to get the number in 6 boxes.

   STRATEGY D

Boxes	1	2	4	6
Envelopes	14	28	56	84

   Explain: Double the number of envelopes in 1 box to get the number in 2 boxes. Double those to get the number in 4 boxes. Add the number in 2 boxes to the number in 4 boxes to get the number in 6 boxes.

2. Which of these strategies do you think is easiest to use? Why? Responses will vary.

CONTINUE THE PROBLEM SOLVING

The intent of pages 4–6 is to build on common strategies while at the same time motivating students to use the ratio table as a viable tool for multiplication and division. The contexts in pages 4–6 enhance this idea. As students work on page 4, you may wish to circulate and monitor students' discussions and recorded answers. Then have students compare and discuss their answers in a class discussion. Refer to the **Teacher Notes: Student Page 4** for more specific ideas about the problems on this page.

Continue to focus on the possible misconceptions mentioned previously as well as the formalization of the intuitive strategies that have been discussed in the notes and illustrated in the problems themselves (doubling, halving, combining the numerators and denominators respectively across columns, etc.).

Focus on these issues as well:

Validate Students' Strategies – When several students use different strategies to solve the same problem, have them discuss how and why their strategies led to the same conclusion.

Allow Waiting Time – When students struggle to explain their reasoning, allow at least 20 seconds for them to organize their thoughts.

TEACHER NOTES: STUDENT PAGE 4

Problem 3: All of the previously mentioned strategies are illustrated by problems 3a–3e. Some problems utilize two strategies. For example, in problem 3c both multiplying by 10 and halving are used. The top row of each ratio table has been completed for students to help guide practice in a variety of the strategies.

Problem 4: Be sure students understand the problem. *Watch for:* Students need to recognize that each floor has 25 windows and that a ratio table can be used to determine how many sets of 25 there are in 138. Students are left to determine the beginning ratios for this table. They may initially struggle to establish the first ratio in the table. *Teaching Strategy:* Help them think of this problem as a multiplication problem. For example, if there are 25 windows on each floor, how many would there be on two floors? This will help them determine the first ratio, from which the others will follow. The two follow-up questions will help you assess whether students actually understand the context of the problem and the way the ratio table could be used to make sense of it.

Student Page 4: Problems and Potential Answers

Section A: Ratio Tables, Multiplication, and Division — Set 2

3. Clearview Glass has a contract to wash windows at the City Hall building. There are 25 windows on each floor of the building. There are 10 floors in all. How many windows will they have to wash if they clean the windows on:

   a) 8 floors of the building?

Floors	1	2	4	8		
Windows	25	50	100	200		

   b) 6 floors of the building?

Floors	1	2	3	6		
Windows	25	50	75	150		

   c) 5 floors of the building?

Floors	1	10	5			
Windows	25	250	125			

   d) 9 floors of the building?

Floors	1	10	9			
Windows	25	250	225			

   e) all 10 floors of the building?

Floors	1	10				
Windows	25	250				

4. Sherri was going to wash the windows on all 10 stories of the building. She started at the top floor. After finishing the 25 windows on the top floor, she was lowered to the ninth floor. After finishing those windows, she was lowered to the next floor down, and so on. She reported that after washing 138 windows the crane broke, so she had to stop. <u>On how many floors did Sherri wash *all* the windows? How many floors and windows are left?</u> Use a ratio table to solve the problem. Then answer the questions

Floors	1	2	3	4	5	6			
Windows	25	50	75	100	125	150			

On how many floors did Sherri wash all the windows? __5__ floors

How many floors and windows are left? 4 complete floors with 100 windows and a partial floor of 12 windows.

4 Book 2: *The Ratio Table*

CONTINUE THE PROBLEM SOLVING

The intent of Student Pages 5–6 is to motivate the use of ratio tables as a computational tool for both multiplication and division. The use of context is an important feature of these problems. Have students work individually to solve the problems on page 5. As they work, circulate and monitor their work and recorded answers. When students finish, have them compare and discuss their answers with a partner. Then have each pair report their conclusions in a class discussion. Refer to the **Teacher Notes: Student Page 5** for more specific ideas about the problems on this page.

As students work and report their conclusions, focus on the following issues:

Allow Processing Time – If students are comfortable with using the ratio table as a tool for multiplication, they may need a few additional moments at the beginning of the division problems to envision the context and to choose the appropriate strategy.

Help Make Connections – Emphasize the inverse relationship between division and multiplication. You may wish to remind students that, for example, if 2 × 3 = 6, then 6 ÷ 2 = 3 and 6 ÷ 3 = 2. You might take the time to reword several problems to show how a slight change in wording can elicit the use of a different operation.

TEACHER NOTES: STUDENT PAGE 5

Problems 1–2: The intent of these problems is to explicitly suggest that ratio tables can be used for multiplication and division. Problem 1 is one that would typically invite students to divide 780 by 60. Do not discourage students from using the traditional division algorithm to solve problem 2. The purpose of these questions is to establish a context whereby the ratio table can be set alongside the traditional division algorithm to show the table's usefulness and ease of application.

Problem 3: Be sure to emphasize that although these problems as stated are represented as division problems, multiplicative reasoning can be used to solve them. *Watch for:* Students may have difficulty at first establishing the initial column in the ratio table. *Teaching Strategy:* You can help students do so by helping them create verbal statements that are embodied in the table. For example, for 3c, you might encourage students to verbalize the following:

"How many groups of 16 are in 256? One group of 16 is 16." (This is the first column in the table.)

Once the first column is established, the table may be developed in a variety of ways. Again, the key to solving these problems is for students to recognize the essence of the problem: what is being asked and how might the solution be approached.

Student Page 5: Problems and Potential Answers

Section A: Ratio Tables, Multiplication, and Division Set 3

A large school complex orders 780 newspapers. Newspapers are delivered in bundles of 60. How many bundles are delivered to the school?

1. Which operation can you use to solve this problem? *Various operations could be used. A common one would be division.*

2. Solve this problem <u>any way you choose</u>. Show your work in the space below.

   Responses will vary.

   Explain your strategy. _____

Since multiplication and division are inverse operations, you can use ratio tables to solve both kinds of problems. You might have answered Problem 1 above by saying that it was a *division problem*. You are right! Can you use a ratio table to solve this division problem? Here is one way to do so…

$\frac{780}{60}$ →

Number of Factors	1	10	2	3	**13**
Product	60	600	120	180	**780**

So… $\frac{780}{60} = 13$

3. Complete the following division problems. *Strategies will vary.*

   a) How many 15's are there in 75? So, 75 ÷ 15 = ☐

Number of Factors	1	10	5			
Product	15	150	75			

   b) How many 20's are there in 840? So, 840 ÷ 20 = ☐

Number of Factors	1	10	20	40	2	42	
Product	20	200	400	800	40	840	

   c) How many 16's are there in 256? So, 256 ÷ 16 = ☐

Number of Factors	1	10	5	15	16		
Product	16	160	80	240	256		

Book 2: *The Ratio Table*

CONTINUE THE PROBLEM SOLVING

Have students work individually to solve the problems on page 6. As they work, circulate and monitor their recorded answers. As students finish each problem, have them compare and discuss their answers with a partner. Then have each pair share their answers in a class discussion of the problem. Refer to the **Teacher Notes: Student Page 6** for more specific ideas about the problems on this page.

As students work and report their conclusions, focus on these issues:

Validate Alternate Solutions – When several students use different strategies to solve the same problem, have them discuss and compare their strategies to see whether they are all correct.

Allow Waiting Time – When students struggle to explain their thinking, allow at least 20 seconds for them to organize their thoughts.

Encourage Language Development – Students need to be reminded about the notion of inverse operations. Multiplication and division might be thought of as inverses of each other, one undoes the other. Addition and subtraction are similarly inverse operations. When learners view multiplication and division as inverse operations, then they can more easily apply the ratio table based on their understanding of a given context in an intuitive and logical way (as opposed to believing there is one method for a particular kind of problem).

Student Page 6: Problems and Potential Answers

Section A: Ratio Tables, Multiplication, and Division — Set 3

4. Blank CD's are shipped in boxes of 40. The music teacher orders 350 blank CD's. How many boxes should she order to make sure she gets at least 350 CD's?

Boxes	1	10	9					
CD's	40	400	360					

Boxes of CD's she should order: __9 boxes__

Explain your strategy: Multiply the number of CDs in 1 box by 10. Then subtract the number of 1 box from the number in ten boxes to get the number in 9 boxes.

5. There are 150 students at Emerson Middle School. Each student needs 3 pencils to start the school year. Pencils are shipped in boxes that contain 12 pencils each. How many boxes of pencils need to be ordered? Use ratio tables to solve this problem.

Students	1	100	50	150				
Pencils	3	300	150	450				

Boxes	1	10	20	40	2	38		
Pencils	12	120	240	480	24	456		

Boxes of pencils needed: __38 boxes__

Explain your strategy: First find the number of pencils needed for 150 students. Multiply the number of pencils for 1 student by 100. Then halve that to get the number of pencils for 50 students. Then add the number of pencils needed by 100 students to the number needed by 50 students to get the number needed by 150 students, which totals to 450 pencils.

Next find the number of boxes needed for 450 pencils. Multiply the number of pencils for 1 box by 10. Double this for the number in 20 boxes. Double this for the number in 40 boxes. Double the number in 1 box to get the number in 2 boxes and subtract that from the number in 40 boxes. The result is 38 boxes, with 456 pencils needed.

TEACHER NOTES: STUDENT PAGE 6

Problem 4: Problem 4 provides more practice with division contexts. *Teaching Strategy:* Continue to encourage students to experiment with various strategies. In this problem, for example, students might multiply by 10, then subtract 1, and, correspondingly, 40.

Problem 5: The solution for this problem requires two steps. Students must first determine how many pencils are required for the pupils in the school. They may immediately recognize that, since each student needs 3 pencils, the total number of pencils is 150 × 3, or 450. Then a second series of computations must be completed to determine how many boxes must be ordered to obtain 450 pencils. Students must work from the given information that one box contains 12 pencils. Ratio tables can be used to solve both of these problems, and their use should be encouraged.

Forward Thinking: A Teaching Opportunity

These problems elicit a kind of proportional reasoning that is common in algebra classes. Take this opportunity to foreshadow ways in which algebraic methods can be used to solve these kinds of problems. For example, recall the first part of problem 5:

If each student needs 3 pencils, and there are 150 students, how many pencils are needed?

In the future, it is likely that students would be expected to solve this problem with a proportion such as A is to B, as C is to D. You may wish to introduce this method:

1 student is to 3 pencils as
150 students is to how many pencils?

You then might wish to represent this as a series of equivalent ratios in the following way:

$$\frac{1}{3} = \frac{150}{?}$$

The task now becomes one of helping students understand the typical process through which these kinds of proportions are solved. To do so, it might be helpful to connect the steps (cross multiply, then divide) to a ratio table. Students may be encouraged to think of the vertical lines in the ratio table that separate the columns (and ratios) as symbols of equality, adjacent columns in a ratio table are equivalent in value. The traditional next step in this problem would be the following:

$$1(x) = (150)(3)$$
$$x = 450$$

The ratio table work students have been doing thus far offers an explanation of the traditional algorithm. That is, in order to go from 1 to 150, one needs to multiply by 150. Likewise, the lower row of the ratio table must also be multiplied by 150 to preserve the equivalent ratio. So 3 × 150 = 450.

SECTION A ASSESSMENT (PAGE 7)

LAUNCH THE ASSESSMENT

Have students turn to the Section A Assessment, page 7. An additional copy is found on page 13 of the Assessment Book. Have students work individually to solve the problems and write their explanations. As they work, circulate to be sure students understand what they need to do for each problem. Be sure that students are completing each part of the problem. For example, in problem 1, students need to explain the strategy used to complete the problem. You may find it helpful to read the directions for all the problems before students begin, discussing the types of responses they should create.

Encourage students to use whatever space they need to explain their thinking. If the space on the page is inadequate, they should use an additional sheet of paper or use the back of the page.

Refer to the **Teacher Notes: Student Page 7** for more specific ideas about the problems on this page.

Evaluate Student Responses

Use the Assessment Rubric on page 12 of the Assessment Book (pictured on page 104 of the Teacher Edition) to evaluate student responses. The Assessment Book has some general suggestions for using the rubric that may be helpful to you.

TEACHER NOTES: STUDENT PAGE 7

Problems 1–3: Each of these problems uses different strategies that students should have encountered throughout Section A. *Watch for:* Students should identify doubling, multiplying by 10, addition, halving, etc.

Problem 4: *Watch for:* Students should demonstrate understanding of techniques useful for solving both multiplication and division with ratio tables.

Student Page 7: Problems and Potential Answers

Section A: Problems for Assessment

Problem: Longfellow Elementary School was going to put in a new gym floor. The gym floor tiles came in boxes of 45 tiles per box. Mr. Sheffield, the gym teacher, ordered 16 boxes of tiles. Three students wanted to know how many tiles that was. Each student used a ratio table to find an answer.

1. Becky solved the problem this way:

Boxes	1	2	3	4	5	6	7	8	16
Tiles	45	90	135	180	225	270	315	360	720

Explain Becky's thinking. She found the first eight multiples of 45. Then she doubled the number of tiles in 8 boxes to get the number in 16 boxes. Or, she could have repeatedly added 45 until she got to 8 boxes. At that point, she could have doubled the number of tiles in 8 boxes to get the number in 16 boxes.

2. Ann solved the problem this way:

Boxes	1	2	4	8	16
Tiles	45	90	180	360	720

Explain Ann's thinking. She doubled the boxes and their respective number of tiles until she got to 16 boxes.

3. Brian solved the problem this way:

Boxes	1	10	2	6	16
Tiles	45	450	90	270	720

Explain Brian's thinking. He multiplied the number of tiles in 1 box by 10. He then doubled the number of tiles in 1 box. Then he multiplied the number in 2 boxes by 3 to get the number in 6 boxes. Finally, he added the number in 10 boxes to the number in 6 boxes to get the number in 16 boxes.

4. Use a ratio table to complete the following:

   a) 12 x 13 = 156

Number of Factors	1	2	3	10	13
Product	12	24	36	120	156

   b) 308 ÷ 14 = 22

Number of Factors	1	10	20	21	22
Product	14	140	280	294	308

   c) 13 x 35 = 455

Number of Factors	1	10	20	30	5	35
Product	13	130	260	390	65	455

Book 2: *The Ratio Table*   7

SCORING GUIDE BOOK 2: THE RATIO TABLE

Section A Assessment
For Use With: Student Book Page 7

PROBLEM DESCRIPTION	SCORING: WHAT TO LOOK FOR	SCORE AND COMMENTS
Problem 1 Explain the thinking behind a given ratio table. Level 4: Synthesis and Evaluation	Do students: • Have an understanding of the way a ratio table works? • Recognize the increasing by one strategy?	 Points:_____ of 2
Problem 2 Explain the thinking behind a given ratio table. Level 4: Synthesis and Evaluation	Do students: • Have an understanding of the way a ratio table works? • Recognize the doubling strategy?	 Points:_____ of 2
Problem 3 Explain the thinking behind a given ratio table. Level 4: Synthesis and Evaluation	Do students: • Have an understanding of the way a ratio table works? • Recognize the (x10) strategy? • Recognize the addition principle?	 Points:_____ of 2
Problem 4a–c Solve multiplication and division problems using a ratio table. Level 1: Comprehension and Knowledge Level 2: Tool Use	Do students: • Understand the function of a ratio table? • Use creative strategies to complete ratio tables? • Accurately compute using ratio tables?	 Points:_____ of 6

TOTAL POINTS:_____ OF 12

Section B: Applications of the Ratio Table

SECTION B PLANNER

THE MATHEMATICS CONTENT AND GOALS

GOALS

Students will:
- Use ratio tables to multiply two-digit numbers.
- Use ratio tables to multiply with numbers that contain decimal points.
- Use ratio tables to find equivalent fractions and reduce fractions to simplest form.

LANGUAGE DEVELOPMENT
Mathematical language in this section includes:

Numerator: The number above the bar in a fraction; it represents the number of parts of the whole or set being considered.

Denominator: The number below the bar in a fraction; it represents the number of parts making up the whole.

Reduce: To find an equivalent fraction by lowering its terms; to simplify a fraction without changing its value.

Simplify: To rename a fraction in a simpler form by dividing its numerator and denominator by a common factor.

Simplest Form: The form of a fraction when its numerator and denominator have no common factor other than 1.

Decimal: The number in the base 10 number system, having one or more places to the right of a decimal point.

Algorithm: A prescribed set of steps used to solve a particular kind of problem.

Fraction: A number used to name a part of a group or a whole. The number below the bar is the denominator, and the number above the bar is the numerator.

Equivalent Fractions: Fractions that have the same value, but are written with different numerals, are equivalent fractions. For example, 1/3 and 2/6 are equivalent fractions.

Column: Ratio tables are organized in rows and columns. A column refers to one vertical set of numbers, with the number of groups on top, and the total number of objects being counted on the bottom.

Cell: One particular entry in a given ratio table; only one number can be in each cell.

The Ratio Table *Teacher Edition*

PACING

The projected pacing for this unit is 3–6 class periods (based on a 45 minute period).

PROBLEM SETS: OVERVIEW

While the majority of the problems in Section A emphasized contexts in which the ratio table might be used to solve contextually based problems that deal with whole numbers, Section B illustrates that the ratio table can also be used as a tool to develop other mathematics. For example, one of the most powerful mathematical applications of the ratio tool is in finding equivalent fractions and simplifying fractions. Much of this section is devoted to this task.

Set 1 (pp. 8–9; problems 1–5)
The problems in Set 1 focus primarily on using ratio tables with decimals. Given problems with benchmark decimals such as 0.25, 0.50, 0.75, and 0.10, students can generally eliminate the decimal within several columns of the ratio table. For example, doubling 0.25 gets 0.50; doubling again eliminates the decimal altogether. Multiplying by multiples of ten also works nicely to move the decimal.

Set 2 (p. 10; problems 1–5)
The problems in Set 2 emphasize ratios that do not have a numerator of 1. In all the previous problems in this book, the first column of the ratio table began with 1 in the first, top cell with some other number in the bottom cell. In these problems, other ratios are used, such as 3 pounds of peaches for $2. The ratio tables work in exactly the same way–the starting point just looks somewhat different. The final problem in this set asks students to work backwards to find a ratio with a numerator of one.

Set 3 (pp. 11–12; problems 1–4)
The problems in this set help students develop both understanding of and facility with equivalent fractions. In short, the fundamental design of a ratio table is exposed as a table that contains all equivalent fractions. In these problems, students must find equivalent fractions, simplify fractions, and reduce fractions to their simplest forms. This work is probably familiar to students. What will very likely be new to them is the use of a ratio table to determine such equivalencies.

CONCEPT DEVELOPMENT (Pages 8–10)

INTRODUCE THE CONCEPT

The purpose of this section of Book 2 is to have students use ratio tables to rename ratios with decimals as equivalent ratios with whole numbers, to do it as efficiently as possible, and to use the ratio table to complete the calculations. The use of the ratio table allows students to do these calculations without having to worry about adjusting their answers to account for the decimal point, as they would when using traditional algorithms, particularly those used in multiplication and division. Many students know that it is important to adjust for the decimal, but they do not know why they are doing so. By using ratio tables, students are more likely to develop better conceptual understanding of operations with decimals and the relative magnitude of results, and are therefore less likely to make careless mistakes with these computations.

ASSESS STUDENTS' PRIOR KNOWLEDGE
Write the following on the board:

$$2 \times 25 = ? \text{ and } 2 \times 2.5 = ?$$

Ask:
What is the major difference between these two number sentences? Is there also a difference in how you would find the answers? What is that difference?

Listen for:
(Students should be aware that the decimal point in the second number sentence means the multiplicand is less than the multiplicand in the first number sentence and will result in a lesser product.)
- The first number sentence has all whole numbers and the second has a whole number and a decimal.
- The first number sentence is easier to multiply.
- You would multiply both the same way, but you would write a decimal point one place to the left in the answer for the second number sentence.

MODEL MATHEMATICAL THINKING
On the board, write 4×12.5 and 2×25. Lead students in a discussion about the relationship between the two problems. Illustrate that the answers are the same because 4 is double 2 and 12.5 is half of 25. Further elicit that multiplying by 2 is the inverse of dividing by 1/2.

Tell students that since they feel that multiplying whole numbers is easier than multiplying decimals, they can use a ratio table to get rid of the decimal and make the multiplication easier. You will likely need to model the process of multiplying decimals by 10, resulting in moving the decimal one place to the right. Next model the thinking for another example by asking, *One pound is about equal to 2.2 kilograms. How many kilograms are equal to 45 pounds?*

Talk Through the Thinking:
We need to multiply 45 by 2.2. How can we get rid of that decimal point as quickly as possible to make it easier to find the answer? What if we doubled 2.2? We would get 4.4. That might help, but we still have a decimal point. Is there any other way to move that decimal point to the right? We can multiply 4.4 by 10. That will give us 44. Once the decimal point is gone, we can use a ratio table to solve the problem. Here is how our solution might look in a ratio table. Draw this ratio table on the board.

Pounds	1	10	5	40	45
Kilograms	2.2	22	11	88	99

Ask:
What was the strategy I used to solve the problem?

Listen for:
- First, you multiplied 2.2 by 10 to get rid of the decimal. You found that 10 pounds is about 22 kilograms.
- Because 5 is half of 10, you found half of 22 kilograms. That means that 5 pounds is about equal to 11 kilograms.
- 40 is 4 × 10, so you multiplied 4 × 22 to get 88. This means that 40 pounds is about equal to 88 kilograms.
- Finally, you added 11 kilograms to 88. So 45 pounds is about equal to 99 kilograms.

LAUNCH THE PROBLEM SOLVING

Have students work individually to solve the problems on page 8. As they work, you may want to circulate and monitor their work and recorded answers. After they finish the page, have them compare and discuss their answers with a partner. Then have each pair share their results in a class discussion. Refer to the **Teacher Notes: Student Page 8** for more specific ideas about the problems on this page.

As students work and report their conclusions, focus on these issues:

Help Make Connections – Reinforce common strategies students have already learned that are helpful when computing with decimals, such as doubling and multiplying by 10 and 100.

Validate Representations – Some students may need to use more columns than are given in their ratio tables when they are converting ratios with a decimal in either the numerator or denominator. This should not be discouraged. In time students will become more proficient with their use of strategies in relation to ratio tables. Have these students compare their ratio tables with those of others and discuss whether their own solutions are correct.

Allow Processing Time – It is very important to allow students ample time as they work on these problems while they are still developing confidence with ratio tables.

Encourage Language Development – Review the definition of decimal before engaging these problems.

TEACHER NOTES: STUDENT PAGE 8

Problem 1: The intent of problem 1 is to begin to draw a contrast between traditional multiplication algorithms with decimals and decimal work with ratio tables. Encourage students to solve the problem in any way. Be sure to discuss the work of a student who used the traditional algorithm as shown on the answer page. *Teaching Strategy:* You may wish to ask students to elaborate on their explanation of the problem, particularly the last step in which the decimal point is moved two spaces to the left. Students typically do not understand why this needs to be done, only that they have to do so. Rich discussion of this problem will help illuminate the ease with which ratio tables can be used to solve computations with simple benchmark decimals.

Problem 2: When working with decimals in ratio tables, the key is to eliminate the decimal as quickly as possible. *Teaching Strategy:* With the benchmark decimals (e.g., 0.25, 0.5, 0.75, and 0.10), it is usually easiest to do so by doubling the decimal until the result is a whole number. It is often easy to eliminate the decimal by multiplying by 10 as well. In this case, by doubling twice in the first two columns of the ratio table, the decimal 0.25 can be eliminated (i.e., 0.25 → 0.50 → 1.0).

Problem 3: *Teaching Strategy:* Strategies will vary, so be sure to engage students in conversation about how they completed their ratio tables. *Watch for:* Some students may continue to add 1.50, while others will use doubling or additive strategies when possible.

Student Page 8: Problems and Potential Answers

Section B: Applications of the Ratio Table Set 1

1. Solve the following problem any way you choose.

    12 x 2.25

    ```
        2.25
      x   12
      ——————
         450
      + 2250
      ——————
       27.00
    ```

    Explain your strategy: _____
    Responses will vary.

2. The multiplication problem above contained a decimal. Maybe you solved it using a set of steps called an algorithm. Algorithms are very helpful, but we need to make sure we understand how they work. For example, in this problem, you might have "moved" the decimal point over two places in the answer. Do you have any idea why you had to do that? While an algorithm like the one you used to multiply two numbers works just fine, you might be surprised how easy it is to use a ratio table to solve the same problem. Look at how the problem is solved using a ratio table.

Number of Factors	1	2	4	12
Product	2.25	4.50	9.00	27.00

    a) Explain this strategy. _____
    Double 2.25 once to get 4.50. Double 4.50 to get 9.00. Multiply 9.00 by 3 to get 27.

    b) Compare the ratio table strategy to the algorithm for multiplication you may already know.
    The ratio table strategy allows you to find the number of 2.25's that are in 27. There are twelve 2.25's in 27.

3. For a summer job, John sells peanuts at the baseball stadium. One package of peanuts costs $1.50. Most people buy more than one package of peanuts at a time. John decides to make a table that will help him quickly determine how much to charge people, depending on how many packages of peanuts they buy. Complete John's ratio table for him.

Peanuts	1	2	3	4	5	6
Cost	$1.50	$3.00	$4.50	$6.00	$7.50	$9.00

Is using a ratio table when you are working with decimals any different from using one when you are working with whole numbers?

Explain your strategy. Answers will vary.

CONTINUE THE PROBLEM SOLVING

Have students work individually to solve the problems on page 9. As they work, you may want to circulate and monitor their work and recorded answers. As students finish each problem, have them compare and discuss their answers with a partner. Then have each pair share their answers in a class discussion of the problem. Refer to the **Teacher Notes: Student Page 9** for more specific ideas about the problems on this page.

As students work and report their conclusions, focus on these issues:

Facilitate Students' Thinking – When several students have differing explanations of the methods used and the strategies they might use to solve the same problem, have them discuss their methods and give examples.

Allow Waiting Time – When students struggle to explain their thinking, allow at least 20 seconds for them to organize their thoughts.

TEACHER NOTES: STUDENT PAGE 9

Problem 4: This problem provides students with further practice with decimals. *Watch for:* Most students will quickly multiply by 10 to find an equivalent decimal, which eliminates the decimal.

Problem 5: These problems force students to examine and use particular strategies. *Teaching Strategy:* Be sure to pause for healthy discussion of the strategies that were structured into the ratio tables as well as the strategies students tend to prefer. The discussion questions at the end of the problem are excellent opportunities to make informal assessments of student understanding.

Student Page 9: Problems and Potential Answers

Section B: Applications of the Ratio Table Set 1

4. A ticket to get into Wet World Water Park costs $3.50. How much do tickets for 10 people cost? How much do they cost for 18 people?

Tickets	1	10	5	2	20	18		
Cost	$3.50	$35.00	$17.50	$7.00	$70.00	$63.00		

10 people? _$35.00_   18 people? _$63.00_

5. Tickets for the school play are $1.75 each. Together, Jenny and Sarah sold 28 tickets. How much money did they raise? _$49.00_

Both Jenny and Sarah started ratio tables but did not finish them. Help Jenny and Sarah complete the tables by filling in the shaded boxes.

Jenny's method

1	2	4	28			
$1.75	$3.50	$7.00	$49.00			

Sarah's method

1	10	20	5	2	30	28
$1.75	$17.50	$35.00	$8.75	$3.50	$52.50	$49.00

What was Jenny's method? She doubled the price of 1 ticket to get the price of 2 tickets. She doubled that to get the price of 4 tickets. Then she multiplied that by 7 to get the price of 28 tickets.

What was Sarah's method?   She multiplied the price of 1 ticket by 10 to get the price of 10 tickets. She doubled that to get the price of 20 tickets. She halved the price of 10 tickets to get the price of 5 tickets. Then she doubled the price of 1 ticket to get the price of 2 tickets. She then added the price of 10 tickets and 20 tickets to get the price of 30 tickets. Finally, she subtracted the price of 2 tickets from 30 tickets to get the price of 28 tickets.

Is one method better than the other? Why or why not? Reponses will vary.

How would you solve this problem? Reponses will vary.

Book 2: *The Ratio Table*

CONTINUE THE PROBLEM SOLVING

Have students work individually to solve the problems on page 10. As they work, circulate and monitor their work and recorded answers. When they finish the page, have students compare and discuss their ratio tables with a partner. Then have each pair share their conclusions in a class discussion of the problems. Refer to the **Teacher Notes: Student Page 10** for more specific ideas about the problems on this page.

As students work and report their conclusions, focus on these issues:

Help Make Connections – Remind students that they can use strategies they learned before, such as doubling and counting on, to help them complete the ratio tables.

Allow Waiting Time – When students struggle to explain their thinking, be sure to allow them ample time to gather and organize their thoughts.

Encourage Language Development – These problems repeatedly make reference to columns, rows, and cells. Be sure to review these definitions with students.

TEACHER NOTES: STUDENT PAGE 10

Problem 1: The problems on this page are different from the previous ones in that the starting ratios are not in a 1-to-x relationship. For example, in this problem, 3 peaches are sold for $2. *Watch for:* At first, students may question whether this problem is in the right form for a ratio table because they have become accustomed to starting problems with a 1 in the top row of the first column. *Teaching Strategy:* If students persist, you can always reduce these fractions such that they do resemble earlier problems. In this problem, for example, if 3 peaches sold for $2, then 1 peach can be sold for 2/3 of a dollar, or $0.66.

Problem 2: Like problem 1, this problem requires students to apply division strategies in which the beginning ratio does not have a numerator of 1.

Problems 3–4: These problems give more practice with fractions that are not unit fractions, which are fractions with a numerator of 1.

Problem 5: Problem 5 does exactly what was referenced above: renaming the initial ratio of 3 : 3.75 as a ratio with a numerator of 1. *Teaching Strategy:* In order to solve this problem in only two additional steps, students should first divide both 3 and 3.75 by 3. This results in a second ratio, 1 : 1.25. At this point students can simply multiply by 10 both to find an equivalent ratio with only whole numbers (this eliminates the decimal) and to solve the problem. Be sure to discuss this problem.

Student Page 10: Problems and Potential Answers

Section B: Applications of the Ratio Table — Set 2

Solve the problems using a ratio table.

1. Joel went to an orchard to pick fruit. Three pounds of peaches sold for $2. How much did Joel have to pay for 12 pounds? $8.00

Pounds of Peaches	3	6	12		
Cost	$2.00	$4.00	$8.00		

2. How much would Joel have to pay for 33 pounds? $22.00

Pounds of Peaches	3	12	24	36	33
Cost	$2.00	$8.00	$16.00	$24.00	$22.00

3. You can buy two watermelons for $3. How many watermelons can you buy if you have only $7.50? _____5_____ watermelons

Watermelons	2	4	1	5	
Cost	$3.00	$6.00	$1.50	$7.50	

4. Four pounds of apples cost $2.50. You have $10 to spend on apples. How many pounds can you buy? _____16_____ pounds

Pounds of Apples	4	8	16		
Cost	$2.50	$5.00	$10.00		

5. Three pounds of cherries cost $3.75. How much do 10 pounds cost? Joanie says she can solve this problem using only <u>three columns</u> in a ratio table. Can you figure out how she did it?

Pounds	3	1	10
Cost	$3.75	$1.25	$12.50

Explain Joanie's solution: She found the price of 1 pound by dividing the price of 3 pounds by 3. Then she multiplied the price of 1 pound by 10 to get the price of 10 pounds.

10   Book 2: *The Ratio Table*

CONCEPT DEVELOPMENT (Pages 11–12)

INTRODUCE THE CONCEPT

Draw this example of a ratio table on the board:

Tickets	3	6	18
Cost	$4	$8	$24

Ask:
Suppose I erase parts of this ratio table like this. [Erase everything but the fraction 3/4.]

$$\frac{3}{4}$$

What is left?

Listen for:
• A fraction; the fraction three fourths.

Redraw the ratio table. Explain that a ratio table is a collection of any number of fractions that have something in common.

Ask:
What do the fractions in the ratio table have in common?

Listen for:
• They all name the same part.
• They are all equivalent fractions.

MODEL MATHEMATICAL THINKING

Have students turn to page 11 in their books. Point out the ratio table at the top of the page. Tell students that a ratio table can be thought of as a collection of equivalent fractions that are organized in a helpful way.

Ask:
Can we make up a problem that could be solved using this ratio table?

Talk Through the Thinking:
Let's look at the fractions in the first three columns in the ratio table. They are 1/2, 2/4, and 4/8. Suppose I had three pizzas, all the same size, and I cut them in different ways. I cut one in half. I cut another into 4 equal slices. I cut a third pizza into 8 equal slices.

[Refer to the diagrams in the student book.] *Which would be the most pizza: 1 out of 2 slices of the first pizza, 2 out of 4 slices of the second pizza, or 4 out of 8 slices of the third pizza? It doesn't matter. Because the pizzas are all the same size, and I cut each of them into equal slices, I would get the same amount of pizza regardless of the equivalent fraction of a pizza I used.*

Ask:
Suppose I had another pizza of the same size and I cut it into 16 equal slices. How many slices would I need to have in order to get the same amount of pizza as with the other pizzas? Why?

Listen for:
• You would need to have 8 slices of pizza.
• You would have 8/16 of the pizza. This pizza is the same size as the others, and it is cut into equal slices. The fraction 8/16 is equivalent to 1/2, 2/4, and 4/8. It names the same part.

LAUNCH THE PROBLEM SOLVING

Have students work individually or in pairs to solve the problems on page 11. As they work, circulate and monitor their discussions and recorded answers. After they finish the page, have students share their conclusions in a class discussion of the problems on the page. Refer to the **Teacher Notes: Student Page 11** for more specific ideas about the problems on this page.

As students work and report their conclusions, focus on these issues:

Look for Misconceptions – Students may confuse the terms equivalent fractions with equal fractions (See the Teacher Notes below).

Facilitate Students' Thinking – Fraction circles, fraction strips, and other visual aids or hands-on manipulatives will greatly enhance students' conceptual understanding of fractional equivalencies.

Allow Waiting Time – When students struggle to explain their thinking, allow ample time for them to organize their thoughts.

Encourage Language Development – Review definitions of fraction and equivalent fractions.

Student Page 11: Problems and Potential Answers

Section B: Applications of the Ratio Table Set 3

The ratio table can also be used to understand fractions.

When you compare columns in a ratio table, you will find something interesting about the way the numbers are related. Look at this ratio table:

1	2	4	8
2	4	8	16

With a friend, discuss how this ratio table was completed.

Now, let's look at each column of the table and then write each as a fraction.

$$\frac{1}{2} \quad \frac{2}{4} \quad \frac{4}{8} \quad \frac{8}{16}$$

What do you notice about these fractions? They are equivalent fractions all with a value of one-half.

Think of it this way. Nick is sharing a pizza with his brother. The top number in the fraction, the **numerator**, is the number of slices Nick eats. The bottom number of the fraction, the **denominator**, is the total number of equal slices when the pizza is first cut. So, take a look at how much pizza Nick could eat for each pizza. The shaded part represents the number of pizza slices that Nick could eat.

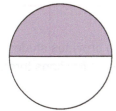 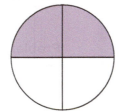 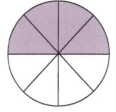

Pizza one: 1 out of 2 slices Pizza two: 2 out of 4 slices Pizza three: 4 out of 8 slices

Could Nick eat the same amount of pizza each time? Yes! Even though he may eat *more slices*, the amount of pizza remains the same. So the fractions 1/2, 2/4, 4/8, and 8/16 all have the same value. When two fractions have the same value, we call them *equivalent fractions*.

A ratio table can help us find and use equivalent fractions. In fact, **every** ratio table is simply a list of equivalent fractions.

1. Find equivalent fractions for 2/3.
Responses will vary. Here are some possible answers:

2	4	8	16	32	64
3	6	12	24	48	96

2. Find equivalent fractions for 3/4.
Responses will vary. Here are some possible answers:

3	6	9	12	21	24
4	8	12	16	28	32

Book 2: *The Ratio Table* 11

TEACHER NOTES: STUDENT PAGE 11

Much of this page is given to an explanation of equivalent fractions. As noted, a ratio table is simply a way to organize equivalent fractions. Students should be comfortable thinking in both directions with ratios: reducing a fraction to simpler terms, such as 2/4 → 1/2, and finding multiples of a given fraction, or raising its terms, such as 2/3 → 4/6. These concepts are developed on this page through problems 1 and 2.

Problems 1-2: *Teaching Strategy:* Be sure to help students understand how the steps they have become comfortable with using for ratio computations in ratio tables can also be used to find equivalent fractions.

> **On the Lookout for Misconceptions**
>
> The most common misconception students bring to the study of fractions has to do with the difference between the terms equivalent and equal. This misconception will be dealt with explicitly in a later book in this series. For now, be aware that students may confuse equivalent fractions with equal fractions.
>
> Students know that 1/2 and 2/4 are equivalent fractions. Yet depending on the context, they may not necessarily refer to equal amounts. Have students imagine two apple pies, one of which is larger than the other. The fractions 1/2 and 2/4 represent the same portion of one pie. But 1/2 of the small pie is quite different in quantity from 2/4 of the large pie. The fractions are equivalent, but the actual amounts are not equal.

CONTINUE THE PROBLEM SOLVING

Have students work individually to solve the problems on page 12. As they work, you may want to circulate and monitor their work and recorded answers. As students finish each problem, have them compare and discuss their answers with a partner. Then have each pair share their answers in a class discussion of the problem. Refer to the **Teacher Notes: Student Page 12** for more specific ideas about the problems on this page.

As students work and report their conclusions, focus on these issues:

Validate Alternate Solutions – When several students use different ratios to lower terms, have them discuss whether the ratios they chose are all correct.

Encourage Language Development – When students are discussing the ratios they used in problem 4, invite them to use terms such as simplest form, and reduce. It is likely that students will need explanations for both of these concepts.

TEACHER NOTES: STUDENT PAGE 12

Problem 3: This problem provides students with practice in finding equivalent fractions through the use of the ratio table.

Problem 4: Problem 4 asks students to work in the reverse direction by simplifying fractions, or lowering their terms. Be sure students understand what is meant by simplest form, or simplest terms. A fraction is in simplest form when it cannot be simplified any further without introducing a decimal in the numerator or the denominator. Other vocabulary you may wish to bring out is the idea of reducing a fraction, or lowering its terms.

Student Page 12: Problems and Potential Answers

Section B: Applications of the Ratio Table — Set 3

1. Use a ratio table to find equivalent fractions for the following:
   Responses will vary. Sample responses are given.

   a) 3/5

3	6	12	24	48
5	10	20	40	80

   b) 4/5

4	8	12	16	20
5	10	15	20	25

   c) 1/4

1	2	3	4	8
4	8	12	16	32

   d) 1/3

1	10	9	19	11
3	30	27	57	33

2. Sometimes you can use a ratio table to **reduce** fractions. That means you can use a ratio table to **simplify** a fraction and *reduce it to its simplest form*. Try to simplify the following fractions as much as you can. Reduce the terms by halving and dividing.

   a)

24	12	6	3
80	40	20	10

   b)

60	6	2
90	9	3

   c)

18	9	3
24	12	4

12 Book 2: *The Ratio Table*

SECTION B ASSESSMENT (PAGES 13–14)

LAUNCH THE ASSESSMENT

Have students turn to the Section B Assessment on page 13. An additional copy is found on page 16 of the Assessment Book. Have students work individually to solve the problems and write their explanations. As they work, circulate to be sure students understand what they need to do for each problem. Be sure that students are completing each part of the problem. For example, for problem 1b, students need to complete a ratio table and explain each step taken. You may find it helpful to read the directions for all the problems with the class before students begin, discussing the types of responses they will need to make for each problem.

Encourage students to use whatever space they need to explain their thinking. If the space on the page is inadequate, they should use an additional sheet of paper or use the back of the page.

Refer to the **Teacher Notes: Assessment Problems for Section B** for more specific ideas about the problems on this page.

Evaluate Student Responses

Use the assessment rubric on page 14 of the Assessment Book (pictured on page 122 of the Teacher Edition) to evaluate student responses. The Assessment Book has some general suggestions for using the rubric that you may find helpful.

TEACHER NOTES: ASSESSMENT PROBLEMS FOR SECTION B

Problem 1: This series of questions enables students to understand that a ratio table may be every bit as efficient as the traditional multiplication algorithm in solving problems. Some students may not be familiar with the traditional method of multiplying two-digit numbers. In such cases, make accommodations for students. While some students may still prefer to use the traditional algorithm they first used for multiplication, there is great advantage to being able to multiply in more than one way. Be sure to pause for healthy discussion of 1d. *Teaching Strategy:* You may wish to give students additional problems of this type, encouraging them to multiply with both the traditional method and ratio tables. After repeated practice and comparison, it should not be surprising to see some students begin to prefer ratio tables to the standard algorithm.

118 **The Ratio Table** *Teacher Edition*

Student Page 13: Problems and Potential Answers

Section B: Problems for Assessment

1. There are 24 sticks of gum in every pack. How many sticks of gum are in 16 packs?

   a) Solve using an algorithm:

   $$\begin{array}{r} 24 \\ \times\ 16 \\ \hline 144 \\ +\ 240 \\ \hline 384 \end{array}$$

   Explain your steps. Multiply the 24 by 6 to get 144. Then multiply the 24 by 10 to get 240. Add the 144 and 240 to get 384.

   b) Complete the ratio table to solve the same problem. How many sticks of gum are in 16 packs?

Packs	1	2	20	4	16
Gum	24	48	480	96	384

   Explain your steps. Double the one 24 to get two 24s, which equals 48. Multiply the two 24s by 10 to get 20 24s, which equals 480. Double the two 24s to get 4 24s, which equals 96. Subtract four 24s from 20 24s to get sixteen 24s, which equals 384.

   c) What happens if we switch the numbers in the first column, and then solve the ratio table? Finish the ratio table.

1	10	20	5	25	24
16	160	320	80	400	384

   Explain your steps. Multiply the one 16 by 10 to get ten 16s, which equals 160. Multiply the ten 16s by 2 to get twenty 16s or 320. Half the ten 16s to get five 16s, which equals 80. Multiply the five 16s by 5 to get twenty-five 16s or 400. Subtract one 16 from twenty-five 16s to get twenty-four 16s, or 384.

   d) Compare these three strategies. Which one do you like best? Why?   Responses will vary.

Book 2: *The Ratio Table*   13

CONTINUE THE ASSESSMENT

Have students turn to the Section B Assessment on page 14. An additional copy is found on page 17 of the Assessment Book. Have students work individually to solve the problems and write their explanations. As they work, circulate to be sure students understand what they need to do for each problem. Be sure that students are completing each part of the problem. For example, for problem 1 students need to complete a ratio table and explain the strategy they used. You may find it helpful to read the directions for all the problems with the class before students begin, discussing the types of responses they will need to make for each problem.

Encourage students to use whatever space they need to explain their thinking. If the space on the page is inadequate, they should use an additional sheet of paper or use the back of the page.

Refer to the **Teacher Notes: Assessment Problems for Section B** for more specific ideas about the problems on this page.

Evaluate Student Responses

Use the assessment rubric on page 15 of the Assessment Book (pictured on page 123 of the Teacher Edition) to evaluate student responses. The Assessment Book has some general suggestions for using the rubric that you may find helpful.

TEACHER NOTES: ASSESSMENT PROBLEMS SECTION B

These assessment problems are designed to elicit a wide range of ratio-table strategies. *Watch for:* As you assess the work of your students on these problems, look for instances in which students can articulate their reasoning for using the common strategies developed in this book.

Student Page 14: Problems and Potential Answers

Section B: Problems for Assessment

2. A ruler costs $1.75. How much money will it take to buy rulers for all 22 students in Mrs. Miller's class?
   $38.50

Students	1	2	20	22			
Cost	$1.75	$3.50	$35.00	$38.50			

   Explain your steps. Double the cost for 1 student to get the cost for 2 students. Multiply this by 10 to get the cost for 20 students. Then add the cost for 2 students and 20 students to get the cost for 22 students.

3. A vendor sells hot dogs at the ballgame, 2 for $1.50. How many hot dogs can you buy with $20? 26
   Use a ratio table to help solve the problem.

Hot Dogs	2	4	8	16	24	26	
Cost	$1.50	$3.00	$6.00	$12.00	$18.00	$19.50	

   Explain your steps. Double the cost of 2 hot dogs to get the cost of 4. Double the cost of 4 to get the cost of 8. Double the cost of 8 to get the cost of 16. Add the cost of 8 and 16 to get the cost of 24. Add the cost of 2 hot dogs to the cost of 24 hot dogs to get the cost of 26 hot dogs, which is the most you can get for $20.

4. Find 6 equivalent fractions for the fraction 3/8. Write the equivalent fractions in a ratio table.
   Responses will vary. A sample response is given.

3	6	9	12	15	18	21	
8	16	24	32	40	48	56	

5. Use a ratio table to reduce the fraction 240/360 to its simplest form.
   Responses will vary. A sample response is given.

240	24	12	4	2			
360	36	18	6	3			

6. Why are all the fractions in a ratio table equivalent fractions?
   Because the same operation is being applied to each number in a column.

SECTION B ASSESSMENT

Section B Assessment
For Use With: Student Book Page 13

PROBLEM DESCRIPTION	SCORING: WHAT TO LOOK FOR	SCORE AND COMMENTS
Problem 1a Solve a multiplication problem using an algorithm. Level 1: Comprehension and Knowledge Level 2: Tool use	Do students: • Understand how an algorithm works? • Implement appropriate strategies in an algorithm? • Articulate their solution strategy?	Points:_____ of 3
Problem 1b Finish a partially completed ratio table. Level 1: Comprehension and Knowledge Level 2: Tool use	Do students: • Have an understanding of the way a ratio table works? • Recognize and subsequently implement appropriate strategies in a ratio table? • Articulate their solution strategy?	Points:_____ of 3
Problem 1c Finish a partially completed ratio table. Level 1: Comprehension and Knowledge Level 2: Tool use	Do students: • Understand how a ratio table works? • Recognize and subsequently implement appropriate strategies in a ratio table? • Articulate their solution strategy?	Points:_____ of 3
Problem 1d Comparison of two strategies. Level 4: Synthesis and Evaluation	Do students: • Understand the function of a ratio table and an algorithm? • Compare different strategy usage within two tables? • Articulate their thinking adequately?	Points:_____ of 3

PAGE ONE, TOTAL POINTS:_____ OF 12

SECTION B ASSESSMENT

Section B Assessment
For Use With: Student Book Page 14

PROBLEM DESCRIPTION	SCORING: WHAT TO LOOK FOR	SCORE AND COMMENTS
Problem 2 Solve a word problem using a ratio table. Level 1: Comprehension and Knowledge Level 2: Tool use	Do students: • Understand how a ratio table works? • Implement the appropriate strategies in a ratio table? • Articulate their solution strategy?	Points: _____ of 3
Problem 3 Solve a word problem using a ratio table. Level 1: Comprehension and Knowledge Level 2: Tool use	Do students: • Understand how a ratio table works? • Implement the appropriate strategies in a ratio table? • Articulate their solution strategy?	Points: _____ of 3
Problem 4 Use ratio tables to find equivalent fractions. Level 1: Comprehension and Knowledge Level 2: Tool use Level 3: Connections and Application	Do students: • Understand how a ratio table works? • Recognize and subsequently implement appropriate strategies in a ratio table? • Articulate their solution strategy? • Have a conceptual understanding of equivalent fractions?	Points: _____ of 3
Problem 5 Use ratio tables to find equivalent fractions. Level 1: Comprehension and Knowledge Level 2: Tool use Level 3: Connections and Application	Do students: • Understand how a ratio table works? • Recognize and subsequently implement appropriate strategies in a ratio table? • Articulate their solution strategy? • Have a conceptual understanding of equivalent fractions?	Points: _____ of 3
Problem 6 Explain equivalent fractions through use of ratio tables. Level 4: Synthesis and Evaluation	Do students: • Understand ratio tables? • Understand equivalent fractions? • Understand the relationship between equivalent fractions and ratio tables?	Points: _____ of 3

PAGE TWO, TOTAL POINTS: _____ OF 15

End-of-Book Assessment (Pages 15–17)

LAUNCH THE ASSESSMENT

Have students turn to the End-of-Book Assessment on page 15. An additional copy is found on page 20 of the Assessment Book. Have students work individually to solve the problems and write their explanations. As they work, circulate to be sure students understand what they need to do for each problem. For example, in problem 1 students need to analyze the ratio table and fill in each cell, maintaining equal ratios, to get to an equal ratio with the given numerator. You may find it helpful to read the directions for all the problems with the class before students begin, discussing the types of responses they will need to make for each problem.

Encourage students to use whatever space they need to explain their strategies. If the space on the page is inadequate, they should use an additional sheet of paper or use the back of the page.

Refer to the **Teacher Notes: End-of-Book Assessment, Student Page 15**, for more specific ideas about the problems on this page.

Evaluate Student Responses

Use the assessment rubric on page 18 of the Assessment Book (pictured on page 130 of the Teacher Edition) to evaluate student responses. The Assessment Book has some general suggestions for using the rubric that you may find helpful.

TEACHER NOTES: END-OF-BOOK ASSESSMENT, STUDENT PAGE 15

Problems 1–6: These problems have been designed specifically to highlight each of the six ratio-table strategies developed throughout this book. *Watch for:* At this point, students should be able to quickly identify and use these strategies.

Problems 7–8: These problems are nearly identical to others presented earlier. They may be used to assess your students' facility with ratio tables, as well as their ability to decipher the meanings, and subsequent problem-solving approaches, of problem contexts.

Student Page 15: Problems and Potential Answers

End-of-Book Assessment

You solved many problems in this book with ratio tables. You probably used familiar strategies like these:

Multiply by 10

1	10
15	150

Multiply

2	6
50	150

Doubling

4	8
15	30

Halving

20	10
30	15

Adding

1	2	3
25	50	75

Subtracting

1	10	9
12	120	108

Find the missing numbers in the ratio tables below. Then write which of the above strategies you used.

1.

1	10	9
18	180	162

Strategy: Subtracting

2.

1	10	5
18	180	90

Strategy: Halving

3.

1	10	20
12	120	240

Strategy: Doubling (or multiplying by 2)

4.

2	12
8	48

Strategy: Multiplying

5.

4	40
18	180

Strategy: Times 10

6.

2	10	12
8	40	48

Strategy: Adding

7. A stamp costs 37 cents. How much does it cost for a book of 20 stamps? 30 stamps?

Stamps	1	10	20	30			
Cents	37	370	740	1110			

8. There are 24 flowers in each box. How many flowers are in 9 boxes?

		Step #1	Step #2	Step #3	Step #4	Step #5
Boxes	1	2	4	10	5	9
Flowers	24	48	96	240	120	216

Describe how each step of the ratio table was determined (e.g., doubling, adding, etc.)

Step 1: Doubled the flowers in 1 box.

Step 2: Doubled the flowers in 2 boxes.

Step 3: Times 10 the number of flowers in 1 box.

Step 4: Halved the number of flowers in 10 boxes.

Step 5: Added the number of flowers in 4 boxes and 5 boxes.

CONTINUE THE ASSESSMENT

Have students turn to the End-of-Book Assessment on page 16. An additional copy is found on page 21 of the Assessment Book. Have students work individually to solve the problems and write their explanations. As they work, circulate to be sure students understand what they need to do for each problem. For example, in problem 10 students need to decide which ratios will help them multiply, which strategies to use to find these ratios, and then fill in the appropriate cells, maintaining equal ratios. You may find it helpful to read the directions for all the problems with the class before students begin, discussing the types of responses they will need to make for each problem.

Encourage students to use whatever space they need to explain their strategies. If the space on the page is inadequate, they should use an additional sheet of paper or use the back of the page.

Refer to the **Teacher Notes: End-of-Book Assessment, Student Page 16**, for more specific ideas about the problems on this page.

Evaluate Student Responses

Use the assessment rubric on pages 18–19 of the Assessment Book (pictured on pages 130–131 of the Teacher Edition) to evaluate student responses. The Assessment Book has some general suggestions for using the rubric that you may find helpful.

TEACHER NOTES: END-OF-BOOK ASSESSMENT, STUDENT PAGE 16

Problem 9: This problem should not be overlooked. *Watch for:* Students' responses to this problem will be a good indicator of the degree to which they understand the purposes and structures of ratio tables and strategies for using them.

Problems 10–11: These problems may be used to assess students' ability to use ratio tables as computational tools.

Problem 12: Problem 12 requires that students pull together all the concepts in this book. It is a rich problem and should not be skipped. That said, it is likely students may find it challenging and will need assistance. Students must first recognize and understand the essential elements of the context of the problem. *Teaching Strategy:* It might help to restate the problem in other words; for example, *Matthew needs a grade of 80% in order to pass the test. The test is 75 problems long. How many correct answers does he need to have on the test to make sure he scores at least 80%? In other words, what is 80% of 75?*

Once this task is clear, students should recognize that the starting ratio for the table is 8/10. By using the ratio table to find the equivalent fraction with a denominator of 75, students should be able to determine that 80% of 75 is 45.

Student Page 16: Problems and Potential Answers

End-of-Book Assessment

9. What are equivalent fractions? Equivalent fractions are fractions that represent the same value.

   How does a ratio table help you find equivalent fractions? In a ratio table, when the same operation is applied to both numbers in a column, equivalent fractions are maintained.

10. Use a ratio table to multiply the following:

    a) 19 x 18 = 342

1	10	9	19		
18	180	162	342		

    b) 22 x 11 = 242

1	2	20	22		
11	22	220	242		

11. Use a ratio table. Reduce each fraction to its simplest form.

    a) 36 ÷ 60

36	18	9	3		
60	30	15	5		

    b) 120 ÷ 160

120	12	6	3		
160	16	8	4		

12. For Matthew to get a B on a test, he needs to answer at least 8 out of every 10 questions correctly. The test has 75 questions. What is the least number of correct answers Matthew needs to get a B? _____60_____ Use a ratio table to help you solve this problem.

Number Correct	8	16	32	48	56	4	60	
Total Problems	10	20	40	60	70	5	75	

CONTINUE THE ASSESSMENT

Have students turn to the End-of-Book Assessment on page 17. An additional copy is found on page 22 of the Assessment Book. Have students work individually to solve the puzzles. As they work, circulate to be sure students understand what they need to do for each problem. For example, for all the puzzles, students need to use all the cells, and only those cells, in each ratio table. You may find it helpful to read the directions for the puzzles with the class before students begin, discussing the types of responses they will need to make for each problem.

Refer to the **Teacher Notes: End-of-Book Assessment, Student Page 17** for more specific ideas about the problems on this page.

Evaluate Student Responses

Use the assessment rubric on page 19 of the Assessment Book (pictured on page 131 of the Teacher Edition) to evaluate student responses. The Assessment Book has some general suggestions for using the rubric that you may find helpful.

TEACHER NOTES: END-OF-BOOK ASSESSMENT, STUDENT PAGE 17

These puzzles were added as a final assessment activity for students. By requiring students to use a limited number of columns in their ratio tables, these problems force them to experiment until they find appropriate strategies. The problems have been designed to elicit a wide range of strategies. Students should be encouraged to develop their own puzzles to be shared with their peers.

Student Page 17: Problems and Potential Answers

End-of-Book Assessment

Ratio Table Puzzles

The ratio tables below are puzzles. Try to solve the puzzles by correctly filling in all the empty cells in each table. You may need to use several strategies, such as doubling, halving, adding, multiplying, and so on.
Occasionally, answers may vary.

1.

1	2	4	8
6	12	24	48

2.

3	6	9	12	18	36
7	14	21	28	42	84

3.

2	20	40	60
5	50	100	150

4.

3	18	15
2	12	10

5.

1	6	18	17
3	18	54	51

Book 2: *The Ratio Table* 17

SCORING GUIDE BOOK 2: THE RATIO TABLE

End-of-Book Assessment
For Use With: Student Book Pages 15–16

PROBLEM DESCRIPTION	SCORING: WHAT TO LOOK FOR	SCORE AND COMMENTS
Problems 1-6 Find the missing values in partially completed ratio tables by recognizing particular strategy use. Level 1: Comprehension and Knowledge Level 2: Tool use	Do students: • Understand how a ratio table works? • Recognize various solution strategies in use? • Implement appropriate strategies in a ratio table?	(#1) Points:_____ of 2 (#2) Points:_____ of 2 (#3) Points:_____ of 2 (#4) Points:_____ of 2 (#5) Points:_____ of 2 (#6) Points:_____ of 2
Problem 7 Use a ratio table to solve a word problem. Level 1: Comprehension and Knowledge Level 2: Tool use Level 3: Connection and Application	Do students: • Understand how a ratio table works? • Use appropriate and varied strategies in a ratio table?	Points:_____ of 3
Problem 8 Finish a partially completed ratio table, and explain each step in the table. Level 1: Comprehension and Knowledge Level 2: Tool use	Do students: • Understand how a ratio table works? • Recognize and subsequently implement appropriate strategies in a ratio table? • Articulate their strategy usage?	Points:_____ of 4
Problem 9 (pg. 16) Define equivalent fractions, and how they are expressed in a ratio table. Level 4: Synthesis and Evaluation	Do students: • Have an understanding of equivalent fractions? • Have an understanding of the way in which ratio tables make use of equivalent fractions?	Points:_____ of 3

PAGE ONE, TOTAL POINTS:_____ OF 22

End-of-Book Assessment (Continued)
For Use With: Student Book Pages 16–17

PROBLEM DESCRIPTION	SCORING: WHAT TO LOOK FOR	SCORE AND COMMENTS
Problems 10a–b Use ratio table to multiply two, two-digit numbers. Level 1: Comprehension and Knowledge Level 2: Tool use	Do students: • Use a ratio table to multiply two-digit numbers? • Use appropriate strategies?	(#10a) Points:_____ of 2 (#10b) Points:_____ of 2
Problems 11a–b Reducing fractions with ratio tables. Level 1: Comprehension and Knowledge Level 2: Tool use	Do students: • Understand how a ratio table works to represent division? • Use appropriate and varied strategies in ratio table?	(#11a) Points:_____ of 2 (#11b) Points:_____ of 2
Problem 12 Use a ratio table to solve a word problem. Level 1: Comprehension and Knowledge Level 2: Tool use Level 3: Connection and Application	Do students: • Understand how a ratio table works? • Recognize and subsequently implement appropriate strategies in a ratio table?	Points:_____ of 2
Ratio Table Puzzles (pg. 17) Solve ratio table puzzles by use of creative proportional strategies. Level 1: Comprehension and Knowledge Level 2: Tool use Level 3: Connection and Application	Do students: • Have an understanding of equivalent fractions? • Understand how ratio tables make use of equivalent fractions?	(#1) Points:_____ of 2 (#2) Points:_____ of 2 (#3) Points:_____ of 2 (#4) Points:_____ of 2 (#5) Points:_____ of 2

PAGE TWO, TOTAL POINTS:_____ OF 20

Book 3:
Knowing Numbers

Book Three Overview: Knowing Numbers

Introduction

This book is the third in a series of eight units that are geared toward helping middle-grades learners acquire both facility with, and understanding of, the basic mathematical procedures and concepts that lay the groundwork for more advanced mathematical study. In particular, this text series cultivates understanding of a number of mathematical tools that children learn to use with facility in various mathematics and real-world contexts.

Book Focus

This book is designed to help students develop a rich sense of numbers, their relationships to each other, how they are manipulated in various operations, and how they can be used to enhance meaning of everyday mathematical contexts. The first two sections of this book review topics that were introduced in *Book One: The Number Line* and *Book Two: The Ratio Table.* Despite the power of these two flexible models, it is also the case that some problem contexts are more suited to other approaches. In this book, students will explore the properties of numbers that will help them develop efficient solution strategies and intuitive methods for carrying out computations.

Sections A and B revisit the number line and ratio tables, respectively. The beginning of Section C: What's that Number? provides students with the opportunity to describe numbers in as many ways as possible. It then uses these informal descriptions to prompt students to consider ways in which numbers can be decomposed and, subsequently, recombined in other contexts. Section D: Making Change uses money to help students become flexible with informal addition and subtraction contexts as they make change for customers, explore receipts, and estimate monetary amounts. Section E: From Adding to Multiplying explores the relationship between multiplication and repeated addition, and includes the introduction of the area model as a method of multiplication. Finally, the unit assessment provides students with multiple opportunities to apply the informal strategies introduced in earlier sections in the context of a real-world scenario.

How to Use this Book

There are two primary sections in every lesson. The lesson starts with a discussion that helps you assess what students already know and a suggestion for how to model the type of mathematical thinking they will be doing on their own. What follows is a resource guide to support the development of concepts and skills as students solve the problems. Throughout the resource guide, you will be provided with insights into the mathematical content of the problems, pedagogical ideas to enhance teaching and learning, samples of anticipated student work, insights about student thinking related to the topics at hand, and ideas about assessment. You will also find a reproduction of the student page that includes answers. This program is meant to be flexible and relies on your craft and knowledge. Toward that end, the resource materials that accompany this text are not intended to be used as a script. Instead, the intention of this program is that you will have a chance to apply your knowledge of students, your own experiences with these mathematical tools, and your intuition about teaching to make this program as effective as possible.

Models of Implementation

This program has been designed to be as flexible as possible. While this series of books may be used as the primary curriculum for the classroom, it was not designed as the full curriculum for any given grade level. Rather, it was crafted to support you as you help students understand the number operations and concepts that precede more advanced work in algebra. You may therefore choose to use this program either as a guide for whole-class explorations or as the text for smaller, pull-out groups of students. In both cases, it is important to note that this program is designed on the principle that students learn mathematics in large measure through interactions with one another. Throughout the books, you will find numerous questions that ask students to explain their thinking. These occasions should not be taken lightly. It is in the sharing and comparing of solution strategies that children begin to build a firm foundation of understanding. The social dynamic of learning mathematics is important to recognize. Participation in mathematical discourse may be the most powerful impetus for learning mathematics available to young learners, and you should take advantage of every opportunity to encourage children to talk about their mathematical thinking and processes. Given a commitment to this principle, this program is likely to be most successful when students are progressing through the problems with their peers.

Addressing Issues of Language

There is no question that one of the greatest challenges facing teachers today is to make instruction relevant and accessible for second language learners. *Inside Math* has been written with this concern in mind. Careful consideration was given to the language that appears in directions, contextually based problems, and other sections of the book where text is necessary. When possible, for example, we have limited new vocabulary to only what is essential to the concepts being presented, and we revisit new vocabulary words and concepts repeatedly throughout the text. To assist teachers in making instruction accessible for English language learners, as well as other students for whom reading presents particular challenges, several supporting features were added to the teacher's edition. First, within the section planner that introduces each new major mathematical concept contained in the book, there is a heading that reads: Language Development. In this section of the overview, new vocabulary words are introduced and defined. Later in the text, when these words and concepts are introduced in a specific lesson, the teacher notes include additional information about pertinent language considerations and vocabulary. These notes appear as Encouraging Language Development under the Concept Development and Continue the Problem Solving headings.

Explaining Thinking

Throughout this series, students will be asked to explain their thinking. The ability to articulate mathematical ideas and solution strategies is a feature of mathematics education that continues to grow in its importance. We see numerous examples in state, national, and international achievement tests in which answers alone are not enough, students must also be able to express their thought processes, give rationale for answers, and articulate steps in any given strategy. In this book there are opportunities for students to do likewise.

As this is often a new and challenging task for students, it is important for teachers to be able to model the process of making thinking explicit. At the beginning of each section in the book, there are suggestions for ways to introduce the content at hand, many of which are suitable candidates for teachers to illustrate what means to explain thinking in an intelligible way. Be aware of both the importance of this feature of the program, as well as the challenge it provides students as they practice this skill for what might be the first time.

Assessment

At the conclusion of each section, you will find several problems that may be used for formative assessments. These problems review key concepts discussed in the previous section. At the end of each book are additional assessment problems that cover the content of the entire book. These problems may be used as a cumulative assessment of student understanding of the key concepts in the book. The teachers' guide contains insights as to how the assessment problems might best be used and what they are intended to measure.

Assessment rubrics and scoring guides for every assessment may be found in Assessment Teacher Edition. Detailed instructions regarding assessment in general, and the use of the program rubrics in particular, are included in the introduction of Assessment Teacher Edition.

Professional Background

The purpose of this book is to provide learners with an opportunity to develop a richer sense of numbers: what they are, how they can be represented, how they can be operated upon, and how they can be used to help us make sense of our lives and the world around us. The importance of helping children acquire this sort of number sense cannot be understated. Confidence with number meanings and relationships is important for the computational skills required to operate successfully with numbers. But there is more to number sense than algorithms. A rich understanding of numbers allows students to make connections, formulate mathematical relationships, make reasonable estimates, and work confidently in contexts that are inherently numerical. Children come to school with many innate ideas and experiences with numbers. Yet it is discouraging to see how many students entering the middle grades can essentially do little more with numbers than to count. This book provides students with ample exposure to activities and number contexts that will support the development of their numeracy and mathematical thinking.

A Framework for Thinking About Number Sense

Given the breadth and depth of the number domain, many definitions of number sense can be found in textbooks, research articles, and teacher support materials. The ideas upon which this text series is based emerge from a fundamental position of thinking about number sense in the following way:

> Number sense includes a good intuition about numbers and their relationships. It develops gradually as a result of exploring numbers, visualizing them in a variety of contexts, and relating them in ways that are not limited by traditional rules and procedures (Howden, 1999).

While using algorithms and procedures is centrally important to the well-prepared mathematics student, we also know that those skills alone are insufficient for children. We need to give our children more: a profound understanding of fundamental number relationships, concepts, operations, representations, rules, and applications.

In recent years, the National Council of Teachers of Mathematics (NCTM), among many other groups, has advocated experiences for students that allow them to "understand numbers, ways of representing numbers, relationships among numbers, and number systems." Moreover, the NCTM advocates the position that "understanding meanings of operations and how they relate to one another" is fundamental to the well-rounded education of children, as is the ability "to compute fluently and make reasonable estimates." Hence, the recommendations of numerous mathematics education researchers and experienced teachers across the nation suggest that our students need to compute with accuracy and efficiency, just as they should also be able to think conceptually about number relations and applications. It is toward this attainable goal that this book is devoted.

The Big Ideas

There are several key ideas developed in this book. The first two sections review two fundamental number tools that were developed in previous books in this program: the number line and ratio tables. Reviews of these two models in Sections A and B are important not only in terms of the way they reinforce earlier learning, but also because inherent in these two mathematical tools are number relationships and concepts (e.g., skip-counting on the number line) that connect nicely with the core concepts developed in the book. Reviews of both the number line and ratio tables set the stage for the primary focal points developed throughout the book.

Big Idea #1: Numbers are Related to Each Other The most salient idea promoted in this book is that numbers are connected to each other. Consider, for example, the number 8. Eight can be thought of as the double of 4, two less than 10, or the sum of 5 and 3. It is even visually represented, and rather easily recognized by most learners, as a pattern of dots in this 10-frame representation.

One can imagine how a well-developed understanding of the number 8 in these various ways can be instrumental in allowing children to attach meaning to related numbers such as 18, 58, or 280. Throughout this book, we will take advantage of students' natural inclination to think of the composition of numbers from other related numbers. Although this term and the related term decomposition are not explicitly introduced to students, they will have plenty of opportunities to use this concept as they manipulate numbers and engage in the problems in the text.

The idea of composition is first introduced explicitly at the beginning of Section C, where students are asked to draw two pictures representing the number 17. While many students will initially choose to draw 17 dots (or boxes, or balls, etc.) in some random arrangement, you should look for an opportunity in their second picture to help them think of 17 as being composed of a group of smaller numbers. Some math educators have advocated the use of this language: "What's inside 17?" Helping students see 17 as being composed of one 10 and one 7 is useful in contexts that require students to combine multidigit numbers. Inherent in this particular decomposition of 17 (and a great strategy in every case) is the idea that we can decompose numbers as tens and ones to illustrate the power of place value in our number system. Thinking of 17 as the combination of 10 and 7 is preferable to breaking 17 into groups of 9 and 8, for example, because the number is now arranged based on place value: one group of 10 and 7 ones.

Keep in mind, of course, that you may need to back up one step to help some understand the significance and value of working with 10 as a starting point. Throughout the text, look for times in which students may "see inside" a number in order to decompose it in such a way that it can most easily be combined with other numbers.

Being able to decompose numbers in this way is essential if we hope to develop students' confidence in mental calculations (and certainly pencil and paper computations as well). Rather quickly in Section C of the text, students are asked to use this idea of decomposition to combine numbers. It is a remarkable moment when students grasp the power of number decomposition as a tool toward success with the four operations. What we want to push them toward is a sophisticated use of number decomposition such that they begin to operate with numerically compatible numbers. Take, for example, the following problem:

$$\begin{array}{r} 27 \\ + 78 \\ \hline \end{array}$$

At first glance, and with the traditional addition algorithm in mind, this is not a trivial problem for those who may not have strong number sense or experience with the addition algorithm. Imagine a context in real life where these two numbers might need to be combined mentally, on the spot. Consider the mental gymnastics necessary to compute this sum using the traditional method. Start in the right hand column, add 7 + 8 = 15, write the 5, regroup the 1 ten, move to the left column, add 2 + 7 = 9, don't forget the regrouped 1 ten from earlier, 9 + 1 = 10, write the 10, final answer, 105.

This problem becomes much easier for the student who can see inside these two numbers: 27 might be thought of as 25 and 2 more. 78 might be thought of as 75 and 3 more, 25 + 75 = 100, and 2 + 3 = 5. Hence, 100 + 5 = 105. A different student with equally strong number sense might think, "27 is close to 30, 78 is close to 80, 30 + 80 = 110. I subtract 3 (because 27 is three less than 30), and subtract 2 more (because 78 is 2 less than 80): 110 – 5 = 105." When a student is able to decompose numbers into more friendly or compatible combinations of numbers, he or she has a huge advantage over students who must rely on algorithms without understanding why they work. If students are comfortable with number decomposition, research has shown repeatedly that they can easily grasp the traditional algorithms and use them effectively. The reverse, however, is not true. Being able to use the algorithm does not necessarily imply the student has rich understanding of what she is doing in the procedure, nor whether the answer she obtains is reasonable.

Throughout Sections C and D of the student book, learners have opportunities to practice this approach of decomposition to compatible numbers. They are asked to think about combinations of 10, the foundation upon which so much of our number system is based. They are also asked to find combinations for 100, and then spend time adding to 100 using decimals and contexts involving money.

Big Idea #2: Operations are Related to Each Other The second major idea in this book is that, just like individual numbers, operations are related. Beginning in Section E, the notion that multiplication can be thought of as repeated addition is developed implicitly. Students begin with an activity where they find combinations of numbers that, when added together, equal a target sum. Students quickly realize, for example, that 3 and 7 make 10, and therefore that combination of 3 and 7 could be used multiple times (repeatedly adding 10) to arrive at a given sum. For example, one might decompose the number 25 into a combination of: (7 + 3) + (7 + 3) + 5 = 25. In the next set of problems, students calculate the cost of flats of stamps that come in various arrangements. Students can draw on their spatial reasoning (area models are effective ways to teach multiplication), as well as the notion of repeatedly adding same-size groups of stamps to determine the costs of the flats. In this diagram taken directly from a problem in Section E, for example, students are encouraged to find efficient strategies for arriving at a cost for the flat of stamps. Students may start by recognizing that two $0.50 stamps equal a dollar. They could then group the stamps in pairs, count the pairs (7 total), and then arrive at an answer of $7 for the flat. Other students might see the first two columns of the stamps as being equal to $2 each. The remaining 3 columns would be half that amount, $1. So 2($2) + 3($1) = $7.

$0.50	$0.50	$0.50	$0.50	$0.50
$0.50	$0.50	$0.50	$0.50	$0.50
$0.50	$0.50			
$0.50	$0.50			

In this way, students can see directly how multiplication simply gives us a more efficient way to add groups of the same number. The informal understanding of multiplication that this specific problem motivates is explicitly developed in problems throughout Section E. As you help students develop understanding of multiplication, do not forget to encourage them to use the decomposition strategies that they developed earlier in the book. Help students see numbers within numbers that can help them effectively combine those numbers, this time with multiplication.

Big Idea #3: Numbers are Inherently Tied to the World Around Us

The final big idea that is worthy of mention in this overview is the notion that numbers, and therefore number sense, are intricately tied to the world in which we live and the problem settings that we must engage. Throughout this book, real-world contexts are used to motivate the development of number sense in general and the specific strategies outlined above that include, for example, decomposition of numbers and finding compatible numbers that make addition and subtraction problems less complicated. Look for opportunities to emphasize how these strategies are the ones that we do use in daily life. They become dynamic strategies that can be applied in various ways, and at various times, as we seek to solve authentic problems that we may face. Throughout this book, and this series, you are encouraged to be flexible with the answers and solution strategies presented by your students. With time, the precision of their approximations and informal strategies will improve, particularly with the use of contextual problems that naturally guide students toward fruitful strategies. Patience with this process now, allowing students to pursue strategies that are supported by their own reasoning, will pay great dividends for the development of their number sense and fluency with operations as they progress as thinkers and users of mathematics.

Section A: A Review of the Number Line

SECTION A PLANNER

THE MATHEMATICS CONTENT AND GOALS

GOALS

Students will:
- Visualize addition and subtraction using the number line as a model.
- Develop understanding and facility with skip-jumping along the number line.
- Apply number-line strategies for addition and subtraction in various problems and contexts.
- Compare different solution strategies for addition and subtraction.
- Develop efficiency in calculating 2- and 3-digit addition and subtraction problems mentally.

LANGUAGE DEVELOPMENT

Mathematical language in this section includes:

Number Line: A number line is a mathematical model that is used to represent points (or coordinates) that are placed correctly, according to a uniform scale, along a continuum. In this book, the open-ended number line, a line that has not been labeled in any preconceived way, is used repeatedly to help students develop understanding of numbers and their relationship to one another. A simpler definition for students might be: "A line with numbers placed in their correct position."

Skip-jump: An interval that is used repeatedly to progress along the number line.

Graph: In this book, graph is used to refer to instances in which students are asked to locate a point on a number line (e.g., graph the number 10 on the number line) or label a point on a number line that already exists (e.g., what is the number value of Point A on the number line?). Several synonyms for graph might also have been used appropriately (e.g., mark, label, or place), but for simplicity, graph is used in each of these various contexts. A simpler definition for students might be to put a number on a number line in the right place.

Multiple: In this book, a multiple is used to refer to a fixed increment that students will use to partition a number line. For example, students might be asked to graph points on a line in multiples of 10: 10, 20, 30, etc. Or they may be asked to identify how many multiples of 5 exist on a given number line. A common synonym for multiple that some students might use is increment. Another mathematical definition of multiple is the product of the given number and another number.

Explain Your Thinking: In this section, students are invited to explain their thinking. You might want to help students recognize that this process is not one that they are likely to be familiar with, but that it is an extremely important skill to develop. They may need practice in learning how to find the salient features of their thinking strategies and time to develop the confidence to articulate those thoughts in a public discussion.

Ratio Table: A collection of equivalent ratios organized in a table.

Target Number: When using a number line, students are sometimes asked to think of a target number on the number line. It might be thought of in other words as a numeric destination on the number line.

PACING

The projected pacing for this unit is 2–3 class periods (based on a 45 minute period).

PROBLEM SETS: OVERVIEW

Set 1 (pp. 1–2; problems 1–6)
These problems review the number line both as a scale and as a computational tool. The first few problems prompt students to think about the relative scales of several number lines by having them place given numbers on the lines and identify given locations. The later problems in this section motivate the use of the number line as a computational aid.

Set 2: (p. 3; problems 1–7)
This stand-alone activity could be used as a formative assessment partway through this unit. In this activity, students are asked to think about the most efficient (i.e., least number of steps) mental strategies for a variety of addition and subtraction problems. Encourage students to compare solution strategies with each other, or engage the class in conversation about the various ways to use the number line. Students could extend this activity by trading their own problem scenarios with each other.

CONCEPT DEVELOPMENT (Pages 1–3)

INTRODUCE THE CONCEPT

ASSESS STUDENTS' PRIOR KNOWLEDGE

Ask:
Which number is closer to 50: 22 or 82? Draw a picture to justify your answer.

Listen for:
- 22 is closer to 50.

Look for:
Students who are comfortable with number lines as visual representations will most likely draw a number line with 50 as the midpoint and both 22 and 82 in their respective locations to the left and right of 50. These students may use skips of 10 and then use smaller increments as they work forward from 50 to 82 and backwards from 50 to 22.

MODEL MATHEMATICAL THINKING

Have students share their pictures of the above problem with a partner. Draw a number line on the board with 50 as the midpoint. Mark the locations of 22 and 82 on the line. As you talk through the thinking, demonstrate on the number line. Then ask, *You used a picture to solve the problem. What other strategy could I use? How can I represent this strategy with a diagram or picture?*

Talk Through the Thinking:
I could use subtraction to solve the problem. I could start by subtracting 50 from 82: 82 – 50 = 32. Then I can model this subtraction on the number line. I can start at 82 and skip back to 50. What would be a good increment to skip with? I know. I can start with skips of 10: 82, 72, 62, 52. That's 3 skips of 10, or 30. Now what can I do? I can skip by 1s back to 50: 52, 51, 50. That's 2 skips of 1, or 2. So I skipped a distance of 32.

Ask:
How can I subtract to find how far 22 is from 50? How can I represent this with a diagram or picture?

Listen for:
- You can subtract: 50 – 22 = 28
- You can start at 50 on the number line. Then you can skip back using two skips of 10 to 30. Then you can skip back using one skip of 5 and three skips of 1 until you reach 22.

LAUNCH THE PROBLEM SOLVING

Have students work individually to solve the problems on page 1. As they work, you may want to circulate and monitor their recorded answers. When everyone has finished, have students share and discuss their answers in a class discussion of the problems. Refer to the **Teacher Notes: Student Page 1** for more specific ideas about the problems on this page.

As students work and report their answers, focus on these issues:

Help Make Connections – Help students understand the connections between these number lines and the ones they may have encountered in Book 1. Encourage them to use previously learned strategies such as doubling and halving to locate numbers on the line.

Allow Processing Time – It is imperative for students to work slowly enough on these problems so that they can develop confidence and facility with number lines.

Validate Representations – When several students use different numbers on their number lines, as in problems 3 and 4, have them compare their work and discuss whether all the representations are valid.

Encourage Language Development – Be sure to review the key definitions presented earlier for use on these pages of activities.

Student Page 1: Problems and Potential Answers

Section A: The Number Line in Review — Set 1

1. Graph the following numbers on both of the two number lines below.

   a) 5   b) 15   c) 18   d) 3   e) 12   f) 9

   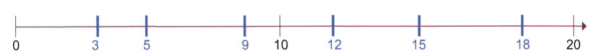

   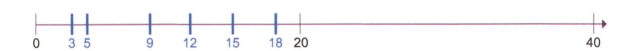

2. Which numbers are represented by the letters on the number line below?

   a) 10   b) 25   c) 40   d) 55   e) 75   f) 90   g) 98

   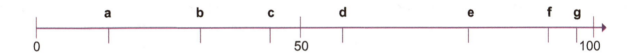

3. Label the number line below. Graph at least five points on the number line in addition to those that are already there. *Include the number 50.*   Answers will vary

4. Draw a number line that **starts with the number 10**, and **ends with the number 60**. Graph the numbers 30 and 50 and **at least two other points** on your number line.   Answers will vary

Book 3: *Knowing Numbers*   1

TEACHER NOTES: STUDENT PAGE 1

Problem 1: This problem is a review of similar problems students may have encountered in *Book 1: The Number Line.* So students will very likely implement strategies that they developed earlier for partitioning the number line, such as halving or doubling. *Watch for:* Check for accuracy as students partition the number lines, and allow them to share the informal strategies they used to place numbers on the line. Also watch for students' ability to adjust to the different scales on the first and second number lines.

Problem 2: *Watch for:* Check for accuracy as students identify points already placed on the number line.

Problems 3–4: These problems will measure students' ability to develop and maintain, or keep constant, the scale of a number line.

TEACHER NOTES: STUDENT PAGE 2

CONTINUE THE PROBLEM SOLVING

Have students work individually to solve the problems on page 2. As they work, you may want to circulate and monitor their recorded answers. As students finish each problem, have them compare and discuss their answers with a partner. Then have each pair share their answers in a class discussion of the problem. Refer to the **Teacher Notes: Student Page 2** for more specific ideas about the problems on this page.

As students work and report their conclusions, focus on these issues:
Validate Representations – Different students will use different target numbers and starting numbers for problem 5. Have them discuss whether all representations are correct.
Help Make Connections – Remind students to use what they have learned about skip-counting to solve the problems on this page.
Allow Waiting Time – When students struggle to explain their thinking, allow them at least 20–30 seconds to organize their thoughts.

Problem 5: Much like the previous two problems, this problem is designed to make students define and then use a particular scale for a number line. Although students will be choosing their own starting points and target values, the process remains the same. *Watch for:* Students must define a starting value and an ending value, then determine ways in which the number line can be partitioned uniformly between those points.

Problem 6: Skip-counting is a technique developed in *Book One: The Number Line.* Students learn to skip along the number line using comfortable intervals such as 10 or 5. Skip-counting on a number line is a technique that, with practice, becomes a helpful strategy for students' mental computations. *Teaching Strategy:* Skip-counting provides a solid foundation for the informal number strategies developed later in this book. So be sure to allow students ample time to discuss their use of this process.

Student Page 2: Problems and Potential Answers

Section A: The Number Line in Review — Set 1

5. Start at zero. Pick any starting multiple and place it in the **start box**. Then choose a **target number** for the **end of your number line**. Skip count by the number in the start box to reach your target number. Challenge yourself to get to the target number <u>by a different method</u>. Try it again (Trial 2) with new start and target numbers. *Responses will vary.*

Trial 1: My Target Number ___

0 [Start Box]

Trial 2: My Target Number ___

0 [Start Box]

6. Use the number lines and skip counting to fill in the box and make the number sentences true.

a) 43 + 87 = **130**

Explain your thinking. *Responses will vary.*

b) 81 - 47 = **34**

Explain your thinking. *Responses will vary.*

c) 66 + **158** = 224

Explain your thinking. *Responses will vary.*

2   Book 3: *Knowing Numbers*

CONTINUE THE PROBLEM SOLVING

Have students work individually to solve the problems on page 3. As they work, you may want to circulate and monitor their recorded answers. As students finish each problem, have them compare and discuss their answers with a partner. Then have each pair share their answers in a class discussion of the problem. Refer to the **Teacher Notes: Student Page 3** for more specific ideas about the problems on this page.

As students work and report their conclusions, focus on these issues:

Validate Representations – When students come up with different solutions to the skip trips, have them discuss which of these solutions involve taking the fewest skip-jumps.

Facilitate Students' Thinking – You may wish to remind students that they can count backward as well as forward on the number lines.

Allow Processing Time – Allow students ample time to determine which skip-trips will take the fewest steps. You might suggest they work out the skip-trips on scratch paper before representing them on the page.

TEACHER NOTES: STUDENT PAGE 3

Students typically enjoy skip-jumping. After they come to understand the process, students may be encouraged to create their own skip-trip parameters and share them with peers. As students try to come up with problems with solutions that their peers might overlook, they will be enriching their own number sense and developing continued expertise and confidence with the number line.

Problems 1–7: Again, this activity is a review of work done in *Book One: The Number Line*. The problems on this page provide important practice for students' development of skip-counting techniques. *Teaching Strategy:* Have students share their solutions with the class. *Watch for:* Be sure students understand what they are supposed to do. They are to begin at the starting point and use skip-jumps of 1, 10, or 100 to arrive at the target in as few jumps as possible. *Teaching Strategy:* Do not over-prepare students for these problems. They will learn best as they discuss and compare their strategies with those of their peers. For example, some students will not immediately consider that it could be more efficient to skip beyond the target and then backtrack, as is the case in problem 7. As students complete these problems, they should be encouraged to create new problems to be solved by their classmates.

Student Page 3: Problems and Potential Answers

Section A: The Number Line in Review — Set 2

SKIP JUMPS

Try to get to the indicated number with as few skip jumps as possible. You may only make skips of 1, 10, or 100. Illustrate your strategies on the number lines. It may take you two tries!

How many skips?

1. **EXAMPLE:** Go from 0 to 23 in the fewest skip jumps possible.

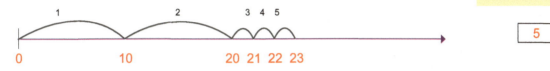

5

2. Go from 0 to 58 in the fewest skip jumps possible.

7

3. Go from 45 to 87 in the fewest skip jumps possible.

6

4. Go from 108 to 240 in the fewest skip jumps possible.

6

5. Go from 56 to 173 in the fewest skip jumps possible.

6

6. Go from 886 to 1100 in the fewest skip jumps possible.

7

7. Go from 10 to 98 in the fewest skip jumps possible.

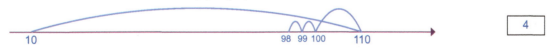

4

Book 3: *Knowing Numbers*   3

SECTION A ASSESSMENT (PAGE 4)

LAUNCH THE ASSESSMENT

Have students turn to the Section A Assessment on page 4. An additional copy is found on page 32 of the Assessment Book. Have students work individually to solve the problems and write their answers. As they work, circulate to be sure students understand what they need to do for each of the problems. Be sure that students are completing each part of the problem. For example, for problem 3, students should not only use the number line to find a sum, they should also write the sum in the space provided and then explain their strategy. You may find it helpful to read the directions for all the problems before students begin, discussing the types of responses they will need to make for each problem.

Encourage students to use whatever space they need to explain their thinking. If the space on the page is inadequate, they should use an additional sheet of paper or use the back of the page.

Refer to the **Teacher Notes: Assessment Problems for Section A** for more specific ideas about the problems on this page.

Evaluate Student Responses

Use the assessment rubric on page 31 of the Assessment Book (pictured on page 152 of the Teacher Edition) to evaluate student responses. The Assessment Book has some general suggestions for using the rubric that you may find helpful.

TEACHER NOTES: ASSESSMENT PROBLEMS FOR SECTION A

The problems on this page are designed to give you an opportunity to assess the progress and the thinking of students about the use of the number line. The content of the problems on this short assessment are also particularly well suited to prepare students for the concepts developed in the remainder of this book.

Student Page 4: Problems and Potential Answers

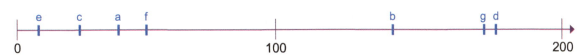

Section A: Problems for Assessment

1. Place these values on the number line below.

   a) 40   b) 140   c) 25   d) 180   e) 10   f) 50   g) 175

   ```
   e  c  a  f              b            g d
   |--|--|--|--|-----------|------------|-|----|
   0           100                          200
   ```

   Explain how you knew where to place each value on the number line.

   a) Almost halfway to 100

   b) Almost halfway between 100 and 200

   c) One fourth of 100

   d) A little more than 3/4 of the way from 100 to 200

   e) 1/10 from zero to 100

   f) Halfway between 0 and 100

   g) 3/4 of the way from 100 and 200

2. Use a number line and skip counting to solve the following problems. Show your steps on the line.
   Answers will vary. Sample answers are given.

   a) 28 + 49

   Jump by 50, then back 1: 28, 78, 77

   b) 33 + 98

   Jump by 100, back by 2: 33, 133, 131

   c) 38 − 14

   Start at 38, subtract 10, subtract 4: 38, 28, 24

   d) 79 − 25

   Start at 79, subtract 20, subtract 5: 79, 59, 54

3. Use the number lines and skip counting. Fill in the boxes to make the number sentences true.

   a) 43 + 56 = **99**

   Explain your thinking. Start at 43, jump 50, jump 5, jump 1.

   b) 91 − 57 = **34**

   Explain your thinking. Start at 91, subtract 60, add 3.

4 Book 3: *Knowing Numbers*

SCORING GUIDE BOOK 3: KNOWING NUMBERS

Section A Assessment
For Use With: Student Book Page 4

PROBLEM DESCRIPTION	SCORING: WHAT TO LOOK FOR	SCORE AND COMMENTS
Problem 1a–g Place numbers on a number line. Level 1: Comprehension and Knowledge Level 2: Tool use	Do students: • Understand the number line, and relative positions of numbers across a range? • Accurately place their values? • Explain their thinking?	Points:_____ of 14
Problem 2a–d Model addition problem on number line using skip-counting. Level 1: Comprehension and Knowledge Level 2: Tool use	Do students: • Use the number line to represent the skip-counting principle? • Use the number line as a tool for addition?	Points:_____ of 8
Problem 3a–b Model addition problem on number line using skip-counting. Level 1: Comprehension and Knowledge Level 2: Tool use	Do students: • Use the number line to represent the skip-counting principle? • Use the number line as a tool for addition? • Articulate their thinking in a way that is sound?	Points:_____ of 4

TOTAL POINTS:_____ OF 26

Section B: The Ratio Table in Review

SECTION B PLANNER

THE MATHEMATICS CONTENT AND GOALS

GOALS
Students will:
- Use ratio tables to think multiplicatively.
- Use ratio tables to solve multiplication and division problems.

> **LANGUAGE DEVELOPMENT**
> **Mathematical language in this section includes:**
> *Ratio:* A proportional relationship between two numbers or quantities.
> *Ratio Table:* A collection of equivalent ratios organized in a table.
> *Multiple:* A number that is the product of a specific number and another number.

PACING
The projected pacing for this unit is 2–3 class periods (based on a 45 minute period).

PROBLEM SETS: OVERVIEW

The ratio table is a flexible tool that students can use to solve a variety of problems. Throughout this section, students will build on the additive strategies developed previously as they organize ratios in a table. The intuitive strategies, skip-counting, doubling, halving, adding, multiplying by 10, etc., developed in Book 1 will be helpful in this section. The use of the ratio table in this section is important in that it will be revisited in subsequent books and used for more complex work with ratios, fractions, percents, and decimals.

Set 1 (pp. 5–6; problems 1–7)
The problems in Set 1 introduce the ratio table. Although the introductory example uses a variety of strategies that will be developed later, the bulk of the problems in this section utilize simple addition to illustrate the progression of ratio tables. Important in this section are occasions for students to compare various strategies. By comparing strategies, students begin to recognize the mathematical principles inherent in the problems.

Set 2 (pp. 7–8; problems 1–3)
Strategies for using ratio tables effectively are presented in this section. Specifically, students are introduced to doubling, multiplying, and halving strategies as well as the additive strategies emphasized in Set 1. Set 2 focuses primarily on multiplicative relationships and develops strategies for both multiplication and division. A partitive approach is taken to help students conceptualize division and to use ratio tables effectively.

CONCEPT DEVELOPMENT (Pages 5–6)

INTRODUCE THE CONCEPT

ASSESS STUDENTS' PRIOR KNOWLEDGE
Write the following on the board: *Fall Clean Up: $1 for Every 4 Bags of Leaves.*

Ask:
Two students earned extra money by raking leaves for their neighbors in the fall. They charged $1 for every 4 bags of leaves they raked. How many bags of leaves would they need to rake for a neighbor who wanted to pay $4? What if the neighbor wanted to pay $5?

Listen for:
(The strategies students would use to solve the problems, particularly whether these strategies involve proportional and/or multiplicative reasoning)
- If I can have 4 bags of leaves raked for $1, then I can have 8 bags of leaves raked for $2. I can double $2 to get $4, and then double 8 bags to get 16 bags of leaves.
- I can multiply $1 by 4 to get $4. Then I would have to multiply 4 bags of leaves by 4 to get 16 bags of leaves.
- If $1 is charged for raking 4 bags of leaves, then I can multiply 5 × $1 to get $5. This means I could also multiply 5 × 4, to get 20 bags of leaves raked for $5.

MODEL MATHEMATICAL THINKING
Model the thinking or a related problem by asking: *Suppose the two students worked for a whole afternoon and raked a total of 14 bags of leaves. How much would they have earned?*

Allow students to think about this problem for 30–45 seconds. Then elicit that this problem is different from the first problem because now the number of bags that were raked is known and they need to find how much money was earned.

Talk Through the Thinking:
We know that $1 will pay for 4 bags of leaves. If we think of this in the other direction, we can say that 4 bags of leaves will cost $1. We know that 3 × 4 = 12. So because 4 bags of leaves costs $1, then 12 bags cost 3 times that much, or $3. And if 4 bags of leaves cost $1, then half that amount, or 2 bags of leaves, would cost half as much as $1, or $0.50. Now, we know that 12 + 2 = 14. So we can add the cost of 12 bags of leaves to the cost of 2 bags of leaves to find how much the students earned.
$3.00 + $0.50 = $3.50.

Draw the table below on the board.

Bags of Leaves	4	2	12	14 (12 + 2)
Amount Earned	$1.00	$0.50	$3.00	$3.50

Ask:
What patterns do you see in this ratio table?

Listen for:
- A doubling/halving pattern.
- Addition of proportional amounts.

154   **Knowing Numbers** *Teacher Edition*

LAUNCH THE PROBLEM SOLVING

Initially, have students work individually to come up with two strategies for solving problem 1. As they work, circulate throughout the room, noting the different strategies students might be using. As you move into a full class discussion of the first problem, be sure to talk through all the strategies that students used. Refer to the **Teacher Notes: Student Page 5** for more specific ideas for each problem on this page.

As students work and report their conclusions, focus on these issues:

Validate Alternate Solutions – Different students may use different strategies to solve problem 1. Have these students compare and discuss their solution strategies to determine whether each is valid.

Allow Waiting Time – When students struggle to explain their thinking, allow them at least 20 seconds to organize their thoughts.

Facilitate Students' Thinking – Many students will initially solve ratio problems by repeated addition. Encourage them to become more sophisticated as they use various strategies (doubling, halving, multiplying by three, combining ratios, etc.).

Encourage Language Development – In order to use ratio tables effectively, it is crucial that students have basic understanding of commonly used computational strategies such as multiplying by 10, or doubling. Each of these key ideas is expressed below. If students are unaware of these ideas, reinforce them prior to beginning this book. Students will become comfortable with these strategies as they use them frequently throughout the text.

- *Multiplying:* It is crucial that students understand multiplication as groups of a given set. For example, 12 x 13 might be thought of as 12 groups of 13. If students understand this fundamental notion of multiplication as repeated addition, they are ready to use ratio tables.
- *Multiplying by 10:* A very common strategy with ratio tables is the process of multiplying by 10. The "groups of" idea is important here. For example, 4 x 10 might be thought of as 4 groups of 10: 10, 20, 30, 40. Larger numbers work the same way: 14 x 10 means, 14 groups of ten: 10, 20, 30… 130, 140. Once students understand the idea of repeatedly adding ten, they will quickly begin to use a shortcut, simply adding a zero to whatever number is being multiplied by ten. For example, **13** x 10 = **13**0.
- *Doubling:* Doubling is also an important strategy for ratio tables. For example, if two cases of juice contain 14 bottles, then four cases (double the amount) would include 14 x 2, or 28 bottles. Make sure you help students with informal methods for doubling. For example, 14 might be thought of as (10 + 4). Therefore, doubling 14 might be thought of as doubling (10 + 4), meaning that we can double the 10 (i.e., 20) and then double the 4 (i.e., 8), which is 20 + 8 = 28.
- *Halving:* Likewise, halving a given amount is also a valuable strategy. For example, if 10 boxes of apples contain 180 apples, then five boxes would contain 90 apples. The same informal strategy may be used to help students divide a given quantity in half. 180 might be thought of as (100 + 80). Half of 100 is 50, and half of 80 is 40. Hence, half of 180 is: 50 + 40 = 90.

Student Page 5: Problems and Potential Answers

Section B: The Ratio Table in Review Set 1

1. Redcliff Elementary School advertises that they will always have a student-to-teacher ratio of 12 to 1. That means for every 12 students, there is 1 teacher. This year, 104 students are enrolled in the school. How many teachers are needed? __9__ Use any method you choose. Explain your answer.

    Responses will vary.

    Explain your thinking. _____

2. The principal used the following strategy to solve the problem.

Teachers	1	10	2	8
Students	12	120	24	96

    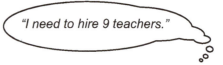
    "I need to hire 9 teachers."

    Explain her strategy. She multiplied the number of students for 1 teacher by 10 to get the number of students for 10 teachers. Then she doubled the number of students for 1 teacher to get the number of students for 2 teachers. Finally, she subtracted the number of students for 2 teachers from the number of students for 10 teachers to get 96 students. She then knew that 8 teachers would not be enough, so she hired 9 teachers.

3. The principal used a ratio table to solve this problem. Compare her strategy to your strategy.
    Responses will vary.

4. Which strategy do you like best? Why?
    Responses will vary.

TEACHER NOTES: STUDENT PAGE 5

The problems on page 5 are all related and are intended to demonstrate the use of ratio tables as a viable option to more traditionally taught computational methods. As was the case with the review pages on number lines, this section should be familiar to students who have completed the second book in this series, *Book 2: The Ratio Table*. If students have not completed *Book 2,* it is likely that they will need additional time to become comfortable with ratio tables.

Problem 1: *Teaching Strategy:* Encourage students to solve this problem using any method they feel comfortable with. Students who have done the work in *Book 2: The Ratio Table* may choose to solve this problem with a ratio table.

Problem 2: This problem engenders the essential working feature of the ratio table—proportional reasoning. *Watch for:* Students should recognize that the original number relationship, 1 teacher for every 12 students, can be preserved in another form by using proportional reasoning. Although the numerator and denominator of a fraction may change, its value remains the same if both the numerator and denominator are increased or decreased by the same proportion. In this case, the common strategy of multiplying by 10 is illustrated, as is a doubling strategy. For example, if 1 teacher is needed for every 12 students, then 10 teachers would be necessary for 120 students.

Problems 3–4: *Teaching Strategy:* Be sure to allow students ample time for discussion of these problems so they can begin to think conceptually about ratio tables.

CONTINUE THE PROBLEM SOLVING

The intent of page 6 is to encourage students to move away from the cumbersome process of single-step, repeated addition. Capitalize on students' eagerness to skip steps and take shortcuts to complete the ratio tables more efficiently.

As students work individually to solve the problems on page 6, circulate and monitor their recorded answers. As they finish each problem, have them compare and discuss their answers with a partner. Then have pairs share their conclusions in a class discussion of the problem. Refer to the **Teacher Notes: Student Page 6** for more specific ideas about the problems on this page.

As students work and report their conclusions, focus on these issues:

Facilitate Students' Thinking – Remind students that they can go back to a ratio that appeared earlier in the ratio table if they are having difficulty.

Help Make Connections – When students begin problem 6, suggest that they ask themselves how they went about solving problem 5. Have them determine whether they can use the same or a similar strategy to solve the problem.

TEACHER NOTES: STUDENT PAGE 6

Problem 5: This problem has two essential components. The first is that students need to recognize that 208 brushes are needed (2 × 104 students). The second is that they need to determine how many packs of paintbrushes are needed if each pack contains 20 brushes. This is where the ratio table helps in solving the problem. *Watch for:* Students should use doubling strategies and multiplicative strategies, such as multiplying by 10.

Problem 6: The solution to problem 6 is contingent on the successful completion of problem 5. Similar strategies will be used.

Problem 7: Ben effectively uses a doubling strategy to eliminate the decimal point and to move toward a successful solution. *Teaching Strategy:* Be sure students understand that going back to use a ratio that appeared earlier in the table is often a fruitful strategy. For the first try, after doubling several times, Ben went back and subtracted the original ratio to find the final ratio in the table. For the second try, Ben multiplied by 10 and then used a halving strategy to come close to the final answer. Be sure to allow students ample time to discuss these strategies.

Student Page 6: Problems and Potential Answers

Section B: The Ratio Table in Review — Set 1

5. The teachers at Redcliff School need to order art supplies for their 104 students. Paintbrushes come in packs of 20. Each student needs 2 <u>paintbrushes</u> at the start of the year. How many packs must the teachers order? _____

Packs	1	2	4	8	12	11		
Brushes	20	40	80	160	240	220		

6. Each pack of paintbrushes costs $8. How much will it cost to supply all 104 students with 2 paintbrushes each?

Packs	1	2	4	8	12	11		
Cost	$8	$16	$32	$64	$96	$88		

Explain your strategy. Responses will vary. _____

7. Ben used the two strategies below to find how much it would cost to order 15 cases of soda at a cost of $4.50 per case. He was not sure if he did it correctly the first time, so he tried again using a different method. Explain his two strategies.

First Try

Cases	1	2	4	8	16	15		
Cost	$4.50	$9.00	$18.00	$36.00	$72.00	$67.50		

Explain Ben's strategy. Ben doubled the cost of 1 case to get the cost of 2 cases. He doubled the cost of 2 cases to get the cost of 4 cases. He doubled the cost of 4 cases to get the cost of 8 cases. He doubled the cost of 8 cases to get the cost of 16 cases. He then subtracted the cost of 1 case from the cost of 16 cases to get the cost of 15 cases.

Second Try

Cases	1	10	5	15				
Cost	$4.50	$45.00	$22.50	$67.50				

Explain Ben's strategy. Ben multiplied the cost of 1 case by 10 to get the cost of 10 cases. He then halved the cost of 10 cases to get the cost of 5 cases. Finally, he added the cost of 10 cases to the cost of 5 cases to get the cost of 15 cases.

CONTINUE THE PROBLEM SOLVING

Have students work individually to solve the problems on page 7. As they work, you may want to circulate and monitor their recorded answers. As students finish each problem, have them compare and discuss their answers with a partner. Then have each pair share their answers in a class discussion of the problem. Refer to the **Teacher Notes: Student Page 7** for more specific ideas about the problems on this page.

As students work and report their conclusions, focus on these issues:

Facilitate Students' Thinking – You may wish to remind students that they can use doubling and halving strategies to complete the ratio tables.

Allow Waiting Time – When students struggle to explain their thinking, allow them ample time to organize their thoughts.

TEACHER NOTES: STUDENT PAGE 7

Problem 1: These practice problems emphasize the usefulness of ratio tables for both multiplication and division. Be sure to emphasize that although these problems as stated are represented as division problems, multiplicative reasoning can be used to solve them. Students may have difficulty at first establishing the initial column in the ratio table. *Teaching Strategy:* You can help them do so by creating verbal statements that are embodied in the table. For example, for 1c, you might encourage students by modeling the following:

How many groups of 16 are in 272? I know that there is one group of 16 in 16. This is the first column in the table.

Once the first column is established, the table may be developed in several ways. The key to solving these problems is for students to understand what they are being asked to find and how might the solution be reasonably approached.

Student Page 7: Problems and Potential Answers

Section B: The Ratio Table in Review — Set 2

Since multiplication and division are inverse operations, ratio tables can be used to solve both kinds of problems. Can you use a ratio table to solve a division problem? Here is one way to do so.

252 ÷ 12 →

Factors	1	10	20	**21**
Product	12	120	240	**252**

So… 252 ÷ 12 = 21

Now let's use a ratio table to multiply 12 × 21.

Factors	1	10	2	12
Product	21	210	42	252

So… 12 × 21 = 252

1. Complete the ratio tables to solve the division problems.

    a) How many 15's are there in 75? 75 ÷ 15 = 5

Factors	1	2	4	5			
Product	15	30	60	75			

    b) How many 20's are there in 620? 620 ÷ 20 = 31

Factors	1	10	20	30	31		
Product	20	200	400	600	620		

    c) How many 16's are there in 272? 272 ÷ 16 = 17

Factors	1	10	5	15	2	17	
Product	16	160	80	240	32	272	

    d) How many 18's are there in 378? 378 ÷ 18 = 21

Factors	1	10	20	21			
Product	18	180	360	378			

CONTINUE THE PROBLEM SOLVING

Have students work individually to solve the problems on page 8. As they work, you may want to circulate and monitor their recorded answers. As students finish each problem, have them compare and discuss their answers with a partner. Then have each pair share their answers in a class discussion of the problem. Refer to the **Teacher Notes: Student Page 8** for more specific ideas about the problems on this page.

As students work and report their conclusions, focus on these issues:

Validate Alternate Strategies – When several students use different strategies to solve the problems, have them discuss whether all their strategies are valid.

Facilitate Students' Thinking – Remind students that when they use ratio tables, they should pay attention to the numbers in both the top and the bottom rows of each column.

Allow Waiting Time – When students struggle to explain their thinking, allow them ample time to organize their thoughts.

TEACHER NOTES: STUDENT PAGE 8

Problem 2: Problem 2 provides students with more practice with ratio tables in the context of a story problem. *Teaching Strategy:* Allow students to discuss both the problem and their solution strategies.

Problem 3: This problem is unique because it asks students to operate based on what they find in both the numerator (the number in the top row of each column) and the denominator (the corresponding number in the bottom row). In many instances, students will focus on manipulating the numerators in the ratio tables. This problem requires them to use proportions that make sense for the denominators. For example, the third column of Method #1 suggests that students should double the denominator in order to eliminate the decimal ($3.50 → $7). *Teaching Strategy:* Be sure to encourage students to discuss their thinking in their determinations whether one method is better than another.

Student Page 8: Problems and Potential Answers

Section B: The Ratio Table in Review Set 2

2. One ticket to the high school basketball game costs $2.50. How much would tickets cost for 10 people? How much would they cost for 18 people?

People	1	10	20	2	18		
Cost	$2.50	$25.00	$50.00	$5.00	$45.00		

10 people? __$25.00__

18 people? __$45.00__

3. Tickets for the ice-cream social cost $1.75 each. The first-grade class sold 36 tickets. How much money did they raise? To find out, complete the ratio tables below by filling in the shaded boxes.

Method #1

Tickets	1	2	4	40	36
Money	$1.75	$3.50	$7.00	$70.00	$63.00

Method #2

Tickets	1	10	20	5	35	36
Money	$1.75	$17.50	$35.00	$8.75	$61.25	$63.00

How much money did they raise? __$63.00__

Describe method #1. Double the cost of 1 ticket to get the cost of 2 tickets. Double the cost of 2 tickets to get the cost of 4 tickets. Multiply the cost of 4 tickets by 10 to get the cost of 40 tickets. Subtract the cost of 4 tickets from the cost of 40 tickets to get the cost of 36 tickets.

Describe method #2. Multiply the cost of 1 ticket by 10 to get the cost of 10 tickets. Double the cost of 10 tickets to get the cost of 20 tickets. Halve the cost of 10 tickets to get the cost of 5 tickets. Add the cost of 10, 20, and 5 tickets to get the cost of 35 tickets. Add the cost of 1 ticket to the cost of 35 tickets to get the cost of 36 tickets.

Is one method better than the other? Why or why not? Responses will vary.

How would you have solved this problem? Responses will vary.

SECTION B ASSESSMENT (PAGE 9)

LAUNCH THE ASSESSMENT
Have students turn to the Section B Assessment on page 9. An additional copy is found on page 33 of the Assessment Book. Have students work individually to solve the problems and write their answers. As they work, circulate to be sure students understand what they need to do for each of the problems. Be sure that students are completing each part of the problem. For these problems, students need to fill in all the blank cells while maintaining equivalent ratios. You may find it helpful to read the directions for all the problems before students begin, discussing the types of responses they will need to make for each problem.

Refer to the **Teacher Notes: Assessment Problems for Section B** for more specific ideas about the problems on this page.

Evaluate Student Responses
Use the assessment rubric on page 32 of the Assessment Book (pictured on page 166 of the Teacher Edition) to evaluate student responses. The Assessment Book has some general suggestions for using the rubric that you may find helpful.

TEACHER NOTES: ASSESSMENT PROBLEMS FOR SECTION B

By requiring students to use a limited number of columns in their ratio tables, these puzzles force students to experiment until they find appropriate strategies. The problems have been designed to elicit a wide range of strategies. You may want to encourage students to create their own, similar puzzles to be shared with their peers.

Student Page 9: Problems and Potential Answers

Section B: Problems for Assessment

Ratio Table Puzzles

The ratio tables below are puzzles. Try to solve each puzzle by filling in the empty cells in the ratio table in exactly the number of columns provided. You may need to use several strategies, such as doubling, halving, adding, multiplying, and so on.

1.
1	2	4	8
4	8	16	32

2.
3	6	12	24	30	36
5	10	20	40	50	60

3.
1	10	20	30	60
2.5	25	50	75	150

4.
5	50	25
2	20	10

5.
3	6	9	15
2	4	6	10

Book 3: *Knowing Numbers*   9

SCORING GUIDE BOOK 3: KNOWING NUMBERS

Section B Assessment
For Use With: Student Book Page 9

PROBLEM DESCRIPTION	SCORING: WHAT TO LOOK FOR	SCORE AND COMMENTS
Problems 1–5 Solve ratio table puzzles by use of creative proportional strategies. Level 1: Comprehension and Knowledge Level 2: Tool use Level 3: Connection and Application	Do students: • Understand equivalent fractions? • Understand how ratio tables make use of equivalent fractions?	(#1) Points:_____of 2 (#2) Points:_____of 2 (#3) Points:_____of 2 (#4) Points:_____of 2 (#5) Points:_____of 2

TOTAL POINTS:_____ OF 10

Section C: What's That Number?

SECTION C PLANNER

THE MATHEMATICS CONTENT AND GOALS

GOALS
Students will:
- Explore multiple ways to represent a given number.
- Develop intuitive strategies for grouping numbers strategically to take advantage of adding with friendly numbers (e.g., finding numbers that add to 10, 20, and 100).

> **LANGUAGE DEVELOPMENT**
> **Mathematical language in this section includes:**
> *Describe/description:* In this section, students are asked to describe a number. This might entail giving the mathematical characteristics of the number, its qualities, or its relationship to other numbers.

PROBLEM SETS: OVERVIEW

Set 1 (pp. 10–11; problems 1–4) This set of problems requires that students represent numbers in several ways. The first few problems in this section are very informal, and through them students should be given the freedom to think broadly about exactly what a number is: an abstract representation of some given quantity. The second half of the problems in this set require students to find combinations of numbers that result in friendly numbers, or numbers that can later be used to add efficiently and quickly. For example, finding combinations of numbers that total 10 or 100 can be helpful for simplifying later computation. The emphasis of this section is to begin developing the skill of adding and subtracting mentally.

Set 2 (p. 12; problems 1–3) This section continues to build students' confidence and flexibility in finding friendly combinations of numbers.

PACING

The projected pacing for this unit is 2–3 class periods (based on a 45 minute period).

CONCEPT DEVELOPMENT (Pages 10-12)

INTRODUCE THE CONCEPT

ASSESS STUDENTS' PRIOR KNOWLEDGE
Draw this table on the board:

	$20 bills	$10 bills	$5 bills	$1 bills
a				24
b		1	2	4
c		1	3	1
d	1			4
e		2		4
f			4	4
g		1	1	6

Ask:
Which of the combinations of bills can you use to make $24? Which combinations can you not use to make $24?

Listen for:
- The combinations in rows a, b, d, e, and f all make $24.
- The combinations in row c ($26) and row g ($21) do not make $24.

Discuss decomposition of numbers in an informal way. You might say something like this: *Sometimes it is easier to work with numbers if we break them apart into smaller numbers so that we are able to see inside the larger numbers. For example, inside $24 I can see $10 + $10 + $4 and $20 + $4. Whether we write $24 as $10 + $10 + $4 or $20 + $4, the value remains the same. When we do see and use these numbers within larger numbers, we should be smart about it. When we look inside larger numbers, it is always a good idea to look for multiples of 10, 100, or even 1,000 if the number is large enough.*

Ask:
What numbers can you see inside 18? Inside 54?

Listen for:
(Any combinations of tens and ones)
- 10 + 8
- 50 + 4

MODEL MATHEMATICAL THINKING
Explain that being able to see the numbers inside other numbers can be useful in addition, especially mental addition. Then model a related example by asking students to suppose we have to add 27 + 12. What smaller numbers can we see inside those numbers that would make the addition easier?

Talk Through the Thinking:
I can see 20 + 7 inside 27 and 10 + 2 inside 12. Now I can easily add the tens: 20 + 10 = 30. Then I can add the ones: 7 + 2 = 9. So if I add all the tens and ones together, 30 + 9, I get a sum of 39.

Ask:
How can you use the same strategy to add 34 + 65?

Listen for:
- I see 30 + 4 inside 34.
- I see 60 + 5 inside 65.
- I add the tens: 30 + 60 = 90. Then I add the ones: 4 + 5 = 9. Then I add all the tens and ones: 90 + 9 = 99.

LAUNCH THE PROBLEM SOLVING

Have students work individually to solve the problems on page 10. You may want to circulate and monitor their recorded answers. As students finish each problem, have them compare and discuss their responses with a partner. Then have each pair share their answers in a class discussion of the problem. Refer to the **Teacher Notes: Student Page 10** for more specific ideas about the problems on this page.

As students work and report their conclusions, focus on these issues:

Facilitate Students' Thinking – If students are having trouble decomposing numbers, you must reteach the concept by beginning with 10. You can ask students to name all the ways they can see inside 10 to find combinations of numbers that have a total of 10, such as 1 + 9, 2 + 8, and 3 + 7.

Validate Alternate Solutions – When students come up with different solutions, such as in problem 1, it is important for them to compare and discuss their solutions with their peers to determine whether all are correct.

Validate Alternate Representations – There may be several different pictures drawn as the solution for problem 3. Have students discuss the various representations to see whether they are all valid.

Allow Processing Time – It will take time for students to feel comfortable with and efficient at decomposing numbers. Allow them ample time to understand this concept.

Validate Multiple Viewpoints – It is important to encourage students to see inside numbers in a way that makes sense to them. Some students may feel comfortable decomposing with 10s, some with larger increments of 10. For example, 43 can be decomposed as 40 + 3 or as 10 + 10 + 10 + 10 + 3. In any case, validate various viewpoints, and encourage students to decompose in powerful ways.

Encourage Language Development – You may wish to introduce the term decomposition to students. Alternatively, it is helpful to use language such as, "What numbers can you see inside 54?"

Student Page 10: Problems and Potential Answers

Section C: What's That Number? Set 1

It is important to be able to think of a number in as many ways as you possibly can. For example, you might describe the number 12 as…

> a combination of one dime and two pennies, or
> 2 x 6, or
> one dozen, or
> the number of days until my birthday.

1. How many different ways can you describe the number 36? (Write at least 10 descriptions!)
   Responses will vary.

1.	6.
2.	7.
3.	8.
4.	9.
5.	10.

2. How many different ways can you describe the number 17? Responses will vary.

3. Draw two pictures that represent the number 17. Responses will vary.

Picture 1	Picture 2

4. Was one of these numbers (36 or 17) easier to describe than the other? Explain. Responses will vary.

10   Book 3: *Knowing Numbers*

TEACHER NOTES: STUDENT PAGE 10

Problem 1: *Watch for:* While students will certainly come up with various number sentences to describe 36, such as 30 + 6, 18 + 18, 40 − 4, 6 × 6, encourage them to think of other unique ways to envision the number. This problem, as is the case with those in the remainder of this book, is intended to get students to think broadly about numbers and make connections between numbers and operations. In this spirit, 36 might represent 3 dozen eggs, the age of a student's mother, the number worn by a favorite football player, etc. *Teaching Strategy:* These kinds of responses should be encouraged because they help students connect numbers to their uses in daily life.

Problem 2: In theory, it should be easier to describe 36 than it should be to describe 17, at least from a mathematical perspective. While 36 has many factors (1, 2, 3, 4, 6, 9, 12, 18, and 36), 17 is prime and has only two: 17 and 1. This comparison between 36 and 17 will be touched upon in problem 4.

Problem 3: Students may have some difficulty knowing exactly what to do to solve this problem. *Watch for:* They might draw three groups of objects that total 17: a plane surface with an area of 17 square units, a picture of base-ten blocks to represent 1 ten and 7 ones. Any of these responses is fine as long as they are thinking about a physical model that represents the numeric value of 17. This concept is called *cardinality*, which is the ability to connect a symbol with its quantitative value.

Problem 4: Answers to this problem will vary. *Watch for:* Look for students to discuss distinctions between the mathematical properties of the respective numbers. As noted above, students will probably have more to say about the different ways in which 36 can be represented than about the ways in which 17 can be represented.

Extension Idea

Play 20 Questions with numbers. Have students take turns thinking of a number. The other students try to guess that number by asking questions that can be answered with either yes or no. The only question students may not ask until the final question is: *Is the number* 24? Students should narrow in on the chosen number by asking questions such as:

- Is the number odd?
- Is the number even?
- Is the number greater than 15?
- Is the number a multiple of 5?

CONTINUE THE PROBLEM SOLVING

The focus of page 11 is number decomposition and addition and subtraction with friendly, or compatible, numbers. In these pages student have opportunities to decompose or see inside numbers, group and add compatible numbers, and arrive at a total.

Have students work individually to solve the problems on page 11. As they work, circulate and monitor their recorded answers. When they finish the page, have them compare and discuss their answers in a class discussion. Refer to the **Teacher Notes: Student Page 11** for more specific ideas about the problems on this page.

As students work and report on their conclusions, focus on these issues:

Facilitate Students' Thinking – Remind students that it may be easier for them to work with the numbers if they look inside them and then work with the smaller numbers they find.

Help Make Connections – Encourage students to decompose and then recombine numbers in various ways to help them see connections among the decompositions.

Allow Processing Time – New ways of computing take time to learn. Allow students time to play with the number combinations they see.

Look for Misconceptions – Some students will initially be uncomfortable operating on the various components of a number by starting with the larger parts. For example, when adding 23 and 34, they may be hesitant to add the 20 and 30 first, only to come back later and add the 3 and the 4. This method (decomposing and adding friendly numbers) is often counter to traditional algorithms that require starting on the right column (the ones), and working left (to the tens, hundreds, etc.). Help students work through this limited conception of addition and subtraction.

Encourage Language Development – Review the notion of a target number. In this case, the students are trying to reach the target of $100.

TEACHER NOTES: STUDENT PAGE 11

Problem 1: Problem 1 marks the beginning of a new focus of activity that will permeate much of the rest of the book. In this problem students will think about combinations of numbers that, when added, total 100. The ability to find numbers that add to friendly numbers such as 10 or 100 is a strategy that students will practice and refine throughout the book. If perfected, this strategy can be an extremely powerful complement to the use of number lines as a mental computational tool.

Watch for: At first, this problem may cause frustration because there are not too many obvious solutions. What some students will come to understand is that it may be easier to work backwards from 100 than to start at 0. They will find, for example, that if they can find items with a total cost of $75, they can simply add a fishing pole for another $25 to meet the $100 requirement. In this way, they will find other target numbers that will be useful on their way to $100.

Problems 2–4: These problems encourage students to grapple with the essence of problem 1, which is that some prices in the table cannot work in combination with other prices to total $100. Perhaps the greatest value of this problem is that it offers students a great deal of practice with informal addition and subtraction, although students will probably not view the problem as such. You will see students exhibit great thinking strategies if you allow them time to discuss these problems with each other.

Student Page 11: Problems and Potential Answers

Section C: What's That Number? — Set 1

Congratulations! You've just won a shopping spree at a sports store! You can spend $100! The only rule is that you must spend exactly $100. Here are the items you can choose from:

A)	Running Shoes	$65	I)	Kneepads	$11
B)	Flashlight	$8	J)	Pocket Knife	$22
C)	Basketball	$18	K)	Rain Jacket	$19
D)	Camera	$35	L)	Climbing Rope	$43
E)	Fishing Pole	$25	M)	Skateboard and Helmet	$88
F)	Hiking Boots	$41	N)	Map	$5
G)	Sleeping Bag	$60	O)	Drink Mix	$29
H)	Scooter	$32	P)	2 Mountain Bike Tires	$51

1. Find at least six combinations of items that total exactly $100. (Answers will vary.)

Combination #1: 1 pair of Running Shoes and 1 Camera (A and D)

Combination #2: 1 pair of Hiking Boots, 2 Mountain Bike Tires, 1 Flashlight (F, P, and B)

Combination #3: 1 Sleeping Bag, 1 Scooter, and 1 Flashlight (G, H, and B)

Combination #4: 1 Sleeping Bag, 1 Pocket Knife, and 1 Basketball (G, J, and C)

Combination #5: 1 Camera, 1 Fishing Pole, 1 Drink Mix, and 1 pair of Kneepads (D, E, O, and I)

Combination #6: 1 Fishing Pole, 1 Map, 2 Mountain Bike Tires, and 1 Rain Jacket (E, N, P, and K)

2. Can you buy the skateboard, helmet, and one other item? Explain.
No; the Skateboard and Helmet cost $88, and there is no way to spend the leftover $12 to total $100.

3. Was it hard to find combinations that totaled $100? Explain.
Responses will vary.

4. Like the skateboard and helmet, were there any other items that were impossible to buy? Explain your answer. Tell how you know. No. All other items can be purchased in some combination with other items.

Book 3: *Knowing Numbers* 11

CONTINUE THE PROBLEM SOLVING

Have students work individually to solve the problems on page 12. As they work, circulate and monitor their work and recorded answers. As students finish each problem, have them compare and discuss their answers with a partner. Then have pairs share their answers in a class discussion of the problem. Refer to the **Teacher Notes: Student Page 12** for more specific ideas for each problem.

As students work and report their conclusions, focus on these issues:

Help Make Connections – Encourage students to group numbers to find friendly sums that they can add together easily.

Allow Processing Time – Be sure to allow students extra time to look for combinations of friendly numbers in these problems.

Allow Waiting Time – When students struggle to explain their thinking, allow them at least 20 seconds to organize their thoughts.

TEACHER NOTES: STUDENT PAGE 12

Problem 1: The purpose of problem 1 is to get students to begin thinking about groups of 10. In other words, what are the combinations of single-digit numbers that have a sum of 10? They are 9 and 1, 8 and 2, 3 and 7, 6 and 4, and 5 and 5. *Watch for:* For this problem most students, if not prompted to use another strategy, will begin adding at the left and continue adding on until they reach the equal sign. One of the primary habits that traditional teaching methods creates when students are faced with horizontal addition is that adding must only be done from left to right. Students who begin to group the addends in friendly combinations, as demonstrated by the student in the example, will find that these kinds of addition problems become easy once they learn to use this strategy fluently.

The opening scenario is a true story often told about the famous mathematician, Carl Friedrich Gauss. A simple Internet search will return a great deal of information about this colorful mathematician of the 18th century.

Problem 2: This problem encourages students to add combinations of numbers that have the friendly sum of 20. Although other totals exist, many combinations of numbers in the table will total 20. Students can then count the number of 20s they found as they narrow in on a final answer.

Problem 3: Gauss quickly realized that 1 + 99 = 100. Likewise, 2 + 98 = 100, as did 3 + 97, 4 + 96, etc. In this way, Gauss also realized that there were 49 pairs of numbers that totaled 100 and that there was one extra 50. Hence, the total was 4,900 + 50, or 4,950. *Teaching Strategy:* This is a great problem in and of itself, so do not rush students to this solution. Allow them to experiment with various combinations of numbers from 1 to 100.

Student Page 12: Problems and Potential Answers

Section C: What's That Number? Set 2

There is a famous story about a young boy who later became a great mathematician. One time he got into trouble at school. As a punishment, his teacher told the boy to add all the numbers from 1 to 99. The teacher thought it would take the boy a long time to finish. But the boy found the correct answer in a few seconds! Incredible! While he certainly was a smart student, he used a very simple strategy. Before you learn what his strategy was, complete this addition problem.

1. 2 + 3 + 8 + 1 + 9 + 7 + 5 + 6 + 4 + 5 = **50**

Here is the work of a student who did the very same problem.

2 + 3 + 8 + 1 + 9 + 7 + 5 + 6 + 4 + 5 =   5 × 10 = 50

Explain this student's thinking. Did the student do this problem the same way you did yours?
He saw 5 pairs of numbers, each adding to 10. 5 × 10= 50. Responses will vary.

2. Mr. Faucett's science students went outside to count insects near the river. The students were supposed to count and record every insect they saw. Here is the data the students collected. Find a quick way to add these numbers to find how many insects were seen by the whole class.

Student #1	14	Student #7	10	Student #13	12
Student #2	16	Student #8	9	Student #14	9
Student #3	11	Student #9	9	Student #15	4
Student #4	4	Student #10	6	Student #16	6
Student #5	12	Student #11	8	Student #17	7
Student #6	2	Student #12	13	Student #18	8

Total Number of Insects:
160

3. Now, read the story at the top of the page again. Do you think you know how the boy added all the numbers from 1 to 99 so quickly? Explain how he did it.
Add 1 to 99, 2 to 98, 3 to 97….49 to 51. There are 49 pairs of numbers each adding to 100. So 49 times 100 is 4900, but there is one 50 not paired. So the total is 4950.

12 Book 3: *Knowing Numbers*

SECTION C ASSESSMENT (PAGE 13)

LAUNCH THE ASSESSMENT
Have students turn to the Section C Assessment on page 13. An additional copy is found on page 35 of the Assessment Book. Have students work individually to solve the problem and write their answers. As they work, circulate to be sure students understand what they need to do. Be sure that students are completing each part of the problem. For problem 1, students should make up a list of numbers, add the numbers, and then explain the strategy they used. You may find it helpful to read the directions before students begin, discussing the type of response they will need to make.

Encourage students to use whatever space they need to explain their thinking. If the space on the page is inadequate, they should use an additional sheet of paper or use the back of the page.

Refer to the **Teacher Notes: Assessment Problems for Section C** for more specific ideas about the problems on this page.

Evaluate Student Responses
Use the assessment rubric on page 34 of the Assessment Book (pictured on page 178 of the Teacher Edition) to evaluate student responses. The Assessment Book has some general suggestions for using the rubric that you may find helpful.

TEACHER NOTES: ASSESSMENT PROBLEMS FOR SECTION C

Problem 1: This problem will give you great insight into whether students have grasped the informal addition method taught in this section. *Watch for:* Students should use friendly numbers (usually numbers that end with zero) as a grouping target. Note in particular which numbers students begin to target as they make up their own addition problems.

Student Page 13: Problems and Potential Answers

Section C: Problems for Assesment

1. If you were given a list of numbers that needed to be added quickly, what strategy would you use? Explain by using your own example. Come up with a list of 15 numbers. Then show how you would quickly add those 15 numbers using some strategies like those you have just practiced. Use the space below to create your list of numbers, to show how you would add them, and to describe your strategy.

   Your List: *Answers will vary.*

   Quickly add the numbers. Show your work.

   Describe your strategy.

Book 3: *Knowing Numbers*

SCORING GUIDE BOOK 3: KNOWING NUMBERS

Section C Assessment
For Use With: Student Book Page 13

PROBLEM DESCRIPTION	SCORING: WHAT TO LOOK FOR	SCORE AND COMMENTS
Problem 1 Describe a process through which numbers can be added quickly using various informal strategies elaborated in the text (decomposition of numbers, grouping in tens, etc.). Level 1: Comprehension and Knowledge Level 2: Tool Use Level 3: Connections and Applications	Do students: • Have an intuitive understanding of addition? • Use their intuition about number families and combinations (e.g., the ten family of number facts)? • Accurately compute and use mental mathematics?	(Solution) Points:_____ of 4 (Strategy explanation) Points:_____ of 4

TOTAL POINTS:_____ OF 8

Section D: Making Change

SECTION D PLANNER

THE MATHEMATICS CONTENT AND GOALS

GOALS
Students will:
- Complete number sentences involving the act of making change.
- Examine various ways to make change, using different combinations of coins and/or bills, for a given amount of money.
- Find friendly combinations of decimals.

LANGUAGE DEVELOPMENT
Mathematical language in this section includes:

Estimate: To approximate an amount; to determine an amount that is as close to the actual as possible.

Combination: Two or more numbers that, when joined together, equal a desired amount.

Friendly Numbers: You may wish to use the term friendly numbers with students. Friendly numbers are ones that combine nicely with other numbers, or can be used quickly and effectively in various computations. Numbers like 10 and 5 are friendly from a computational point of view.

PROBLEM SETS: OVERVIEW

Set 1 (pp. 14–15; problems 1–4)
In this set of problems, students are provided with repeated practice in deciphering contexts that require exchanges of money. Sometimes students will have to find the correct change, given the price charged and money collected. At other times, students will have to look at the amount of change given to determine the cost of an item. As in the previous sections, informal and intuitive strategies for combining numbers are encouraged. The second group of problems in this set explicitly asks students to use various combinations of coins to come up with the correct change in a transaction. Students must then discuss which amounts of change seem most reasonable.

Set 2 (p. 16; problems 1–6)
This set of problems focuses on the development of student confidence in making estimates and on the strategies used to find friendly combinations of decimals in the form of money.

PACING
The projected pacing for this unit is 2–3 class periods (based on a 45 minute period).

Knowing Numbers *Teacher Edition* **179**

CONCEPT DEVELOPMENT (Page 14–16)

INTRODUCE THE CONCEPT

ASSESS STUDENTS' PRIOR KNOWLEDGE

On the board write, *Add the following numbers in your head: 25 42 35 48.*

Ask:
What strategy did you use to add mentally?

Listen for:
(Students to talk about decomposing, or "seeing inside," the numbers and adding in ways that are efficient and build on their knowledge of compatible numbers. For example, students might first add 25 and 35 [20 + 30 = 50; 5 + 5 = 10] and then add 42 and 48 [40 + 40 = 80; 2 + 8 = 10]. Then they might add the following: 50 + 10 + 80 + 10 = 150. Some students might suggest combining 25 + 35 and 42 + 48 by decomposing the numbers.)

MODEL MATHEMATICAL THINKING

Model the thinking for a related example by asking, *How can I add these decimals: 0.25, 0.42, 0.35, 0.48?*

Talk Through the Thinking:
I think this problem can be done like the way we did the first one. I can think about the decimals as money amounts: 25 cents plus 42 cents plus 35 cents plus 48 cents. Let's figure out where to start. Well, 25 cents and 35 cents can be added by first combining the 20 and the 30 and then combining the 5 and 5. So I can add these together to get 60 cents. Next I can add 42 cents and 48 cents. That's 40 + 40 combined with 8 + 2. That gives us 90 cents. Now I can add the two totals, 60 cents and 90 cents. If I take 10 cents from the 60 cents I can add it to 90 cents and get 100 cents, which is 1 dollar. Then I add the leftover 50 cents for a final total of 1 dollar and 50 cents. This is written as $1.50. So to find the decimal sum, I can erase the dollar sign and have a decimal total of 1.50.

Ask:
What strategies are the same for both problems?

Listen for:
- Seeing inside the numbers: 25 = 20 + 5; 35 = 30 + 5; 42 = 40 + 2; 48 = 40 + 8.
- Finding ways to combine the numbers to get friendly sums: 25 + 35 = 60; 48 + 42 = 90.

LAUNCH THE PROBLEM SOLVING

Have students work individually to solve the problems on page 14. As they work, circulate and monitor their work and recorded answers. As students finish each problem, have them compare and discuss their answers with a partner. Then have pairs share their answers in a class discussion of the problem. Refer to the **Teacher Notes: Student Page 14** for more specific ideas for each problem.

As students work and report their conclusions, focus on these issues:

Help Make Connections – Remind students that the processes of seeing inside numbers and the addition of friendly numbers are the same with decimals as with whole numbers.

Allow Waiting Time – When students struggle to explain their thinking, allow them at least 20 seconds to organize their thoughts.

Student Page 14: Problems and Potential Answers

Section D: Making Change — Set 1

1. A supermarket manager found an error in the accounting records for the day. He said that the error must have occurred when one of the cashiers gave the wrong change to a customer. Below are some of the transactions that he checked. Fill in the shaded boxes with the correct money amounts.

	Price of Item	Amount Paid by Customer	Amount of Change
A)	$0.85	$1.00	$0.15
B)	$1.96	$2.01	$0.05
C)	$2.17	$2.25	$0.08
D)	$0.67	$0.75	$0.08
E)	$1.75	$2.10	$0.35
F)	$0.89	$5.00	$4.11
G)	$9.99	$20.00	$10.01
H)	$2.86	$3.01	$0.15
I)	$30.25	$50.00	$19.75

2. The manager also found that some receipts had been torn, leaving it hard to tell exactly what the prices of the items were. Look at the receipts below. Help the manager figure out the missing pieces.

   a) The total on this receipt is missing. Is there an easy way to add the numbers to find the total?

   $7.99

   ```
   apples     $0.95
   rice       $0.65
   crackers   $0.41
   milk       $1.99
   juice      $2.19
   gum        $0.35
   pasta      $1.05
   chips      $0.40
   TOTAL
   ```

   Total: $7.99

   b) Three items are listed on this receipt, but only one price is visible. What could have been the prices of the two missing items? Come up with three possible combinations.
   Reponses will vary.

   ```
   bread
   peanut butter
   cheese      $2.40
   TOTAL       $6.25
   ```

   #1 Bread = $2.00   Peanut Butter = $1.85
   #2 Bread = $1.50   Peanut Butter = $2.35
   #3 Bread = $1.75   Peanut Butter = $2.10

   c)
   ```
   Yogurt (3)
   butter     $1.31
   soda       $0.99
   TOTAL      $4.25
   ```

   The price of each yogurt was the same. How much was the price of one yogurt?

   Total: $1.95

   1 yogurt = $ $0.65

Explain your steps: Explanations will vary.

14   Book 3: Knowing Numbers

TEACHER NOTES: STUDENT PAGE 14

Problem 1: This problem gives students multiple opportunities to compute amounts of change mentally. In some cases, students will have to work backwards to solve the problem. For example, they might have to find the amount given to the cashier by adding the price and the change given back. These problems are good examples of the inverse relationship that exists between addition and subtraction. Students will use a variety of strategies to solve these problems.

Problem 2: The intent of these problems is to have students find sums of numbers without the use of a calculator and to find combinations of numbers that add to friendly sums. *Teaching Strategy:* For problem 2a for example, encourage students to scan the list of numbers before beginning to add; this is a helpful strategy that should be emphasized. When they do so, they should recognize that $1.05 + $0.95 = $2.00. This strategy should be repeated until the list is reduced to a smaller number of values that can be combined more easily.

Many correct answers exist to problem 2b. Students should first understand that the bread and peanut butter together must cost $3.85. Any number of combinations will work. *Watch for:* Be sure to check for reasonable answers; it is unlikely, for example, that the peanut butter would cost $0.01 while the bread costs the remaining $3.84.

Problem 2c is slightly more sophisticated in that it requires students first to find the missing total. They then divide that quantity by 3 to find the cost of one single container of yogurt. Students may wish to discuss this problem with peers.

CONTINUE THE PROBLEM SOLVING

Have students work individually to solve the problems on page 15. As they work, you may want to circulate and monitor their recorded answers. As students finish each problem, have them compare and discuss their answers with a partner. Then have each pair share their answers in a class discussion of the problem. Refer to the *Teacher Notes: Student Page 15* for more specific ideas about the problems on this page.

As students work and report their conclusions, focus on these issues:
Help Make Connections – Some students are familiar with making an organized list to solve problems. Suggest that students use this strategy to help them find all the combinations of coins that have a total of $0.37.
Allow Waiting Time – When students struggle to explain their thinking, be sure to allow them ample time to organize their thoughts.

TEACHER NOTES: STUDENT PAGE 15

Problem 3: There are several ways to solve this problem. *Teaching Strategy:* Be sure to take advantage of this opportunity to have students discuss and agree on the total number of distinct solutions. They should be encouraged to make a table to help organize their solution strategies. Encourage students to look for and work in patterns. For example, they will find it helpful to exhaust all possible combinations starting with one coin before starting with another. If Q = quarters, D = dimes, N = nickels, and P = pennies, then 33 cents can be made:

1Q, 1N, 3P	3D, 3P	2D, 2N, 3P
1Q, 8P		2D, 1N, 8P

Problem 4: *Watch for:* It is most likely that the cashier would return either 1Q, 1N, 3P (fewest number of coins) or 3D, 3P (fewest different kinds of coins). *Teaching Strategy:* Let students discuss this problem and defend their opinions.

Student Page 15: Problems and Potential Answers

Section D: Making Change Set 1

3. John bought several items at the store. The total cost was $9.67. He gave the cashier a $10 bill. How much money did John receive in change? __$0.33__

<u>How many different ways</u> are there to represent this amount of change if you can use quarters, dimes, nickels, and pennies? Keep track of all of your solutions in the table below.

Quarter	Dime	Nickel	Penny
$0.25	$0.10	$0.05	$0.01

Quarter	Dime	Nickel	Penny
1		1	3
1			8
	3		3
	2	2	3
	2	1	8
	2		13
	1	4	3
	1	3	8
	1	2	13
	1	1	18
	1		23
		6	3
		5	8
		4	13
		3	18
		2	23
		1	28
			33

4. Of all of the combinations you just discovered, which combination of coins would John have most likely received? Why? 1 quarter, 1 nickel, and 3 pennies because it is the least number of coins; OR 3 dimes and 3 pennies because it is the least number of different kinds of coins.

CONTINUE THE PROBLEM SOLVING

Have students work individually to solve the problems on page 16. As they work, you may want to circulate and monitor their recorded answers. As students finish each problem, have them compare and discuss their answers with a partner. Then have each pair share their answers in a class discussion of the problem. Refer to the **Teacher Notes: Student Page 16** for more specific ideas about the problems on this page.

As students work and report their conclusions, focus on these issues:

Facilitate Students' Thinking – Remind students that an estimate is not an exact answer. Instead, it tells about how much or about how many.

Validate Alternate Solutions – When students use different strategies to solve the same problem, have them share their strategies with their peers.

Allow Waiting Time – When students struggle to explain their thinking, allow them ample time to organize their thoughts.

TEACHER NOTES: STUDENT PAGE 16

Problems 1–6: *Teaching Strategy:* Emphasize that students should quickly estimate the sum of these numbers mentally. The reason that you should ask them to work quickly is not about developing computational speed (an often over-emphasized trait), but to ensure that they estimate rather than compute the actual sum. These problems are designed to help students quickly recognize numbers that combine to an approximate total. For problem 1 for example, students can move from left to right, grouping adjacent numbers: $0.80 + $1.25 is about $2; $0.45 + $0.60 is about $1; $0.20 + $0.78 is about $1. So the total of this set of numbers is about $4.

Problems 5 and 6 ask students to explain their thinking patterns. *Teaching Strategy:* Be sure to use these opportunities to have students share solution strategies. Each of these problems has several combinations that are easy to find, and through such sharing, the activities enrich students' understanding.

Student Page 16: Problems and Potential Answers

Section D: Making Change Set 2

A local bank is sponsoring a contest for students to help them learn how to estimate sums accurately. Each participant in the contest will have 15 seconds to estimate how much it will cost to buy a set of objects. The prize for first place is a bicycle. To help prepare for the contest, your teacher gives you some practice. Try to estimate the sums below as quickly as you can while still being accurate! <u>Do not try to find the exact answers.</u> Instead, try your best to make a quick estimate.   Exact values are given.

1. $0.80 + $1.25 + $0.45 + $0.60 + $0.20 + $0.78 ➡ estimate $4.08

2. $0.15 + $0.25 + $0.85 + $1.25 + $0.50 ➡ estimate $3.00

3. $1.05 + $0.75 + $0.33 + $0.05 + $0.60 + $0.10 + $0.10 ➡ estimate $2.98

4. $18 + $25 + $60 + $32 + $25 + $40 ➡ estimate $200.00

5. $22.50 + $0.75 + $8.00 + $1.25 + $0.40 + $5.10 ➡ estimate $38.00

Explain your solution strategy for problem 5. Responses will vary.
_____
_____
_____

6. $1.25 + $1.25 + $1.25 + $0.75 + $0.75 + $0.75 + $0.50 + $0.50 + $0.25 ➡ estimate $7.25

Explain your solution strategy for problem 6. Responses will vary.
_____
_____
_____

16   Book 3: *Knowing Numbers*

SECTION D ASSESSMENT (PAGE 17)

LAUNCH THE ASSESSMENT

Have students turn to the Section D Assessment on page 17. An additional copy is found on page 38 of the Assessment Book. Have students work individually to solve the problems and write their answers. As they work, circulate to be sure students understand what they need to do for each of the problems. Be sure that students are completing each part of the problem. For example, for problem 1c, students should refer to the information in the introductory paragraph and then determine which combinations of the given coins will let them park for 1 hour. You may find it helpful to read the directions for all the problems before students begin, discussing the types of responses they will need to make for each problem.

Refer to the **Teacher Notes: Assessment Problems for Section D** for more specific ideas about the problems on this page.

Evaluate Student Responses

Use the assessment rubric on page 37 of the Assessment Book (pictured on page 188 of the Teacher Edition) to evaluate student responses. The Assessment Book has some general suggestions for using the rubric that you may find helpful.

TEACHER NOTES: ASSESSMENT PROBLEMS FOR SECTION D

Problem 1: For this problem, students need to become invested in the context. *Teaching Strategy:* It is important to help students note the distinction between the amount of time they might get, given a certain combination of coins, and the relative value of each coin. Problem 1a asks students to decide which coin would be the best one to use based on the number of minutes it buys on the meter, given its value as a monetary unit. Students should understand equivalent values, such as the fact that both 1 quarter and 5 nickels have a value of 25 cents. Through this understanding, they will realize that 1 quarter can buy 15 minutes, while 5 nickels–the equivalent value–can buy 40 minutes.

Problem 2b asks students to compare various combinations. *Watch for:* Not only does this problem encourage practice with multiple addition computations, it also requires a depth of reasoning as students try to keep straight both the number of coins used, and the possible variations of time allotted.

Problem 2c is great for students to use for practicing problem-solving skills while, at the same time, they recognize and develop the use of patterns to solve the problem.

Student Page 17: Problems and Potential Answers

Section D: Problems for Assessment

1. A parking meter takes quarters, dimes, and nickels. For each different coin you put in the meter, you buy a different length of time. If you put one quarter in the meter, you get to park for 15 minutes. For one dime you get to park for 12 minutes, and for one nickel you get to park for 8 minutes.

   a) Which coin gives you the best deal (not necessarily the most time)?

   Explain. The nickel gives you the most time for the money.

   b) If you had 5 coins in your pocket (nickels, dimes and/or quarters), what is the greatest amount of time you could buy from the meter? _____ The least amount of time? _____
   5 quarters; 15 × 5 = 75 minutes   5 nickels; 8 × 5 = 40 minutes

   Explain. _____

   c) If you had 5 quarters, 10 dimes, and 10 nickels in your pocket, how many different combinations of coins could you use to pay for exactly one hour (60 minutes)? Come up with at least 3 different combinations.

   4 quarters
   3 dimes, 3 nickels
   1 dime, 6 nickels
   5 dimes

Book 3: *Knowing Numbers*   17

SECTION D ASSESSMENT

Section D Assessment
For Use With: Student Book Page 17

PROBLEM DESCRIPTION	SCORING: WHAT TO LOOK FOR	SCORE AND COMMENTS
Problem 1a Solve a problem using quarters, dimes, and nickels. Determine the best time-per-coin ratio from the given problem context (coins in a parking meter). Level 1: Connection and Application	Do students: • Understand the value of coins? • Understand the use of ratios to compare time to monetary value? • Articulate their thinking and solution strategy?	 Points:_____of 3
Problem 1b Use information from the context to compute the amount of time given 5 coins. Level 1: Connection and Application	Do students: • Read the problem context and understand the mathematical application? • Compute values based on coins? • Use ratios to determine minutes with respect to coin value? • Articulate their thinking accurately?	 Points:_____of 3
Problem 1c Find different combinations of coins. Level 1: Connection and Application	Do students: • Understand the value of coins? • Complete arithmetic operations to arrive at 60 minutes worth of time? • Use varied and productive strategies/combinations?	 Points:_____of 3

TOTAL POINTS:_____ OF 9

Section E: From Adding to Multiplying

SECTION E PLANNER

THE MATHEMATICS CONTENT AND GOALS

GOALS
Students will:
- Manipulate numbers and operations to obtain a desired value.
- Apply visual, geometric models to the completion of contextually-based multiplication problems.
- Use informal strategies to practice multiplication (repeated addition) of numbers.

LANGUAGE DEVELOPMENT
Mathematical language in this section includes:
Combination: Two or more numbers that, when joined together, equal a desired amount.

PACING
The projected pacing for this unit is 3–4 class periods (based on a 45 minute period).

PROBLEM SETS: OVERVIEW

The problems in this section encourage students to combine multiplicative and additive reasoning in the same problem context. To help them do so, a visual model of multiplication, counting rows of objects, is utilized. As students become comfortable with these problems, they may visualize the numbers and operations in them as rows of tiles or as representing the area of a rectangular region.

Set 1 (p. 18; problems 1–6)
In this set students will enjoy playing a game in which they try to reach a target number by manipulating both the numbers and operations. For example, to obtain a total of 17 using the numbers 2, 3, and 4, students might add 2 + 3 twice for a total of 10, then add 3, and then add 4. Some of these problems are extremely challenging. Students will appreciate the opportunity to create their own problems with which they can challenge their peers.

Set 2 (pp. 19–20; problems 1–6)
The problems in Set 2 utilize a visual (geometric) model/representation to promote the idea of repeated addition, or multiplication. Students should continue to look for informal strategies for adding numbers. In the context of pricing flats of tiles, students get opportunities to develop effective strategies for combining multiple repetitions of the same number.

Set 3 (p. 21; problems 1–4)
This set of problems requires students to problem-solve their way through contexts that juggle multiple concepts and operations. As students think through possible scenarios of ordering tiles, they must keep in mind not only the number of tiles they are ordering, but also whether the tiles can be ordered within the financial constraints presented in the problem. In other words, students need to do the very practical work of balancing quantity with unit cost.

Knowing Numbers *Teacher Edition*   **189**

CONCEPT DEVELOPMENT (Pages 18–20)

INTRODUCE THE CONCEPT

ASSESS STUDENTS' PRIOR KNOWLEDGE
The intent of pages 18–20 is to help students understand the connection between adding like numbers repeatedly (repeated addition) and multiplication. You might begin by pointing out that adding, subtracting, multiplying, and dividing are the four operations. Some people think that each operation is very different from the others. Other people think these operations are related.
Write on the board: Multiplication is repeated addition.

Ask:
What does this sentence mean? Please talk about its meaning with a partner for a moment before you answer. Give an example.

Listen for:
- If you add the same number a given number of times, the answer is the same as it would be if you multiplied that number by the number of times it is added. For example, $2 + 2 + 2 = 6$ and $3 \times 2 = 6$.

MODEL MATHEMATICAL THINKING
Lead the class in a discussion of the relationship between multiplication and repeated addition. Point out that multiplication is a way to make large addition problems easier to compute. Then model the thinking for another example by asking, *How can we use what we already know about seeing inside numbers to multiply 4×12?*

Talk Through the Thinking:
In problems we did earlier, we learned how helpful it can be to see inside larger numbers in order to add them. We can use the same thinking in multiplication. I know that 4×12 means 4 groups of 12. I can see inside 12 and know it is the same as $10 + 2$. So 4×12 is the same as $4 \times (10 + 2)$. I could use words to say that 4 groups of 12 is the same as 4 groups of 10 plus 2, or 4 groups of 10 plus 4 groups of 2. Here is how I can draw a picture of this problem: (Draw the following picture on the board.)

4 Groups of 12

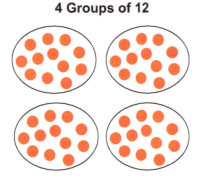

4 Groups of 10 and 4 Groups of 2

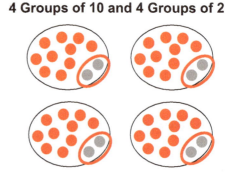

I see that 4 groups of 10 is 40; and 4 groups of 2 is 8. This is a total of 48.
So $4 \times 12 = 4 \times (10 + 2) = (4 \times 10) + (4 \times 2) = 40 + 8 = 48$.

Ask:
Suppose we had to multiply 5×23. How could we use the same thinking to find the answer?

Listen for:
- 23 is the same as $20 + 3$, so 5×23 is the same as $5 \times (20 + 3)$, or $(5 \times 20) + (5 \times 3)$.
- $5 \times 20 = 100$, $5 \times 3 = 15$, and $100 + 15 = 115$. So $5 \times 23 = 115$.

LAUNCH THE PROBLEM SOLVING

Have students work individually to solve the problems on page 18. As they work, you might circulate and monitor their recorded answers. As students finish each problem, have them compare and discuss their answers with a partner. Then have each pair share their answers in a class discussion of the problem. Refer to the **Teacher Notes: Student Page 18** for more specific ideas about each of the problems on this page.

As students work and report their conclusions, focus on these issues:

Allow Processing Time – Some students may need more time to process the techniques needed to solve the problems on this page. Remind them that if their first solution does not work, they can try again.

Look for Misconceptions – The most common misconception is due to a lack of understanding of the distributive property. Students may not believe that 12×4 is the same as $(10 \times 4) + (2 \times 4)$. Drawings are helpful in this regard. A second misconception has to do with order of operations. Be sure to use parentheses to help students steer clear of order of operations mistakes.

Facilitate Students' Thinking – Encourage students to use drawings to help illustrate the distributive property, also support students who pick friendly numbers for these operations as they decompose and use the distributive property.

Encourage Language Development – Remind students of the notion of a combination of numbers (i.e., two or more numbers that, when joined together, equal a desired amount). Also students will be asked to work toward a target number in these problems. Remind them that this target is a desired ending point that they must work toward as they explore various number combinations.

TEACHER NOTES: STUDENT PAGE 18

Problems 1–6: Some of these problems are harder than they might seem at first. *Teaching Strategy:* Encourage students first to try to get in the ballpark and then make small adjustments until they determine a combination of numbers that results in the desired target. *Watch for:* Be sure students understand that the order in which they write the numbers does not matter. This is not necessarily true when multiplication/division operations are combined with addition and subtraction in the same operational string. You may wish to extend this activity by having students generate their own number lists and target sums to be shared with and solved by their peers.

Student Page 18: Problems and Potential Answers

Section E: From Adding to Multiplying — Set 1

Add or subtract, in any combination, the numbers in each set below to reach the target number. Each number must be used at least once. You may use the same number more than once. Try to reach the target in as few steps as possible.

Example: List: 4, 5, 6 → Target = **25**

Solution 1: 4 + 6 + 4 + 6 + 5 = **25**

Solution 2: 5 + 6 + 5 + 5 + 4 = **25**

Solution 3: 5 + 5 + 5 + 5 + 5 + 5 + 5 − 6 − 4 = **25**

One possible solution for each is given.

1. List: 3, 8, 7, 6 → Target: 39

    Solution: 3 + 7 + 7 + 8 + 8 + 6 = 39

2. List: 3, 4, 5, 6, → Target: 42

    Solution: 4 + 6 + 4 + 6 + 3 + 5 + 3 + 5 + 6 = 42

3. List: 4, 5, 11, 16 → Target: 53

    Solution: 4 + 5 + 11 + 4 + 16 + 4 + 4 + 5 = 53

4. List: 6, 9, 13, 15, 12 → Target: 68

    Solution: 13 + 12 + 15 + 6 + 9 + 13 = 68

5. List: 14, 15, 16, 17 → Target: 81

    Solution: 14 + 15 + 16 + 17 + 16 + 17 − 14 = 81

6. List: 3, 7, 11, 17 → Target: 49

    Solution: 3 + 7 + 3 + 17 + 11 + 11 − 3 = 49

Book 3: *Knowing Numbers*

CONTINUE THE PROBLEM SOLVING

Have students work individually to solve the problems on page 19. As they work, you may want to circulate and monitor their recorded answers. As students finish each problem, have them compare and discuss their answers with a partner. Then have each pair share their answers in a class discussion of the problem. Refer to the **Teacher Notes: Student Page 19** for more specific ideas about the problems on this page.

As students work and report their conclusions, focus on these issues:

Allow Waiting Time – When students struggle to explain their thinking, allow them ample time to organize their thoughts.

Validate Alternate Solutions – Have students compare and discuss their solution strategies.

Facilitate Students' Thinking – Encourage students to think of these problems in terms of multiplication. Encourage the use of an area model as a contextual anchor for multiplication.

Validate Representations – Look for students to select friendly combinations of numbers to add repeatedly (multiply). For example, they may see that four $0.50 tiles is the same as $2, and then count accordingly.

TEACHER NOTES: STUDENT PAGE 19

As noted in the summary of this section, these problems will encourage students to combine multiplicative and additive reasoning in the same problem context. As students become comfortable with these problems, they may visualize the numbers and operations in them as rows of tiles or as representing the area of a rectangular region. Whatever the case, students should not be counting individual tiles. Instead, they should be combining the tiles in efficient ways to determine the costs of the various flats of tiles.

Problem 1: Students may initially count individual tiles for this problem. *Teaching Strategy:* As they share their thinking, move them away from this counting strategy to strategies that require them to combine quantities and think multiplicatively.

Problems 2–4: Some students will choose to break this flat into two parts and then add the respective amounts to find the final answer. That is a perfectly fine strategy. Others might subtract out the dead space that would have existed if the flat of tiles formed one rectangle. For example, in problem 2, students might recognize that a full flat would have had 5 columns and 5 rows. Since each column would have a total of $2, the entire flat would have been $10 (5 × 2). But the lower right-hand corner is missing. This missing corner would have had a value of $3. So one solution would be to subtract $3 from $10 for a total of $7.

Teaching Strategy: It is important for students to share these variations in strategies with the class. Be sure to discuss strategy use for problems 3 and 4 in particular.

Student Page 19: Problems and Potential Answers

Section E: From Adding to Multiplying — Set 2

The Tile Shop sells tiles of all kinds for different prices. To make shipping and calculating easier, many tiles of the same kind are sold in flats like the one shown below.

Example Flat of Tiles: $0.50 per tile

$0.50	$0.50	$0.50	$0.50	$0.50
$0.50	$0.50	$0.50	$0.50	$0.50
$0.50	$0.50	$0.50	$0.50	$0.50
$0.50	$0.50	$0.50	$0.50	$0.50

1. How much would it cost to order this flat of tiles?
   Cost. $10.00
   Explain your strategy. *Explanations will vary.*

$0.50	$0.50	$0.50	$0.50	$0.50
$0.50	$0.50	$0.50	$0.50	$0.50
$0.50	$0.50			
$0.50	$0.50			

2. Sometimes a customer does not want a whole flat of tiles. How much would this many tiles cost?
   Cost. $7.00
   Explain your strategy. *Explanations will vary.*

5¢	5¢	5¢	5¢	5¢	5¢	5¢	5¢	5¢	5¢
5¢	5¢	5¢	5¢	5¢	5¢	5¢	5¢	5¢	5¢
5¢	5¢	5¢	5¢	5¢	5¢	5¢	5¢	5¢	5¢
5¢	5¢	5¢	5¢	5¢	5¢	5¢	5¢	5¢	5¢
5¢	5¢	5¢	5¢						

3. How much would this set of plastic tiles cost?
   Cost. $2.20
   Explain your strategy. *Explanations will vary.*

4. Imagine that you work for the Tile Shop. Customers ask for the prices of the sets of tiles below. What is the price of each set? Explain your strategy for each.

a)

16¢	16¢	16¢	16¢
16¢	16¢	16¢	16¢
16¢			

Cost: $1.44   Explain. *Explanations will vary.*

b)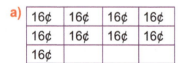

25¢	25¢	25¢	25¢	25¢	25¢	25¢	25¢
25¢	25¢	25¢	25¢	25¢	25¢	25¢	25¢
	25¢	25¢	25¢	25¢	25¢	25¢	25¢
							25¢

Cost: $6.75   Explain. *Explanations will vary.*

Book 3: *Knowing Numbers*

CONTINUE THE PROBLEM SOLVING

Have students work individually to solve the problems on page 20. As they work, you may want to circulate and monitor their recorded answers. As students finish each problem, have them compare and discuss their answers with a partner. Then have each pair share their answers in a class discussion of the problem. Refer to the **Teacher Notes: Student Page 20** for more specific ideas about the problems on this page.

As students work and report their conclusions, focus on these issues:

Validate Alternate Strategies – Students may use several different strategies to solve the problems on student page 20. Be sure to have them compare and discuss their strategies.

Help Make Connections – For problem 6, remind students that these arrangements are similar to the ones in the problems they just completed. You may want to allow students who are struggling to draw pictures.

Allow Waiting Time – When students struggle to explain their thinking, be sure to allow them ample time to organize their thoughts.

Student Page 20: Problems and Potential Answers

Section E: From Adding to Multiplying — Set 2

5. What is the cost of each of the following flats?

   a) | $1.30 | $1.30 | $1.30 |

   Cost: $3.90   Explain: Explanations will vary.

   b) | 80¢ | 80¢ | 80¢ | 80¢ |
      | 80¢ | 80¢ | 80¢ | |
      | 80¢ | 80¢ | 80¢ | |

   Cost: $8.00   Explain: Explanations will vary.

   c) | 75¢ | 75¢ | 75¢ | 75¢ |
      | 75¢ | 75¢ | 75¢ | 75¢ |

   Cost: $6.00   Explain: Explanations will vary.

6. How much would each of the following flats cost?

   a) Flat size: 10 rows by 10 columns
      Tile cost: $0.32 per tile
      Total cost: $32.00

   b) Flat size: 8 rows by 8 columns
      Tile cost: 25 cents per tile
      Total cost: $16.00

   c) Flat size: 10 rows by 10 columns
      Tile cost: $1.25 per tile
      Total cost: $125.00

   d) Flat size: 6 rows by 4 columns
      Tile cost: $2.40 per tile
      Total cost: $57.60

   e) Describe two strategies you have found helpful in solving these problems.
      Responses will vary.

Book 3: *Knowing Numbers*

TEACHER NOTES: STUDENT PAGE 20

Problem 5: *Watch for:* These problems will elicit more of the same strategies as used for those on the previous page. Students may also want or need to use innovative addition strategies, such as grouping, that they practiced earlier in the book.

Problem 6: These problems now require students to visualize the configurations of tiles, compute the total number of tiles per flat, and then distribute the cost per tile appropriately. Problems 6a and 6c should be somewhat easier for students because the total number of tiles is 100. *Teaching Strategy:* Allow students ample time to discuss their approaches.

CONCEPT DEVELOPMENT (Page 21)

INTRODUCE THE CONCEPT

ASSESS STUDENTS' PRIOR KNOWLEDGE
Write on the board: Triple Scoop, $2; Double Scoop, $1.50; Single Scoop, $1.

Ask:
On a class field trip to a dairy, 10 students wanted a triple scoop of ice cream. Four students wanted a double scoop, and 9 students wanted a single scoop. How much did the ice cream cost for all the students?

Listen for:
(Students to separate the problem into steps: [10 × $2] + [4 × $1.50] + [9 × $1])
- The ice cream cost $35.

MODEL MATHEMATICAL THINKING
Model the thinking for another example by asking, *Jared sold his action figures at a garage sale. He sold 6 action figures for $3 each, 4 action figures for $2.50 each, and 5 action figures for $2 each. How much did he earn from the sale of all the action figures?*

Talk Through the Thinking:
The question is asking for the total earnings from all the action figures: 6 + 4 + 5 equals 15 action figures in all. But there are three different prices, $3, $2.50, and $2. So there are three parts to this problem. For the first part, I see that Jared sold 6 figures for $3 each. To find the cost of these figures, I can multiply 6 × $3. That's $18 for the most expensive ones. Next Jared sold 4 figures for $2.50 each. This is harder to multiply. So I'll break apart the $2.50 into dollars and cents: 4 × $2 = $8, and 4 × $0.50 = $2. So the total cost of the $2.50 action figures is $8 + $2, or $10. Now we have 6 action figures at $18 and 4 figures at $10. Now for the least expensive action figures. Jared sold 5 of these for $2 each: 5 × $2 = 10. Now we add all the costs together: $18 + $10 + $10 = $38. Jared earned $38 from the sale of all the action figures.

Ask:
Suppose Jared also sold 6 toy trucks for $1.25 each. How much would he have earned from the sale of the toy trucks? How much would he have earned from the sale of all the action figures and the toy trucks combined?

Listen for:
- He would have earned $7.50 from the sale of the toy trucks.
- He would have earned $45.50 from the sale of all the action figures and the toy trucks combined.

LAUNCH THE PROBLEM SOLVING

Have students work individually to solve the problems on page 21. As they work, circulate to monitor their recorded answers. As students finish each problem, have them compare and discuss their answers with a partner. Then have them share their answers in a class discussion of the problem. Refer to the **Teacher Notes: Student Page 21** for more specific ideas of each problem on the page.

As students work and report their conclusions, focus on these issues:

Help Make Connections – Remind students that they can use ratio tables to help them with problems 1–3.

Facilitate Students' Thinking – Students may come up with different ways to represent these multi-step problems. You may wish to encourage some students to draw pictures.

Allow Waiting Time – When students struggle to explain their thinking, allow them ample time to organize their thoughts.

Explaining Thinking – In these problems, students will be asked to explain their thinking. Remind students of your expectation that they provide written descriptions of their solution strategies.

Student Page 21: Problems and Potential Answers

Section E: From Adding to Multiplying — Set 3

At the Tile Shop, Karen decides that she likes the way that red, blue, and gray tiles look when placed next to each other. She has $20 to spend on the tiles. The red tiles cost $1.20 each. The blue tiles cost $1.80 each. The gray tiles cost $2.50 each.

1. Karen needs 18 tiles to tile her bathroom countertop. Does she have enough money to buy 18 red tiles? How do you know? Explain.
   No, she can only buy 16 of the red tiles, which would cost her $19.20.

2. For $20, how many gray tiles could she order? How many blue tiles could she order?

   Gray Tiles 8   Blue Tiles 11

   Show your work here.

3. Karen knows she is going to have to spend more money to get the tile arrangement she wants. She orders 10 red tiles, 12 blue tiles, and 8 gray tiles. How much money will these tiles cost?

   Total Cost: $53.60

   Show your work here.

   Red tiles: $12.00
   Blue tiles: $21.60
   Gray tiles: $20.00

4. Karen needs 10 blue tiles and 12 red tiles for her kitchen. She has $40 to spend on tiles.
   • How much do the red and blue tiles cost together? $32.40
   • How much money does she have left? $7.60

   With the extra money, how many gray tiles can she buy? Remember that each gray tile costs $2.50.

   Show your work, and explain your answer. **Gray tiles she can buy** _____

   Explain.
   She can buy 3 gray tiles. 10 blue tiles cost $18.00. 12 red tiles cost $14.40. This is a total of $32.40. So she will have $7.60 left to spend on gray tiles, which are $2.50 each. She can only spend $7.50 more (3 × $2.50) without going over the $7.60.

Book 3: *Knowing Numbers*   21

TEACHER NOTES: STUDENT PAGE 21

Problem 1: Problem 1 is fairly complex because it requires students to juggle several bits of information. Karen is limited to $20 and needs a total of 18 tiles. *Watch for:* Students will approach this problem in different ways because it lends itself to the application of a ratio table. Eventually students should realize that even with the least expensive tile ($1.20), she does not have enough money to purchase 18 tiles.

Problem 2: *Teaching Strategy:* Students should be encouraged to use a ratio table to solve this problem.

Problem 3: Problem 3 requires students to compute the costs for the red tiles, the blue tiles, and the gray tiles then add the totals. *Teaching Strategy:* Either a ratio table or other informal strategies for grouping numbers should be encouraged.

Problem 4: This problem is a multi-step problem. Students must first determine the amount spent on the red and blue tiles and then decide how much of the original $40 is left. Next they must determine how many of the gray tiles they can purchase. Remind the students to explain their thinking. *Teaching Strategy:* Encourage students to share their solution strategies and approaches for this problem.

SECTION E ASSESSMENT (PAGE 22)

LAUNCH THE ASSESSMENT

Have students turn to the Section E Assessment on page 22. An additional copy is found on page 40 of the Assessment Book. Have students work individually to solve the problems and write their answers. As they work, circulate to be sure students understand what they need to do for each of the problems. Be sure that students are completing each part of the problem. For example, for problem 4, students must determine the cost of the postage stamps, then explain the strategy they used to do so. You may find it helpful to read the directions for all the problems before students begin, discussing the types of responses they will need to make for each problem.

Encourage students to use whatever space they need to explain their thinking. If the space on the page is inadequate, they should use an additional sheet of paper or use the back of the page.

Refer to the **Teacher Notes: Assessment Problems for Section E** for more specific ideas about the problems on this page.

Evaluate Student Responses

Use the assessment rubric on page 39 of the Assessment Book (pictured on page 203 of the Teacher Edition) to evaluate student responses. The Assessment Book has some general suggestions for using the rubric that you may find helpful.

TEACHER NOTES: ASSESSMENT PROBLEMS FOR SECTION E

These assessment problems will encourage students' use of informal counting/grouping strategies.

Student Page 22: Problems and Potential Answers

Section E: Problems for Assessment

Add or subtract, in any combination, the numbers in each set below to reach the target number. Each number must be used at least once. You may use the same number more than once. Try to reach the target in as few steps as possible.

1. List: 3, 6, 7, 8, 9 → Target: 58

   Solution: 3 + 6 + 7 + 8 + 9 + 9 + 9 + 7 = 58

2. List: 11, 12, 13 → Target: 72

   Solution: 11 + 12 + 13 + 11 + 12 + 13 = 72

3. List: 6, 9, 11, 13 → Target: 61

   Solution: 6 + 9 + 11 + 13 + 11 + 11 = 61

4. How much does the sheet of postage stamps below cost? Cost: $7.70

   Explain your strategy. Explanations will vary.

$0.35	$0.35	$0.35	$0.35	$0.35	$0.35
$0.35	$0.35	$0.35	$0.35	$0.35	$0.35
$0.35	$0.35	$0.35	$0.35	$0.35	$0.35
$0.35	$0.35	$0.35	$0.35		

Book 3: *Knowing Numbers*

SCORING GUIDE BOOK 3: KNOWING NUMBERS

Section E Assessment
For Use With: Student Book Page 22

PROBLEM DESCRIPTION	SCORING: WHAT TO LOOK FOR	SCORE AND COMMENTS
Problems 1–3 Use number combinations (addition and subtraction) to reach a target number. Level 3: Comprehension and Knowledge Level 2: Tool use	Do students: • Understand addition and subtraction? • Repetitively use common facts (e.g., anchoring on 10s)? • Demonstrate accurate computation?	(#1) Points:_____ of 2 (#2) Points:_____ of 2 (#3) Points:_____ of 2
Problem 4 Use groupings (repeated addition) to determine the cost of a sheet of stamps. Level 1: Connection and Application Level 4: Synthesis and Evaluation	Do students: • Recognize and use friendly combinations (e.g., 0.35 + 0.35 = 0.70; 0.70 x 10 = 7)? • Use patterns (both geometric and arithmetic) to help solve the problem? • Explain their thinking?	Points:_____ of 4

TOTAL POINTS:_____ OF 10

End-of-Book Assessment (Pages 23–25)

LAUNCH THE ASSESSMENT

Have students turn to the End-of-Book Assessment on page 23. An additional copy is found on page 43 of the Assessment Book. Have students work individually to solve the problems and write their answers. As they work, circulate to be sure students understand what they need to do. For example, for this page, students must read and understand the list of materials and the price list and then estimate the cost of the tree house. You may find it helpful to read the directions before students begin, discussing the types of responses they will need to make.

This is a challenging series of questions. You may need to spend several minutes introducing the problem context to students. Be prepared for this assessment to take a significant amount of time. For that reason, it might be good to allow students to work in groups on these problems.

Refer to the **Teacher Notes: End-of-Book Assessment, Student Page 23** for more specific ideas about the problems on this page.

Evaluate Student Responses

Use the assessment rubric on page 41 of the Assessment Book (pictured on page 210 of the Teacher Edition) to evaluate student responses. The Assessment Book has some general suggestions for using the rubric that you may find helpful.

TEACHER NOTES: END-OF-BOOK ASSSESSMENT, STUDENT PAGE 23

Students will need to apply many of the skills developed in this book to solve this contextually based problem situation.

Problem 1: *Watch for:* Be sure students are truly making an estimate and not computing an actual answer for this first problem. This is not to say that they will not have to make some calculations along the way to reach their final estimate. For example, they need to determine how many sheets of plywood they need to have a total of 108 square feet. *Teaching Strategy:* Students may need some assistance on this particular element of the problem since area has not been covered explicitly thus far in the book series. Also be sure to encourage students to elaborate on the solution strategy they used to find the estimate.

Student Page 23: Problems and Potential Answers

End-of-Book Assessment

The Tree House

Your class decides to build a tree house for the playground. After drawing up your plans, you decide on the following materials list.

> **TREE HOUSE MATERIALS: WHAT WE NEED TO BUY**
>
> <u>2-by-4's</u>   8 ft long *(We need 3.)*
>   4 ft long *(We need 5.)*
>   2 ft long *(We need 8.)*
>
> <u>Plywood</u>   108 square feet
>
> <u>Screws</u>   3-inch wood screws *(We need 0.5 pound.)*
>   2-inch wood screws *(We need 0.75 pound.)*
>   1.25-inch wood screws *(We need 0.5 pound.)*
>
> <u>Rope</u>   25 feet

Once you get to the hardware store, you are given this price list.

> **PRICE LIST PROJECT: TREE HOUSE**
>
> <u>2-by-4's</u>   8-foot ➡ $2.50
>   12-foot ➡ $3.25
>   16-foot ➡ $4.00
>
> <u>Plywood</u>   4 ft x 8 ft sheet of plywood ➡ $16
>
> <u>Screws</u>   3-inch ➡ $3/pound
>   2-inch ➡ $2/pound
>   1.25-inch ➡ $1.80/pound
>
> <u>Rope</u> $3.60 for 10 feet

1. ***Without doing any calculations,*** estimate how much it is going to cost to build the tree house. <u>Explain your strategy</u> for making your estimate. Remember, this should be a "ballpark" figure – a guess that is reasonably close. Estimate: _____

   Explain. *Responses will vary.* _____
   _____
   _____

Book 3: *Knowing Numbers*   23

CONTINUE THE ASSESSMENT

Have students turn to the End-of-Book Assessment on page 24. An additional copy is found on page 44 of the Assessment Book. Have students work individually to solve the problems and write their answers. As they work, circulate to be sure students understand what they need to do for each of the problems. Be sure students are completing each part of the problem. For example, for problem 3, students should be able to think of a less expensive plan to buy the 2-by-4s and then explain their strategy. You may find it helpful to read the directions before students begin, discussing the types of responses they will need to make.

Encourage students to use whatever space they need to explain their thinking. If the space on the page is inadequate, they should use an additional sheet of paper or use the back of the page.

Refer to the **Teacher Notes: End-of-Book Assessment, Student Page 24** for more specific ideas about the problems on this page.

Evaluate Student Responses
Use the assessment rubric on pages 41–42 of the Assessment Book (pictured on pages 210–211 of the Teacher Edition) to evaluate student responses. The Assessment Book has some general suggestions for using the rubric that you may find helpful.

TEACHER NOTES: END-OF-BOOK ASSSESSMENT, STUDENT PAGE 24

Problem 2: This problem requires students to use a systematic approach to determine how many smaller lengths can be cut from a longer piece of wood. For example, an 8-foot 2-by-4 can be cut into four 2-foot sections. The second part of the problem calls for students to go back and apply the cost of each 2-by-4 to the number of boards needed.

Problem 3: The solution to problem 3 depends on the successful completion of problem 2; so you need to make sure students understand their work for problem 2 before tackling this problem. *Teaching Strategy:* The key to this problem is to eliminate any wasted wood. *Watch for:* Students should key in on the fifth board, which has a length of 4 feet. If one board of 12 feet was purchased, it could be subdivided into three 4-foot lengths. Doing so would reduce the waste of 4 feet that was generated in the previous solution, in which only 8-foot-long 2-by-4s were used.

Problems 4–5: Students must similarly apply informal strategies to determine the appropriate costs per unit measure.

Student Page 24: Problems and Potential Answers

> **End-of-Book Assessment**

2. Remember that you need 2-by-4 boards in the following lengths: 3 that are 8 feet long, 5 that are 4 feet long, and 8 that are 2 feet long. Charles suggests that you should just buy a bunch of 8-foot boards and cut them to size. How many 8-foot boards would you need to get all the different lengths? _____
   We need eight 8-foot boards.

   How much would these boards cost? $20.00

3. Sally thinks there is a way to get all the 2-by-4 lengths you need for less money. Do you agree? Can you come up with a less expensive plan for the 2-by-4's? Explain. _____
   Yes. You can buy four 16-foot boards for $16.00
   Or
   Yes. You can buy one 12-foot board and three 16-foot boards for a total cost of $15.25

4. Remember that you need 3 different sizes of screws. You need 0.5 pound of the 3-inch screws, 0.75 pound of the 2-inch screws, and 0.5 pound of the 1.25-inch screws. How much will all the screws cost? Check the supply list for prices. Show your work.
   Cost: $3.90

   3-inch: 0.5 × $3 = $1.50
   2-inch: 0.75 × $2 = $1.50
   1.25 inch: 0.5 × $1.80 = $0.90

5. How much will the rope cost? Remember that you need **25 feet** of rope. Cost: $9.00
   Show your work.

24 Book 3: *Knowing Numbers*

CONTINUE THE ASSESSMENT

Have students turn to the End-of-Book Assessment on page 25. An additional copy is found on page 45 of the Assessment Book. Have students work individually to solve the problems and write their answers. As they work, circulate to be sure students understand what they need to do for each of the problems. For example, for problem 7, students must use all the previous problems in this assessment to find the total cost of the tree house. You may find it helpful to read the directions for all the problems before students begin, discussing the types of responses they will need to make.

Encourage students to use whatever space they need to explain their thinking. If the space on the page is inadequate, they should use an additional sheet of paper or use the back of the page.

Refer to the **Teacher Notes: End-of-Book Assessment, Page 25** for more specific ideas about the problems on this page.

Evaluate Student Responses

Use the assessment rubric on page 42 of the Assessment Book (pictured on page 211 of the Teacher Edition) to evaluate student responses. The Assessment Book has some general suggestions for using the rubric that you may find helpful.

TEACHER NOTES: END-OF-BOOK ASSSESSMENT, STUDENT PAGE 25

Problem 6: Students may choose to use a ratio table to solve this problem. They may have already done something similar for problem 1 of the assessment, where they needed to estimate the total cost of the job.

Problem 7: This problem summarizes students' work on the assessment. Be sure they are given ample time to articulate their solution strategies and methods for determining the total cost of the tree house.

Student Page 25: Problems and Potential Answers

> **End-of-Book Assessment**

6. The plywood is going to be tricky. It comes in sheets that are 4 feet wide and 8 feet long. What is the square footage of one sheet of plywood? _____32_____ square feet

If you need 108 square feet of plywood for the floors, walls, and roof, how many sheets of plywood will you have to buy? _____4 sheets_____ Show your work.

How much will the plywood cost in all? _____$64.00_____ Show your work.

7. Use the information from the previous problems. Come up with a total cost for the project. What is the least amount of money you will have to spend to build the tree house?

Least amount of money: _____$92.15_____ Show your work.

2-by-4's: $15.25
screws: $3.90
rope: $9.00
plywood: $64.00

Explain your solution strategy for problem 7. _____Explanations will vary._____

Book 3: *Knowing Numbers*

SCORING GUIDE BOOK 3: KNOWING NUMBERS

End-of-Book Assessment
For Use With: Student Book Pages 23–24

PROBLEM DESCRIPTION	SCORING: WHAT TO LOOK FOR	SCORE AND COMMENTS
Problem 1 Estimate the cost of building a tree house from a given supply and price list. Level 3: Connections and Application Level 4: Synthesis and Evaluation	Do students: • Have a general understanding of estimation? • Have the ability to round to the nearest dollar? • Have the ability to compute total costs based on unit cost and number of items? • Articulate their strategy?	Points:_____ of 4
Problem 2 Multiplying unit dimensions and unit costs to estimate supplies needed and costs of supplies. Level 3: Connections and Application Level 4: Synthesis and Evaluation	Do students: • Understand the use of unit measurements? • Demonstrate their facility with number combinations to determine number of board feet needed vs. fixed lengths (8 feet) of the 2x4s? • Determine total cost accurately based on individual unit cost and projected need? • Articulate their thinking?	Points:_____ of 4
Problem 3 Obtain the necessary linear feet of 2x4s by using (buying and then cutting) boards of different lengths to obtain desired linear feet. Level 3: Connections and Application Level 4: Synthesis and Evaluation	Do students: • Understand the use of unit measurements? • Demonstrate facility with number combinations to determine number of board feet needed vs. fixed lengths (8, 12, or 16 feet) of the 2x4s? • Determine total cost accurately based on individual unit cost and projected need? • Articulate their thinking?	Points:_____ of 4
Problem 4 Calculate total costs of screws needed based on unit prices. Level 3: Connections and Application Level 4: Synthesis and Evaluation	Do students: • Understand different unit prices? • Calculate total price based on unit price and quantity needed? • Articulate their thinking?	Points:_____ of 4

TOTAL POINTS:_____ OF 16

SCORING GUIDE BOOK 3: KNOWING NUMBERS

End-of-Book Assessment (Continued)
For Use With: Student Book Pages 24–25

PROBLEM DESCRIPTION	SCORING: WHAT TO LOOK FOR	SCORE AND COMMENTS
Problem 5 Estimate the cost of building a tree house from a given supply and price list. Level 3: Connections and Application Level 4: Synthesis and Evaluation	Do students: • Understand unit price per foot? • Calculate total price based on unit price and quantity needed? • Articulate their thinking?	Points:_____ of 2
Problem 6 Calculate square footage of plywood (4x8) sheet; use square footage to calculate material needed and cost. Level 3: Connections and Application Level 4: Synthesis and Evaluation	Do students: • Understand use of unit measurements? • Demonstrate their facility with area concept to determine number of square feet for one sheet of plywood (4x8=32 feet)? • Determine total cost accurately based on individual unit cost and projected need? • Articulate their thinking?	Points:_____ of 4
Problem 7 Determine total cost estimate for the project based on previous calculations. Level 3: Connections and Application Level 4: Synthesis and Evaluation	Do students: • Understand the use of unit measurements? • Understand cost per unit? • Determine total cost accurately based on individual unit cost and projected need? • Articulate their thinking?	Points:_____ of 4

PAGE TWO, TOTAL POINTS:_____ OF 10

Book 4:
Multiplication and Division

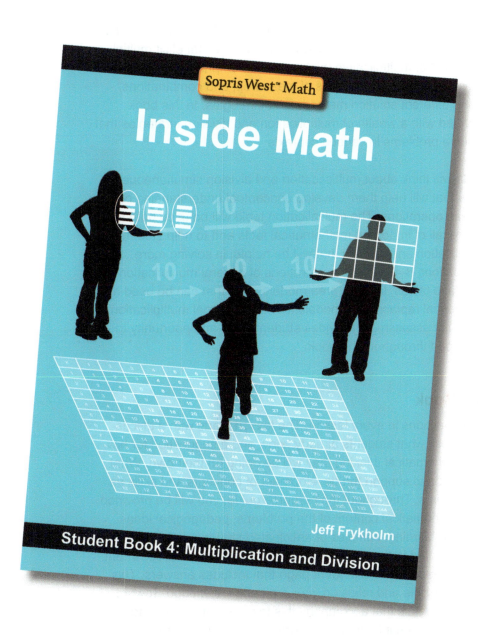

Book Four Overview: Multiplication and Division

Introduction

This book is the fourth in a series of eight that are geared toward helping middle-grades learners acquire both facility with, and understanding of, the basic mathematical procedures and concepts that lay the groundwork for more advanced mathematical study. In particular, this series cultivates understanding of a number of mathematical tools that children learn to use with facility in various mathematical and real-world contexts.

Book Focus

Book 4 is designed to help students develop a rich understanding of multiplication and division through the use of problem contexts and methods that elicit multiplicative thinking. Four kinds of multiplicative thinking will be emphasized: repeated addition, multiplicative comparisons, products of measures, and combinations. Each of these leads to different solution methods and strategies. In this book students will be provided with a wealth of multiplication and division strategies that they can call on to solve problems in various contexts.

In Section A, students will think about multiplication and division simultaneously as they view contexts that will help them develop conceptual understanding of the meanings behind these operations. The multiplication table will be used both to strengthen students' recall of important mathematical facts and to help students see patterns in multiplication and division that will be helpful in solving more complex problems. Sections B–G include explorations of several multiplication and division models (ratio tables, lattices, area models, etc.) that can be used as viable options and potential replacement models for the traditional multiplication algorithm. Finally, the unit assessment provides students with an opportunity to revisit the tools developed throughout the book.

How to Use this Book

There are two primary sections in every lesson. The lesson starts with a discussion that helps you assess what students already know and a suggestion for how to model the type of mathematical thinking they will be doing on their own. What follows is a resource guide to support the development of concepts and skills as students solve the problems. Throughout the resource guide, you will be provided with insights into the mathematical content of the problems, pedagogical ideas to enhance teaching and learning, samples of anticipated student work, insights about student thinking related to the topics at hand, and ideas about assessment. You will also find a reproduction of the student page that includes answers. This program is meant to be flexible and relies on your craft and knowledge. Toward that end, the resource materials that accompany this text are not intended to be used as a script. Instead, the intention of this program is that you will have a chance to apply your knowledge of students, your own experiences with these mathematical tools, and your intuition about teaching to make this program as effective as possible.

Models of Implementation

This program has been designed to be as flexible as possible. While this series of books may be used as the primary curriculum for the classroom, it was not designed as the full curriculum for any given grade level. Rather, it was crafted to support you as you help students understand the number operations and concepts that precede more advanced work in algebra. You may therefore choose to use this program either as a guide for whole-class explorations or as the text for smaller, pull-out groups of students. In both cases, it is important to note that this program is designed on the principle that students learn mathematics in large measure through interactions with one another. Throughout the books, you will find numerous questions that ask students to explain their thinking. These occasions should not be taken lightly. It is in the sharing and comparing of solution strategies that children begin to build a firm foundation of understanding. The social dynamic of learning mathematics is important to recognize. Participation in mathematical discourse may be the most powerful impetus for learning mathematics available to young learners, and you should take advantage of every opportunity to encourage children to talk about their mathematical thinking and processes. Given a commitment to this principle, this program is likely to be most successful when students are progressing through the problems with their peers.

Addressing Issues of Language

There is no question that one of the greatest challenges facing teachers today is to make instruction relevant and accessible for second language learners. *Inside Math* has been written with this concern in mind. Careful consideration was given to the language that appears in directions, contextually based problems, and other sections of the book where text is necessary. When possible, for example, we have limited new vocabulary to only what is essential to the concepts being presented, and we revisit new vocabulary words and concepts repeatedly throughout the text. To assist teachers in making instruction accessible for English language learners, as well as other students for whom reading presents particular challenges, several supporting features were added to the teacher's edition. First, within the section planner that introduces each new major mathematical concept contained in the book, there is a heading that reads: Language Development. In this section of the overview, new vocabulary words are introduced and defined. Later in the text, when these words and concepts are introduced in a specific lesson, the teacher notes include additional information about pertinent language considerations and vocabulary. These notes appear as Encouraging Language Development under the Concept Development and Continue the Problem Solving headings.

Explaining Thinking

Throughout this series, students will be instructed to explain their thinking. The ability to articulate mathematical ideas and solution strategies is a feature of mathematics education that continues to grow in its importance. We see numerous examples in state, national, and international achievement tests in which answers alone are not enough; students must also be able to express their thought processes, give rationale for answers, and articulate steps in any given strategy. In this book, there are opportunities for students to do likewise.

As this is often a new and challenging task for students, it is important for teachers to be able to model the process of making thinking explicit. At the beginning of each section in the book, there are suggestions for ways to introduce the content at hand, many of which are suitable candidates for teachers to illustrate what means to explain thinking in an intelligible way. Be aware of both the importance of this feature of the program, as well as the challenge it might provide students as they practice this skill for what might be the first time.

Assessment

At the conclusion of each section, you will find several problems that may be used for formative assessments. These problems review key concepts discussed in the previous section. At the end of each book are additional assessment problems that cover the content of the entire book. These problems may be used as a cumulative assessment of student understanding of the key concepts in the book. The teachers' guide contains insights as to how the assessment problems might best be used and what they are intended to measure.

Assessment rubrics and scoring guides for every assessment may be found in Assessment Teacher Edition. Detailed instructions regarding assessment in general, and the use of the program rubrics in particular, are included in the introduction of Assessment Teacher Edition.

Professional Background

The first three books in this series were devoted largely to developing students' number sense so that they would be able to work with numbers in sophisticated and meaningful ways. This book builds on this foundation, focusing on some of the computational skills (primarily multiplication and division) that are often viewed as one of the primary objectives of K–8 mathematics. While recent advances in the field of mathematics education, such as research on teaching strategies, understandings of cognition, and curriculum innovation have suggested a more balanced and broader view of priorities for math in the upper elementary and middle grades, there is no doubt that computational proficiency remains a central part of the K–8 curriculum.

This entire program, and this book in particular, is based on the premise that no single method or algorithm should be forced on children as the only way to complete a given problem. Instead, a rich and sophisticated sense of numbers and an understanding of the operations themselves allow students to select, adapt, and flexibly use the solution strategy that most appropriately fits the context and numbers in the problem. The goal of mathematics education, and of this book, is to help students develop over time a range of flexible methods, skills, and mental strategies that will serve them well as they face mathematical problems in their daily lives. The opportunities to develop this kind of flexible, multiplicative reasoning are abundant and serve as the goal of this book.

Multiplication and Division: The Big Ideas

Big Idea #1: Number Decomposition and the Distributive Property
A thorough understanding of multiplication requires students to be confident in breaking apart and combining numbers in creative ways. In an earlier book, students were invited to see inside numbers so that a number such as 43 could be thought of as 40 and 3 more. This sort of number decomposition requires a good understanding of place value, a concept fundamental to multiplication. For multiplication, the ability to decompose numbers toward the goal of working with compatible numbers, numbers that are easy to compute with mentally, is coupled with the distributive property. For example:

$$4 \times 43 \text{ might be thought of as } 4 \times (40 + 3),$$
$$\text{which leads to } (4 \times 40) + (4 \times 3).$$

Big Idea #2: Representations of Multiplication and Division There are many ways to visualize multiplication and division and various ways to compute products and quotients. Several of these visual representations, including the area model, ratio tables, partial products, the lattice method, and the traditional method, are presented throughout this book.

Big Idea #3: Invented Strategies Are Essential The knowledge and confidence with number relationships that students bring to number operations allow them to work efficiently with numbers. This takes place not only through the use of traditional and time-tested algorithms, but also in ways that make logical sense to students. Throughout this book, students will be encouraged to work with strategies that resonate with the problem context. Students are led toward invented strategies, those that are non-traditional, flexible, and personalized, that they may ultimately choose as their preferred approaches depending on how they read and understand the problem context.

Envisioning Multiplication

Section A of this book is devoted to helping students grasp the breadth of contexts that are multiplicative in nature. For example, the problem, "I rode my bike at a rate of 10 miles per hour for 3 hours. How many miles did I ride?" might lead a child to think of multiplication as repeated addition. Alternatively, we might see multiplication and division in terms of sets. For example: Fifteen cookies are to be shared among 5 children. How many cookies will each child receive? This sort of problem leads students to partition into equal groups, or sets. We might think of multiplication as a permutation: A new car can be ordered in 2 exterior colors and 3 interior colors. How many combinations are there? Finally, we might think of multiplication visually, as an area model: A patio is 8 feet wide and 12 feet long. How many 1-foot-square tiles will it take to cover its surface? Each of these problem contexts elicits a different kind of thinking, a different visual model. So we should not be surprised if students choose to solve these problems with different models or algorithms. The intent of the first set of exercises in this book is to help students develop a rich understanding of multiplicative contexts.

The Basic Facts

There is no question that students who do not have a grasp of the basic, single-digit multiplication facts will be at a disadvantage with each new level of mathematics curriculum they encounter. While few people would argue the value of ready recall of 7 × 8, for example, there is some debate about how students who have not mastered basic facts might develop such proficiency. Teachers who draw on students' number sense and understanding of addition and subtraction to help them see and use patterns in the multiplication table will realize greater student success, and more quickly, than those who emphasize rote memorization. The multiplication table itself contains many interesting patterns, curious number connections, and symmetry. Research has shown that taking a week simply to explore the multiplication table often does more to help students master the facts than the flash card approach commonly used by teachers and parents to drill the basic facts. Moreover, when students uncover strategies that help them build on facts they already know, mastering the facts becomes a much less daunting task.

The 60 Second Times Test exercise of the past has outlived its usefulness. Other, better ideas are now well known, some of which are presented in this text.

Partial Products and Strategy Models

Once the basic facts are relatively well understood, students can rapidly advance in their understanding of and computational fluency with multi-digit multiplication. Fundamental to nearly all multiplication algorithms or solution strategies is the idea of partial products. As noted earlier, this strategy rests heavily on students' ability to see numbers within numbers, and to decompose numbers so that they are more easily manipulated. For example, students might choose one of any number of representations and strategies to begin to find the product of 3×23. Several of these strategies are briefly explained below, some of which receive explicit attention in the text. Throughout, note the degree to which partial products are central to the strategies.

Strategy 1: Mental Math

Students who have had sufficient experiences with informal strategies for addition and subtraction are more likely to be able to solve multiplication problems using regrouping strategies and repeated addition. The italicized paragraph below could very well be the literal thinking of a child who is comfortable decomposing numbers and adding friendly groups of ten. Note the partial products that surface in the child's explanation.

"3×23 means 3 groups of 23. I know what 3 groups of 20 is: $3 \times 20 = 60$ [a partial product]. *Now I have to go back and collect the rest: 3 groups of 3 is 9* [second partial product]. *So $60 + 9 = 69$.*"

Strategy 2: Computation with Partial Products and the Distributive Property

Students who are able to do mental calculations like the one highlighted above are likely to be able to take the strategy one step further. They will be able to represent their calculations with symbols and steps that more closely mirror both traditional strategies for multiplication and the formal definition of the distributive property.

$$3 \times 23 \rightarrow 3 \times (20 + 3) \rightarrow (3 \times 20) + (3 \times 3) \rightarrow 60 + 9 = 69$$

Strategy 3: Vertical Computation with Partial Products

```
   23
 ×  3
 ───
    9  → 3 × 3
   60  → 3 × 20
 ───
   69
```

> The same partial products used above can be organized into vertical alignment to match the traditional multi-digit multiplication algorithm. Note, however, that unlike in the traditional algorithm, each partial product, and the steps from which they come, is transparent.

Strategy 4: Area Model
The area model is derived from an array model, in which like units are stacked or lined up in rows. This model may be the most conceptually comprehensible multiplication strategy for young learners. This strategy builds on spatial reasoning, a preferred learning style for more than half of all young children, and it clearly isolates the partial products essential to the completed solution. If teachers introduce this model with small numbers (e.g., 3 × 4), students can literally count tiles or cells, further solidifying their conceptual understanding of area as a parallel construct to multiplication and division.

Multi-Digit Multiplication

As students become comfortable with the idea of partial products and the various representations that make use of them, they will be able to tackle more complex, multi-digit problems with confidence. A significant portion of this book is devoted to this pursuit. Throughout the book, whether using area models, ratio tables, the lattice method, or the traditional algorithm, the degree to which students can see the partial products inherent in the problem will likely determine their success with the strategies. Important to this book is to provide students with opportunities to compare, side-by-side, the various representations and solution strategies. Have students note in particular how the partial products appear in each problem and how each strategy structure may fit a problem context. Consider the following representations of 24 × 32:

Strategy 1: Area Model

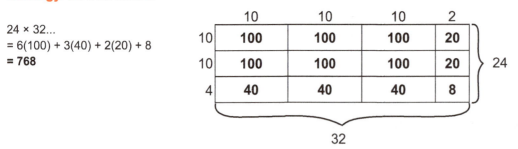

Strategy 2: Ratio Table
In earlier books we learned that the ratio table can be used as a model for multiplication. In this case the partial products are based less on number decomposition and more on proportional reasoning. Either way, it is valuable to emphasize the point that students are making smaller problems out of a larger one. Note also in this strategy the importance of number sense with

respect to addition, doubling, multiplying by 10, etc. For these reasons, the ratio table is an excellent model to present to students, given its emphases on number fluency and proportional reasoning.

1	10	20	2	4	24	
32	320	640	64	128	768	

Strategy 3: Partial Products and the Traditional Method

This book highlights the connections between parts of the traditional method and various elements of partial-product solution strategies. It would be a good idea to show students these two strategies side by side and then ask them to find the connections between them. If this is the first time students have seen the traditional algorithm used in the United States, greater attention must be given to the steps.

Partial Product Elaborated

```
   32
  ×24
    8  (4 × 2)
  120  (4 × 30)
   40  (20 × 2)
  600  (20 × 30)
  768
```

Traditional Method

```
   32
  ×24
  128
  640
  768
```

With greater numbers that lead to greater partial products, it becomes necessary to regroup when using the traditional method. When helping students compare these two strategies, be sure to illustrate and emphasize the connections between steps, having students make special note of where the regrouped numbers appear in the partial-product approach as well as where they occur in the traditional method. It bears repeating that the fundamental process of decomposing numbers (seeing a number inside another number), and using those number components to work more simply toward partial products, is the key to understanding multiplication strategies, models, and algorithms.

Section A: Thinking About Multiplication and Division

SECTION A PLANNER

THE MATHEMATICS CONTENT AND GOALS

GOALS
Students will:
- Recognize that different contexts elicit different kinds of multiplicative thinking.
- Understand the relationship between multiplication and division.

LANGUAGE DEVELOPMENT
Mathematical language in this section includes:

Repeated Addition: The process of adding the same number repeatedly a certain number of times.

Combination: An unordered arrangement of objects.

Area: The number of square units needed to cover a surface.

Multiplication Problem Types: Listed below are the four primary types of multiplication problems highlighted in this text. Be sure to familiarize students with these different conceptions of multiplication. It is not necessary to focus explicitly on the names of these different kinds of problems. Instead, emphasize to your students the different contexts that are multiplicative in nature.

- *Repeated addition problems:* Multiplication understood as the process of repeatedly adding equal sets or groups.
- *Comparison problems:* One number is expressed as a certain number of times as great as another number. For example, 15 is described as 3 times as great as 5 rather than 10 more than 5.
- *Area problems:* A spatial-visual representation in which the number of squares covering a region can be counted.
- *Combination problems:* Problems that involve counting ordered pairs from two sets, where the first element is taken from the first set and the second element is taken from the second set.

PACING
The projected pacing for this section is 1 class period (based on a 45 minute period).

PROBLEM SETS: OVERVIEW

Set 1 (pp. 1–3; problems 1–3)
These problems are designed to help students recognize different kinds of problem contexts that will require multiplication to find a solution. Four kinds of multiplication problems are presented:
- repeated addition problems
- comparison problems
- area problems
- combination problems

CONCEPT DEVELOPMENT (Pages 1–3)

INTRODUCE THE CONCEPT

ASSESS STUDENTS' PRIOR KNOWLEDGE
In this first section of the book, students are exposed to various multiplicative contexts that prompt them to think about the nature of multiplication. Begin with a discussion about multiplication.

Ask:
Suppose you had to explain multiplication to a friend who didn't know what it meant. What would you tell your friend? First, write down some thoughts about this question. Then share your ideas with a partner.

Have a whole-class discussion of the question. As students talk, write a list of the descriptions of multiplication on the board.

Listen for:
(Students may suggest repeated addition as a description. They may mention the multiplication, or times, table. They may also refer to the multiplication algorithm. Some students may suggest that multiplication is a way to combine equal groups.)

MODEL MATHEMATICAL THINKING
Begin a discussion about multiplication by telling the following story:
Thousands of years ago, people learned to cooperate with people from other villages or tribes through trading. To do this, they needed numbers to count with so they could keep track of the objects they were trading and to be sure they did not get cheated. As the villages and tribes got larger, so did the amount of objects they traded. To make it easier to tell how many objects a village was trading, the people learned how to group them and then count the groups. Now, suppose 4 families in a small tribe were in charge of bead-making, and they each contributed 32 beads for trading. How could we find how many beads in all the tribe could trade?

Talk Through the Thinking:
I suppose I could draw 4 circles to stand for the families and then place 32 dots in each circle to stand for the beads. Then I could count all the dots, one by one, to find how many beads in all. This would take a long time. I can also add 32 four times. 32 + 32 + 32 + 32 = 128. That's the correct answer.

Ask:
Are there other ways to find how many beads in all? What are the other ways?

Listen for:
- You could multiply 4 × 32 like this:

$$\begin{array}{r} 32 \\ \times\,4 \\ \hline 128 \end{array}$$

- You could make a ratio table and use adding on and doubling.

Families	1	2	4
Beads	32	64	128

LAUNCH THE PROBLEM SOLVING

There are no problems on page 1. Instead, students are introduced to four common representations of multiplication. Have students read the page and discuss these representations with a partner. Then have pairs share their thoughts in a class discussion. Refer to the discussion **Representations of Multiplication** for further examples.

As students discuss their conclusions and share their thoughts, focus on these issues:

Allow Waiting Time – When students struggle to explain their thinking, be sure to allow them at least 20 seconds to organize their thoughts.

Encourage Language Development – As students discuss page 1, encourage them to use the appropriate terms for the types of multiplication problems presented.

Student Page 1: Problems and Potential Answers

Section A: Thinking about Multiplication and Division — Set 1

There are many ways to think about multiplication and division. Here are four different kinds of multiplication problems:

Type 1: Repeated Addition Problems

For example: Mark has 4 packs of gum. There are six sticks of gum in each pack. How many sticks of gum does he have?

This problem can be solved by adding: $6 + 6 + 6 + 6 = 24$

Type 2: Comparison Problems

For example: Jenny collected 6 cans for recycling. Sarah collected 4 times as many cans as Jenny. How many cans did Sarah collect?

This problem can also be solved by adding, but we think about it in a different way:

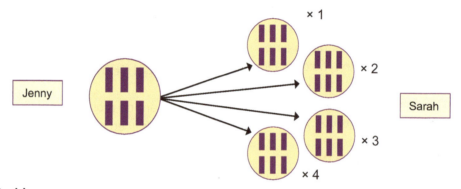

Type 3: Area Problems

For example: A rug is 5 feet long and 3 feet wide. What is its area?

This problem can be solved with a diagram:

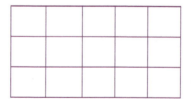

Type 4: Combination Problems

For example: Nikki has 2 shorts, and 3 shirts. How many different outfits can she wear?

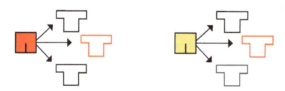

Book 4: *Multiplication and Division*

REPRESENTATIONS OF MULTIPLICATION

The four common representations of multiplication on this page include:

Repeated Addition Problems

Example: Each crayon box holds 12 crayons. I have 3 crayon boxes. How many crayons do I have?

The above example illustrates the most common representation of multiplication encountered by elementary-level students. Such problems require students to repeatedly add equal groups and can be modeled with manipulatives.

Comparison Problems

Example: Paul scored 4 times as many goals as Eddie. Eddie scored 3 goals. How many did Paul score?

This example also illustrates a common elementary school representation of multiplication. Although this kind of problem can be solved by repeated addition, the mental visualization of the problem is quite different because it involves the comparison of two distinct quantities.

Array and Area Problems

Example: A rectangular parking lot has 5 rows with 10 spaces in each row. How many parking spaces are in the lot?

Area representations for multiplication are common in geometry, but may not be frequently used to help students learn how to multiply. The area model for multiplication is important and will be more fully developed in this text. It can be used as a viable method for understanding multiplication and multiplying 2- and 3-digit numbers. A simpler version of the area model is the array model, which models rectangular displays of non-contiguous objects. Both models will be used.

Combination Problems

Example: Susan has 2 pairs of shoes, 3 pairs of slacks, and 2 shirts. How many different outfits can she wear?

Combination problems do not appear as frequently as the others in elementary texts. Yet they do offer students a unique way to think about multiplication. These kinds of problems will be visited later in the book as students learn about combinations and permutations.

CONTINUE THE PROBLEM SOLVING

Pages 2–3 focus on representations, or models, of different multiplication contexts. Through observation of these models, students can explore the meanings of multiplication. Do not overlook this work. One of the key ideas in this book is that students can choose from a number of invented strategies that they think best helps them solve a given problem.

Have students work individually to solve the problem on page 2. As they work, circulate and monitor their recorded answers. When students finish the page, have them compare and discuss their answers with a partner. Then have each pair share their answers in a class discussion. Refer to the **Teacher Notes: Student Page 2** for more specific ideas about the problems on this page.

As students work and report their conclusions, focus on these issues:

Allow Processing Time – Allow ample time for students to assimilate these different representations of multiplication and to determine the kinds of models that represent the different problems.

Facilitate Students' Thinking – Remind students that they have already seen several models for different multiplication problems. Encourage them to remember the representations for each kind of problem.

Encourage Language Development – Recall definitions of the primary categories of multiplication problems highlighted in this section.

TEACHER NOTES: STUDENT PAGE 2

Problem 1: This problem asks students to make the connection between the problems that represent the four types of multiplication problems introduced on page 1 and their respective visual depictions. *Watch for:* Students should be able to match the objects described in the problems with the abstract representation of the objects in the diagrams. Verbal cues in the problems should help students correctly match the problem with the model. The models themselves are suggestive of ways in which these problems can be solved. However, if a student does not make the connection between statement 2 and diagram 2, for example, you may need to point out that the bars don't have to look like fish to stand for fish.

Student Page 2: Problems and Potential Answers

Section A: Thinking about Multiplication and Division Set 1

1. Match each statement with the diagram that best fits the solution.

Statement 1: I rode my bike 10 miles an hour for 6 hours. How many miles did I ride?

Statement 2: I have 3 fish tanks. There are 4 fish in each tank. How many fish do I have?

Statement 3: A tabletop that is 4 feet long and 3 feet wide is covered with 1-foot-square tiles. How many tiles cover the tabletop?

Statement 4: A soccer team has 2 jersey colors, 2 shorts colors, and 2 socks colors. How many uniform combinations are there?

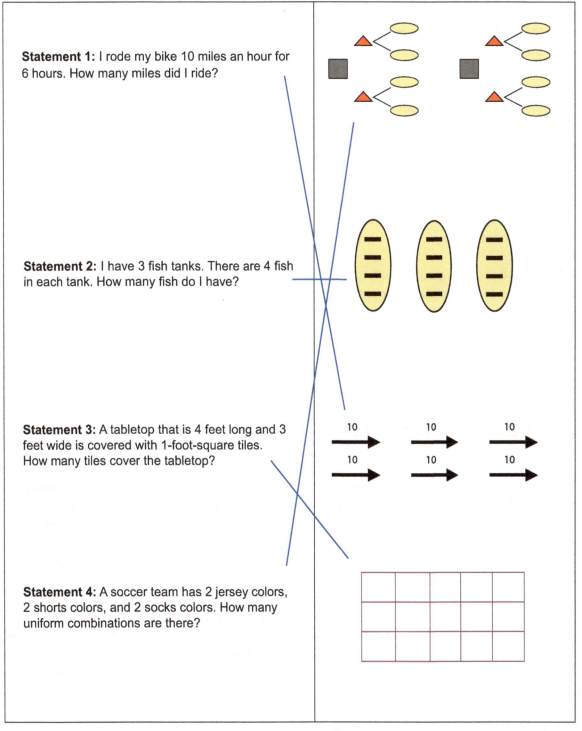

2   Book 4: *Multiplication and Division*

CONTINUE THE PROBLEM SOLVING

Have students read the introductory portion of page 3 individually before calling for a class discussion of the information. Then have students work individually to solve the problems on page 3. As they work, circulate and monitor their recorded answers. When students finish each problem, have them compare and discuss their answers with a partner. Then have each pair share their answers in a class discussion of the problem. Refer to the **Teacher Notes: Student Page 3** for more specific ideas about these problems.

As students work and report their conclusions, focus on these issues:

Facilitate Students' Thinking – To emphasize the relationship between multiplication and division, remind students how these operations are related. You might give the example that because $2 \times 5 = 10$, then $10 \div 2 = 5$ and $10 \div 5 = 2$.

Validate Representations – You may wish to encourage students to draw pictures for problem 2. If so, have students compare and discuss their pictures and how well they represent their problems.

TEACHER NOTES: STUDENT PAGE 3

The primary objective of this page is to help students recognize the inverse relationship between multiplication and division. The key point is that in both division and multiplication, there exists a unique relationship between three numbers. For example, with the multiplication fact $3 \times 4 = 12$, we may need to:
Find the product (the result unknown) of the factors: $3 \times 4 = ?$
Or
We may know the result, but not one of the factors: $? \times 4 = 12$.

The latter case might now be considered a division problem. Students should be fluent in expressing these kinds of number relationships in both multiplicative and divisional contexts.

Problem 2: The two parts to this problem ask students to use what they know to rewrite a multiplication problem as a division problem. *Teaching Strategy:* Be sure to emphasize that the three numbers in each problem are related to each other in a certain way and that this relationship can be expressed either by division or by multiplication.

Problem 3: *Watch for:* Make sure the problem contexts are different for each type of problem and that the contexts match the problem type. You may want to ask students to draw pictorial representations of their problems.

Student Page 3: Problems and Potential Answers

Section A: Thinking about Multiplication and Division Set 1

Sometimes it is helpful to think about multiplication and division at the same time. The problems on the previous page are also division problems, depending on how you look at them. Look at this example…

I rode my bike 10 miles an hour for 6 hours. How many miles did I ride?
Could be changed to a division problem in this way:
I rode my bike for 6 hours and traveled a total of 60 miles. How fast was I riding?

2. Change each of these multiplication problems into a division problem by rewriting the statement. (There is more than one way to do this.) Answers may vary. Sample answers are given.

   a) **I have 3 fish tanks. There are 4 fish in each tank. How many fish do I have?**
      Rewrite as a division problem.

      I have 12 fish. An equal number of fish are in each of 3 fish tanks. How many fish are in each tank?

   b) **A tabletop that is 4 feet long and 3 feet wide is covered with 1-foot-square tiles. How many tiles cover the tabletop?** Rewrite as a division problem:

      A 4-foot long tabletop is covered with 12 tiles. Each tile is a 1-foot square. How wide is the tabletop?

3. Remember the four types of multiplication problems from the first page? Make up your own multiplication problem for each type. Write your problems in the spaces below. Answers will vary.

   a) Repeated Addition _____

   b) Comparison _____

   c) Area _____

   d) Combination _____

Book 4: *Multiplication and Division*

Section B: The Multiplication Table

SECTION B PLANNER

THE MATHEMATICS CONTENT AND GOALS

GOALS

Students will:

- Discover patterns in the multiplication, or times, table and use these patterns to develop more intuitive multiplication sense.
- Use patterns in the times table to master the basic multiplication facts.

LANGUAGE DEVELOPMENT

Mathematical language in this section includes:

Pattern: In this section, students are asked to look for patterns in the multiplication table. What is meant by the use of patterns in this context is the repeated occurrence of various phenomena in the position, size, value, and/or arrangement of numbers as they appear in the table. For example, one pattern students could discover is that every odd number is surrounded by even numbers. All numbers in the 5s row end in either 0 or 5.

Multiple: In this section, students are asked to identify multiples given numbers throughout the times table. A mathematical definition of multiple is the product of the given number and another number. For example, the multiples of 6 include: 6, 12, 18, 24, etc.

PACING

The projected pacing for this section is 2 class periods (based on a 45 minute period).

PROBLEM SETS: OVERVIEW

Set 1 (pp. 4–7; problems 1–3)

The intent of the problems in Set 1 is to encourage students to discover and appreciate the patterns that exist in the multiplication (times) table. When students investigate the multiplication table and discover interesting patterns, there is a much greater chance that they will be able to develop their own intuitive strategies to help them master basic multiplication facts. It is important to spend enough time on the multiplication table so that students can begin to discover the many interesting number relationships and patterns it contains. Some examples are that every odd number is surrounded by even numbers; numbers on a diagonal increase and decrease in regular increments; and there is a line of reflection from the top left to bottom right corners. There are many number patterns and relationships students will find if given the chance. These discoveries are important for the development of their confidence and their mastery of the basic facts.

CONCEPT DEVELOPMENT (PAGES 4–6)

INTRODUCE THE CONCEPT

ASSESS STUDENTS' PRIOR KNOWLEDGE

Many students continue to have difficulty mastering multiplication facts well into middle school and beyond. Pages 4–6 allow students to revisit the times, or multiplication, table in a non-threatening way. Although instant recall of multiplication facts is desirable, it is probably more realistic to give students strategies for quickly finding the product of two numbers. Such strategies include using the commutative property of multiplication, building on a fact they can recall instantly, or using a pattern to help students find a reasonable answer.

On an overhead projector, place a transparency of the multiplication table after first removing the top row and the first column at the left as shown, or give each student a copy of the same.

1	2	3	4	5	6	7	8	9	10	11	12
2	4	6	8	10	12	14	16	18	20	22	24
3	6	9	12	15	18	21	24	27	30	33	36
4	8	12	16	20	24	28	32	36	40	44	48
5	10	15	20	25	30	35	40	45	50	55	60
6	12	18	24	30	36	42	48	54	60	66	72
7	14	21	28	35	42	49	56	63	70	77	84
8	16	24	32	40	48	56	64	72	80	88	96
9	18	27	36	45	54	63	72	81	90	99	108
10	20	30	40	50	60	70	80	90	100	110	120
11	12	33	44	55	66	77	88	99	110	121	132
12	24	36	48	60	72	84	96	108	120	132	144

Ask:
What do you think the numbers in this table represent? Do you see any patterns in the table that might help you answer the question?

Listen for:
Students should recognize that the numbers in the table are the multiplication facts for 1–12. Students may cite several different patterns to justify this thinking, such as the first row just counts by 1s; the second row consists of all even numbers in order; the third row are all the multiples of 3 through 3 × 12, the fourth row all the multiples of 4 through 4 × 12, etc.

MODEL MATHEMATICAL THINKING
Model the thinking for finding other patterns in the table by asking, *Can you see any other patterns in this table?* As you talk through the thinking, indicate the position and the numbers on the transparency.

Talk Through the Thinking
I wonder whether the same number appears more than once in the table in a pattern. If I look in a diagonal line from the top right down to the same number on the left, there are repeated numbers. Let's start at 8 in the top row and draw a line to the 8 in the first column on the left. Next to each 8 is 14, next to each 14 is 18, and next to each 18 is 20. So along this diagonal line are two 8s, then two 14s, then two 18s and then two 20s.

Ask:
Look in a diagonal line from the 9 in the top row to the 9 in the first column at the left. How is this pattern like the one for 8s? How is it different?

Listen for:
- It is like the one for 8s because the same numbers are next to each other.
- It is different because there is only one middle number, 25.
- The numbers in the cells are in fact answers to various multiplication facts.

LAUNCH THE PROBLEM SOLVING

Have students work individually to look for patterns in the multiplication table on page 4. When they finish, have them compare and discuss their responses with a partner. Then have each pair share their answers in a class discussion. Refer to the **Teacher Notes: Student Page 4** for more specific ideas about the problems on this page.

As students work and report their conclusions, focus on these issues:

Allow Processing Time – The more time students spend on this problem, the more discoveries they will make. This can help them solidify their mastery of multiplication facts.

Validate Alternate Solutions – Students may see a variety of patterns in the table. Have them share these patterns with the class and discuss whether all the patterns do, in fact, appear in the table.

Help Make Connections – When possible, help students see the connections between their patterns and the multiplication facts.

TEACHER NOTES: STUDENT PAGE 4

Problem 1: Allow students at least 15 minutes to work on this problem. They will make many interesting discoveries. Students may notice that the numbers in some rows or columns increase by certain amounts, end in a particular digit, or have a special relationship with adjacent cells. Some students may notice patterns with odd and even numbers. Others may notice interesting patterns along the diagonals. As students report their discoveries, encourage them to explain why that particular phenomenon occurs.

An Example of Student Thinking

Sixth Grade Thinking

> A pattern I found is when you first look up in the top left corner of the times table, you see 1 × 1 = 1. If you go diagonally down, you see that 2 × 2 = 4. The difference between the product of these two equations is 3. When you do 3 × 3 = 9, the difference between 2 × 2 = 4 & 3 × 3 = 9 is 5. The difference always goes up by 2 in odd numbers.

Fourth Grade Thinking

> go down to the 10th row, as you go akras it increases by 10.

Student Page 4: Problems and Potential Answers

Section B: The Multiplication Table Set 1

Do you remember learning all of your multiplication facts? You probably used a multiplication table like the one below. That is a lot to remember! Or, is it?

X	1	2	3	4	5	6	7	8	9	10	11	12
1	1	2	3	4	5	6	7	8	9	10	11	12
2	2	4	6	8	10	12	14	16	18	20	22	24
3	3	6	9	12	15	18	21	24	27	30	33	36
4	4	8	12	16	20	24	28	32	36	40	44	48
5	5	10	15	20	25	30	35	40	45	50	55	60
6	6	12	18	24	30	36	42	48	54	60	66	72
7	7	14	21	28	35	42	49	56	63	70	77	84
8	8	16	24	32	40	48	56	64	72	80	88	96
9	9	18	27	36	45	54	63	72	81	90	99	108
10	10	20	30	40	50	60	70	80	90	100	110	120
11	11	22	33	44	55	66	77	88	99	110	121	132
12	12	24	36	48	60	72	84	96	108	120	132	144

1. This multiplication table is interesting to study. There are many patterns in the table that will help you quickly recall all the facts up to 12 × 12. Take a few minutes to explore the table. Write down any interesting patterns you see in the space below. *Responses will vary*

4 Book 4: *Multiplication and Division*

CONTINUE THE PROBLEM SOLVING

Page 5 focuses on some particular patterns that will help students with multiplication facts for 4, 6, and 8. Continue to have students explore patterns in the multiplication table.

Have students work individually to solve the problem on page 5. As they work, circulate and monitor their work and recorded answers. As students finish the problem, have them compare and discuss their answers with a partner. Then have each pair share their answers in a class discussion. Refer to the **Teacher Notes: Student Page 5** for more specific ideas about the problems on this page.

As students work and report their conclusions, focus on these issues:

Facilitate Students' Thinking – As students study and shade the multiplication tables, encourage them to think of the multiplication facts that result in each product. For example, when they shade 16, they can think 2×8, 8×2, or 4×4.

Allow Waiting Time – When students struggle to explain their thinking, allow them at least 20 seconds to organize their thoughts.

Encourage Language Development – The recognition of patterns within the multiplication table, and the subsequent opportunity students have to articulate the nuances of these patterns, are extremely significant. Allow students time to articulate their thinking as they explain the patterns that they identified. It may take them some time to formulate the thoughts and find the words, but this is important developmental work.

TEACHER NOTES: STUDENT PAGE 5

Problem 2: *Watch for:* Students may understand that every multiple of 8 is also a multiple of 4, although the reverse is not true. For students who do not recognize this relationship, partner them with peers and have each write the opposite set of multiples (or have both students shade multiples of both 4 and 8). You might duplicate this table and have students find patterns in the multiples of other numbers. *Teaching Strategy:* Be sure to help students recognize patterns that occur horizontally, as well as the patterns that occur up and down the vertical columns. The time invested in uncovering patterns with this exercise will pay dividends later on for students who continue to struggle with the multiplication facts. In fact, you may wish to have students shade the multiples of every number from 2 through 10, particularly those students who obviously struggle with recall of multiplication facts. The more students develop the ability to recognize and predict patterns of multiples, the more they will be able to draw on their intuition as they learn and use the multiplication facts.

Student Page 5: Problems and Potential Answers

Section B: The Multiplication Table — Set 1

2. Let's look at some patterns. You get an interesting design when you shade in all the multiples of 6 in the table. These are all the numbers you would name if you counted by 6's (like... 6, 12, 18... and so on).

X	1	2	3	4	5	6	7	8	9	10	11	12
1	1	2	3	4	5	6	7	8	9	10	11	12
2	2	4	6	8	10	12	14	16	18	20	22	24
3	3	6	9	12	15	18	21	24	27	30	33	36
4	4	8	12	16	20	24	28	32	36	40	44	48
5	5	10	15	20	25	30	35	40	45	50	55	60
6	6	12	18	24	30	36	42	48	54	60	66	72
7	7	14	21	28	35	42	49	56	63	70	77	84
8	8	16	24	32	40	48	56	64	72	80	88	96
9	9	18	27	36	45	54	63	72	81	90	99	108
10	10	20	30	40	50	60	70	80	90	100	110	120
11	11	22	33	44	55	66	77	88	99	110	121	132
12	12	24	36	48	60	72	84	96	108	120	132	144

What patterns would you find if you counted by 4's? By 8's? Choose one, and shade the correct boxes in the table below.

Multiples of 4

X	1	2	3	4	5	6	7	8	9	10	11	12
1	1	2	3	4	5	6	7	8	9	10	11	12
2	2	4	6	8	10	12	14	16	18	20	22	24
3	3	6	9	12	15	18	21	24	27	30	33	36
4	4	8	12	16	20	24	28	32	36	40	44	48
5	5	10	15	20	25	30	35	40	45	50	55	60
6	6	12	18	24	30	36	42	48	54	60	66	72
7	7	14	21	28	35	42	49	56	63	70	77	84
8	8	16	24	32	40	48	56	64	72	80	88	96
9	9	18	27	36	45	54	63	72	81	90	99	108
10	10	20	30	40	50	60	70	80	90	100	110	120
11	11	22	33	44	55	66	77	88	99	110	121	132
12	12	24	36	48	60	72	84	96	108	120	132	144

Book 4: *Multiplication and Division*

CONTINUE THE PROBLEM SOLVING

Page 6 focuses on other patterns in the multiplication table. Students may find these several specific patterns inherent in the times table particularly interesting. As stated in the Teacher Notes on the following page, it is most important as you lead students through these problems to encourage them to determine why these patterns are true. When they can do so, they will have a strong grasp of the function of the times table and the related facts therein.

Have students work individually to solve the problems on page 6. As they work, circulate and monitor their recorded answers. As students finish each problem, have them compare and discuss their answers with a partner. Then have each pair share their answers in a class discussion of the problem. Refer to the **Teacher Notes: Student Page 6** for more information and further suggestions.

As students work and report their conclusions, focus on these issues:

Facilitate Students' Thinking – Help students make the connection between patterns in the times table and basic multiplication facts.

Validate Alternate Solutions – When students come up with varying responses, have them compare and discuss their responses to determine whether all are correct.

TEACHER NOTES: STUDENT PAGE 6

Problem 3: This problem specifically helps to illustrate several unique characteristics of the multiplication table.

a) Each odd number is surrounded by all even numbers. This phenomenon can be traced to something students may have noticed in their informal examinations of the multiplication table. When multiplying, three options exist: 1) an odd times an odd; 2) an even times an even; or 3) an odd times an even. The only case in which the product of two factors is odd is when the two factors being multiplied are themselves odd. Relate this to repeated addition. The only way to get an odd-number sum is to add an even and an odd. So when we multiply an odd times an odd, for example 3 × 5, what we are really doing is adding 5 three times. Any number plus itself is even (e.g., 5 + 5 = 10). If we continue, adding an odd (5) to an even (10) results in an odd answer (10 + 5 = 15). Now back to the original question, Why is every odd number surrounded by even numbers? This is true because the only way to get an odd product is to multiply an odd by an odd. No matter which adjacent cell one selects, the product will be the result of an odd times an even or an even times an even. *Teaching Strategy:* To emphasize this fact, select one or two odd entries in the table, and look at the combinations of numbers that lead to the products of the adjacent cells.

b) The diagonal line from upper left to lower right is the squares diagonal: all the numbers in these cells are square numbers. This leads to a great opportunity to introduce some important mathematical concepts. First, the squares diagonal is a line of reflection, which hints at the notion of symmetry. The portion of the table to the left of the squares diagonal is the mirror image of the portion of the table to its right. The reason for this is that multiplication is commutative, which is a significant concept for students to embrace. For example, 4 × 3 (4 groups of 3) results in the same quantity as 3 × 4 (3 groups of 4). *Teaching Strategy:* To begin a discussion about the commutative property of multiplication, ask students to locate a particular cell, for example the cell containing the product of 8 × 4. Then ask them to find the cell containing the product of 4 × 8. Do this with several other number pairs. Students soon will see the relationship and notice that these products are on the same diagonal, which is perpendicular to the squares diagonal. They may also notice that each of the products is the same vertical distance from the squares diagonal.

c) This interesting relationship intrigues many students. It can easily be explained when students look at the smaller products that comprise the larger problem. In the given example, the outlined rectangle has in its corners 10, 20, 24, and 12. This problem suggests that for any rectangle students can outline on the times table, the products of the opposite corners will be equal. In this case, 10 × 24 = 20 × 12 = 240. *Teaching Strategy:* Help students by exploring where each of these corners came from: 10 is found by multiplying 2 × 5; 24 is found by multiplying 6 × 4; 20 is found by multiplying 5 × 4; and 12 is found by multiplying 2 × 6. When students combine these products according to the rule, they find that the products of the opposite corners are equal. So in this case, 10 × 24 = 20 × 12.

Student Page 6: Problems and Potential Answers

Section B: The Multiplication Table Set 1

3. Did you know . . .

   a) that every odd number is surrounded by even numbers? Check it out for yourself.

   Write an explanation for why this is so.
   Answers will vary. See teacher notes for explanation. All numbers adjacent to an odd number on the table have at least one even factor.

   b) that if you start in any box in the top row and go down and to the left diagonally, the diagonal line will act like a mirror? That is, you will see the same numbers repeated on both sides of the line.

   Explain why that is so. Answers will vary. See teacher notes for explanation.

   c) that if you choose any four boxes that make up the corners of a rectangle and then multiply the *opposite* corners together, you will get the same answer? *(See the gray box in the table.)* Find another example that works, and then explain **why** the process will always work.

   Explain.
   The factors of each pair of opposite corners are the same

   An example from the gray box: 10 × 24 = 20 × 12

X	1	2	3	4	5	6	7	8	9	10	11	12
1	1	2	3	4	5	6	7	8	9	10	11	12
2	2	4	6	8	10	12	14	16	18	20	22	24
3	3	6	9	12	15	18	21	24	27	30	33	36
4	4	8	12	16	20	24	28	32	36	40	44	48
5	5	10	15	20	25	30	35	40	45	50	55	60
6	6	12	18	24	30	36	42	48	54	60	66	72
7	7	14	21	28	35	42	49	56	63	70	77	84
8	8	16	24	32	40	48	56	64	72	80	88	96
9	9	18	27	36	45	54	63	72	81	90	99	108
10	10	20	30	40	50	60	70	80	90	100	110	120
11	11	22	33	44	55	66	77	88	99	110	121	132
12	12	24	36	48	60	72	84	96	108	120	132	144

6 Book 4: *Multiplication and Division*

CONCEPT DEVELOPMENT (PAGE 7)

INTRODUCE THE CONCEPT

ASSESS STUDENTS' PRIOR KNOWLEDGE
The goal of page 7 is to help students build on the multiplication facts they already know to learn other facts that they cannot immediately recall. Two strategies are often helpful. The first is using the commutative property of multiplication, using the fact that the order of the factors does not affect the product. The second is adding on or subtracting one group to a neighbor fact that is already known.

Ask:
How does knowing that $7 \times 10 = 70$ help you to find 10×7?

Listen for:
(Student understanding that changing the order of the factors does not change the product.)

MODEL MATHEMATICAL THINKING
Model the thinking for another example by asking, *How does knowing the product of 6×8 help us to find the product of 7×8?*

Talk Through the Thinking
Let me see. I know that $6 \times 8 = 48$. I think it means 6 groups of 8. So if 6×8 means 6 groups of 8, 7×8 means 7 groups of 8. I know 7 groups of 8 is one more group of 8 than 6 groups of 8. So I can add 1 group of 8 to the product of 6×8. $48 + 8 = 56$. So $7 \times 8 = 56$.

Explain that the facts $7 \times 8 = 56$ and $6 \times 8 = 48$ are next door neighbors and that students can use neighboring facts to find products.

Ask:
How can you use $6 \times 8 = 48$ to find 5×8?

Listen for:
- 5 groups of 8 is one less group of 8 than 6 groups of 8.
- I can subtract one group of 8 from 48 to find 5×8: $48 - 8 = 40$. So $5 \times 8 = 40$.

LAUNCH THE PROBLEM SOLVING

Have students work individually on page 7. You may wish to circulate and monitor their recorded answers. As students finish the page, have them compare and discuss the multiplication table and their answers with a partner. Then have each pair share their conclusions in a class discussion. Refer to the **Teacher Notes: Student Page 7** for more specific ideas about the problems on this page.

As students work and report their conclusions, focus on these issues:

Facilitate Students' Thinking – You may wish to remind students that changing the order of the factors does not change the product. Also if students catch on to the idea of expanding the multiplication table to multiply greater numbers, you could ask them how they would do this to multiply by 200 or 300 or by thousands.

Allow Processing Time – Processing time for the multiplication facts is important. Normally, students are considered to have mastered a multiplication fact if they can recall its answer within three seconds. A lot of good thinking can take place in 3–5 seconds. Allow students time to develop strategies for finding the answers.

Allow Waiting Time – When students struggle to explain their thinking, allow them ample time to organize their thoughts.

Help Make Connections – Make connections among particular fact strategies that students can use. For example, if students understand how to find 7×5 by thinking about 6×5 and then adding another 5, you can point out that this would be a way to find 11×5.

Reinforce Using Representations – Sometimes students benefit from seeing multiplication facts in array models (area models). You may wish to draw pictures to show, for example, 6×8 or another fact that is causing trouble. The pictures themselves will contain structures and visuals to help students arrive at an answer.

TEACHER NOTES: STUDENT PAGE 7

After the previous informal explorations with the multiplication table, students who are still uncomfortable with all the multiplication facts can now turn to the table to help them recall the facts. What does it mean to have mastery of the multiplication table? Of course, instant recall of multiplication facts is desirable. With time and proper exposure, nearly all students develop instant recall. But how soon can students be expected to have instant recall of the facts? There is notable research to suggest that overemphasizing recall of the facts at an early age can actually inhibit students' understanding of the mathematics of multiplication.

What is meant by mastery of the facts? A good rule of thumb is that 3–5 seconds is probably enough time for students to find the correct answer to a single-digit multiplication problem, assuming that greater efficiency comes with time. There are few situations in life in which it is crucial that young learners be able to recall a multiplication fact in less time. Taking the pressure of time off students will lead them to have greater confidence in both their intuitive ability to discern these facts and their overall efficacy as learners and doers of mathematics. The 60-second multiplication facts tests of the past have long been known to leave indelible and negative impressions on students. If students can solve single-digit multiplication problems in a few seconds using any number of intuitive strategies, they will be further ahead in understanding than students who are forced to simply memorize all the multiplication facts. Let your students use informal strategies to solve multiplication problems. With repeated practice and exposure, they will become more efficient without the inhibitions that many adults have today because of the way in which they were intimidated by the facts. The strategies outlined below will help students toward this end.

The purpose of page 7 is to help students realize that they already know many multiplication facts. The typical strategy teachers employ is to start at the ones and then progress sequentially through the nines. Unfortunately, much of what students already know about multiplication gets overlooked when following this teaching plan. *Teaching Strategy:* Start with the facts students already know because they can then use + 1 strategies to expand their command of the facts. For example, many students already can count by 5s. If they know, for example, that 5 groups of 6 is 30, then they also know that, because of the commutative property, 6 groups of 5 is also 30; then it is trivial for students to simply add one more 6 to 30 in order to compute the product of 6 × 6. The thinking might go as follows: *I know that 5 groups of 6 is 30. So 6 groups of 6 means that I just need to add one more 6 to 30. So 6 groups of 6 is 36.*

Research has indicated that the following facts are either known by students or can be taught as strategies: the 0s, the 1s, the 2s, the 5s, the 10s, the squares, the 9s. When students are comfortable with these facts, then they can also easily compute nearby facts +1 or – 1. For example, if students know the square fact of 4 × 4 = 16, then they can easily compute 4 × 5 (this is an example of an add one more fact) or 4 × 3 (this is an example of a one less fact).

Extension Activity: Give each student a blank multiplication table. Ask students to begin by shading the products they already know. They might start by shading half of the table because it has symmetry. Then start with the facts for 1s, 2s, 5s, etc. Soon, much of the tables will be shaded, and the number of facts remaining to be learned will be much less daunting to students.

Student Page 7: Problems and Potential Answers

Section B: The Multiplication Table — Set 1

The multiplication table can help you learn the multiplication facts. Instead of starting with the 1's, and working your way to the 12's, look at the big picture – the whole table. You probably know more than you think you do. For starters, you don't have to memorize every answer. You only need to learn the answers in half the table! You probably knew this already, but the right half of the table (in yellow) is the mirror image of the area to the left of the red boxes. The red boxes form a diagonal line down the middle, called the "square numbers line." It separates two identical sets of multiplication facts.

X	1	2	3	4	5	6	7	8	9	10	11	12
1	1	2	3	4	5	6	7	8	9	10	11	12
2	2	4	6	8	10	12	14	16	18	20	22	24
3	3	6	9	12	15	18	21	24	27	30	33	36
4	4	8	12	16	20	24	28	32	36	40	44	48
5	5	10	15	20	25	30	35	40	45	50	55	60
6	6	12	18	24	30	36	42	48	54	60	66	72
7	7	14	21	28	35	42	49	56	63	70	77	84
8	8	16	24	32	40	48	56	64	72	80	88	96
9	9	18	27	36	45	54	63	72	81	90	99	108
10	10	20	30	40	50	60	70	80	90	100	110	120
11	11	22	33	44	55	66	77	88	99	110	121	132
12	12	24	36	48	60	72	84	96	108	120	132	144

There are some other helpful facts you probably already know. Shade or circle the row and column for each of these numbers in the light yellow boxes: 1, 2, 5, 10.

If you know these facts, you can figure out the ones that are right next door. So, if you know that 5 × 5 is 25, then you can tell that 5 × **6** is 25 *plus* one more 5, or 30! Shade the following boxes:

The twos +1. For example, if 2 × 5 = 10, then **3** × 5 would be 10 **plus** one more 5 ➔ 15!
The fives +1 and -1. For example, if 5 × 8 = 40, then **4** × 8 would be 40 **minus** one less 8 ➔ 32!
The tens +1 and -1. For example, if 10 × 6 = 60, then **11** × 6 would be 60 **plus** one more 6 ➔ 66!

Are there other boxes that you already know and can shade in?

Responses will vary.

Book 4: *Multiplication and Division*

SECTIONS A and B ASSESSMENT (PAGE 8)

LAUNCH THE ASSESSMENT

Have students turn to the Section A and B Assessment on page 8. An additional copy is found on page 55 of the Assessment Book. Have students work individually to solve the problems and write their answers. As they work, circulate to be sure students understand what they need to do for each problem, and be sure that they are completing each part of the problem. For example, in problem 3 students need to rewrite a problem in two different ways. You may find it helpful to read the directions for all the problems before students begin, discussing the types of responses they will need to make for each problem. Refer to the **Teacher Notes: Assessment Problems for Sections A and B** for more specific ideas about the problems on this page.

Evaluate Student Responses

Use the assessment rubric on page 54 of the Assessment Book (pictured on page 244 of the Teacher Edition) to evaluate student responses. The Assessment Book has some general suggestions for using the rubric that you may find helpful.

TEACHER NOTES: ASSESSMENT PROBLEMS FOR SECTIONS A AND B

These problems are designed to help teachers determine whether students are grasping basic concepts related to multiplication and division.

Problems 1–2: Drawing pictures will help students conceptualize these representations of multiplication.

Student Page 8: Problems and Potential Answers

Sections A and B: Problems for Assessment

1. How many **single-scoop** ice cream cones would be possible with 3 kinds of cones and 4 flavors of ice cream? Explain your answer. Pictures can be part of your explanation.

   > 3 cones times 4 flavors equals 12 possibilities for a single scoop ice cream cone.

2. How many **double-scoop** ice cream cones would be possible with 2 kinds of cones and 3 flavors of ice cream?

   > 2 cones times 3 flavors for the first scoop times 3 flavors for the second scoop equals 18 possibilities for a double-scoop cone.

3. Any multiplication problem can be rewritten as a division problem. For example, the following problem could be rewritten in several ways. Each way keeps the same relationships of the numbers in the original problem.

   > **John picked 3 baskets of apples. Andreas picked 4 times as many baskets as John. How many baskets did Andreas pick?**

   This could be rewritten in the following way as a division problem:

   > **Andreas picked 12 baskets of apples. He picked 4 times as many as John. How many baskets did John pick?**

   Or...

   > **Andreas picked 12 baskets of apples, and John only picked 4. How many times as many baskets did Andreas pick than John picked**

   Rewrite this multiplication problem in two ways. Use the previous example as a model.

   > **This month, Joel saved 5 times as much money as he did last month. Last month he saved $7. How much money did Joel save this month?**

   > Joel saved $35 this month. This is 5 times as much money as he saved last month. How much did Joel save last month?
   > Or...
   > Joel saved $35 this month. Last month he saved $7. How many times more money did Joel save this month compared to last month?

8   Book 4: *Multiplication and Division*

SCORING GUIDE BOOK 4: MULTIPLICATION AND DIVISION

Sections A and B Assessment
For Use With: Student Book Page 8

PROBLEM DESCRIPTION	SCORING: WHAT TO LOOK FOR	SCORE AND COMMENTS
Problem 1 How many single scoop ice cream cone possibilities are there with 3 cones and 4 flavors? Level 1: Comprehension and Knowledge Level 2: Tool use	Do students: • Have an understanding of combinations? • Use counting principles to determine total number of combinations? • Use words and pictures to articulate thinking?	Points:_____ of 4
Problem 2 How many double scoop combinations are possible with two cones, and 3 flavors? Level 1: Comprehension and Knowledge Level 2: Tool use	Do students: • Have an understanding of combinations? • Use counting principles to determine total number of combinations? • Use words and pictures to articulate thinking?	Points:_____ of 4
Problem 3 Rewrite a problem statement (expressed as a division problem) using multiplication. Level 1: Comprehension and Knowledge	Do students: • Have an understanding of the relationship between multiplication and division? • Have the ability to look at a model and transfer to a new context? • Accurately express a multiplicative relationship?	Points:_____ of 2

TOTAL POINTS:_____ OF 10

Section C: Area Models of Multiplication

SECTION C PLANNER

THE MATHEMATICS CONTENT AND GOALS

GOALS
Students will:
- Understand the connection between multiplication as an operation and area models as representations of multiplication.
- Use the area model to visualize products of two numbers.
- Use the area model to help understand both decomposition of numbers and the distributive property of multiplication over addition.

> **LANGUAGE DEVELOPMENT**
> **Mathematical language in this section includes:**
> *Area Model:* The area model is a spatial-visual representation of multiplication in which students can count the number of square units necessary to cover, or tile, a given region. With this kind of model, students explore the connection between the area of a rectangular region and the product of its dimensions (length × width). In other words, to determine the answer to 4 × 5, students can create a rectangular region that is 4 × 5 units and then count the number of square units within the outline of the rectangle.

PACING

The projected pacing for this section is 1–2 class periods (based on a 45 minute period).

PROBLEM SETS: OVERVIEW

Set 1 (pp. 9–12; problems 1–4)
The problems in this set are intended to help students not only develop facility with a representational model for multiplication computation, but also to use that model to better understand what multiplication really is. The area model was introduced in the initial section of this book as one of four ways to represent multiplication. Key to the area model is an understanding of two primary concepts: 1) Numbers can be decomposed into the sum of smaller numbers; and 2) The distributive property can be used to break down one large multiplication problem into several smaller ones. Each of these concepts will be explained in the subsequent pages of this section.

CONCEPT DEVELOPMENT (Pages 9-12)

INTRODUCE THE CONCEPT

ASSESS STUDENTS' PRIOR KNOWLEDGE

Area models are powerful representations of multiplication. Using area models requires that students have a good understanding of both decomposition of numbers and the distributive property. These models give students a visual picture of these two ideas.

Ask:
Suppose we wanted to put wall-to-wall carpet on the floor of a rectangular room. We would have to call a carpet store. The first question they would ask is, "How much carpet do you need?" What would we need to know to be able to answer the question? How would we find the answer?

Listen for:
- We would need to know the area of the floor in square feet or square yards.
- We would find the answer by multiplying the length of the room by its width.

MODEL MATHEMATICAL THINKING

Model the thinking for another example by presenting this problem. *Michael is making an artistic, rectangular tile design. He is using tiles that are 1-inch squares. How many tiles will he need to make a design that is 5 inches wide and 14 inches long?*
As you talk through the problem, draw each picture on the board.

Talk Through the Thinking:
I think a picture would help me to solve this problem.

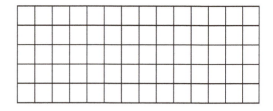

We know that each tile is a 1-inch square. This picture shows a rectangle that has 5 rows of tiles, for a width of 5 inches. Each row is 14 tiles, or 14 inches, long. I could continue to write the numbers in order on the tiles until I get to the very last tile. That would take quite a while, I know. I can look inside 14 to break it apart to make it easier to multiply: 14 = 10 + 4. So I could change my picture to look like this:

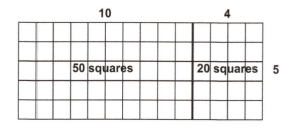

Now I can multiply easily. I can multiply the 10 by 5 and then I can multiply 4 by 5. Then I can write each answer in the correct box in the picture. Let's see where this takes me.

So now we have 50 and 20. We can add these together to find how many tiles Michael will need: 50 + 20 = 70. Michael will need 70 tiles to make his design.

Ask:
Suppose Michael's design was 8 inches long and 33 inches wide. Look at my first picture. How many rows would there be? How many columns? Then how could I break apart 33 to make it easier to multiply? What would you do?

Listen for:
- There would be 8 rows and 33 columns.
- You could break apart 33 as 10 + 10 + 10 + 3.
- Then I would find:
  $(8 \times 10) + (8 \times 10) + (8 \times 10) + (8 \times 3)$

Have students read page 9. When they are finished, have them compare and discuss their thoughts about the area model with a partner. Then have each pair share their conclusions in a class discussion. Refer to **Decomposition, Distribution, and the Area Model** for more information about this method.

As students discuss and report their conclusions, focus on these issues:

Help Make Connections – If students do not remember they can do so, remind them that they can look inside numbers to make them easier to compute. Providing graph paper for students to use on these problems will be helpful as they consider ways to decompose the factors for each product.

Allow Waiting Time – When students struggle to explain their thinking, be sure to allow them ample time to organize their thoughts.

TEACHER NOTES: STUDENT PAGE 9

Decomposition, Distribution, and the Area Model

Decomposition
Earlier in the curriculum, a method of breaking apart numbers, decomposing numbers, by looking inside was developed. To subitize is another term used to describe this action. It is important for students to understand that any number greater than 0 can be expressed as the sum of smaller numbers. For example, we might think of 15 as the sum of 10 + 5, or 36 as the sum of 10 + 10 + 10 + 5 + 1. Once this has been established in students' minds, the next consideration is whether the process of decomposing numbers can assist students with operations other than addition. In the case of multiplication, it turns out that it can.

Distribution
What makes decomposition of numbers important is the way that it can be combined with the distributive property in order to compute with large numbers in a flexible and powerful way. Fundamental to the area model is the understanding that, for example, 3 × 15 can be thought of in the following manner:

3 × 15 → 3 groups of 15 → 15 + 15 + 15 = 45

You might use manipulatives to demonstrate how to rewrite 3 × 15. Students could make 3 stacks of 15 counters each, then rearrange the counters into 3 stacks of 10 counters each and 3 stacks of 5 counters each.

So 3 × 15 → 3 × (10 + 5) → 3 groups of 10 plus 3 groups of 5 → 10 + 10 + 10 + 5 + 5 + 5 = 45.

This idea is represented in the area model of multiplication. Instead of using stacks of counters, the quantity of each number to be multiplied is represented as a dimension of a rectangle. From this point, students are led to discover that the whole area of the rectangle is simply the sum of the areas of smaller regions within the rectangle.

Be sure to pause at the question at the bottom of page 9. Students should be encouraged to break down the rectangle into comfortable numbers. For example, breaking 15 into 10 and 5 is a good idea because students are comfortable working with those benchmark numbers. Breaking 15 into 7 and 8 would be less helpful to many students, but it is still mathematically correct.

Student Page 9: Problems and Potential Answers

Section C: Area Models of Multiplication Set 1

Earlier, you learned that one kind of multiplication problem could be expressed as a rectangle. For example, if a rug is 4 feet long and 2 feet wide, it has an area of 8 square feet (4 × 2 = 8)

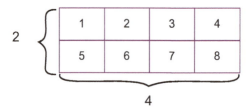

We can use this same idea to compute multiplication problems with greater numbers. For example, let's look at the problem 12 × 4.

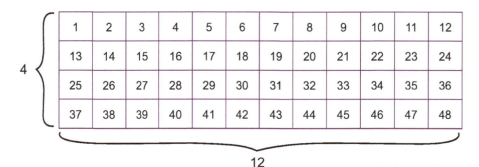

That works, but would you really want to count every square for a problem like, for example, 23 × 48? Probably not! You can still use the same idea if you learn how to break apart larger numbers into smaller ones. Suppose you do want to find 23 × 48. How can you break apart the numbers so that you can get a series of smaller, easier numbers that you can compute more easily? Let's find out.

The outside boundary would look something like this.

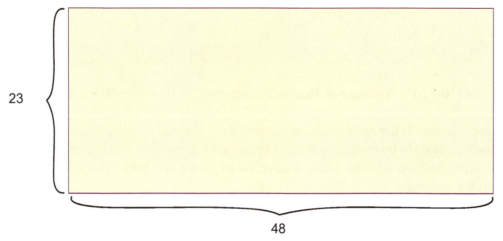

How can we think about breaking this large rectangle into smaller ones?

Book 4: *Multiplication and Division*   9

CONTINUE THE PROBLEM SOLVING

Page 10 is a continuation of the ideas initially set forth on Student Page 9. Have students read this page individually. When they have finished reading, have them discuss the ideas on the page with a partner. Then have each pair share their thoughts in a class discussion. Refer to the discussion **The Area Model** for more specific ideas for this page.

As students discuss their thoughts and conclusions, focus on these issues:

Allow Processing Time – Because the area model for multiplication is a new representation for many students, be sure to allow ample time for students to grasp how the model relates to the numbers being multiplied.

Facilitate Students' Thinking – Encourage students to think in place-value terms when reading page 10. Remind them that 2-digit numbers can be broken apart into tens and ones.

Look for Misconceptions – Be sure that students recognize the principle of conservation of area. This means that a given area can be partitioned into smaller subsections without changing the total area of the original figure.

Validate Representations – Students may choose different ways to decompose the numbers, so their visual representations may differ. Have students discuss these representations to determine whether all are valid.

TEACHER NOTES: STUDENT PAGE 10

The Area Model

The diagrams on page 10 help students see and understand the concepts of decomposition and distribution discussed earlier. At this point, students may also begin to recognize that the decomposition strategies are chosen deliberately in order to take advantage of utilizing multiplication facts that are easier than others.

Multiplying by 10 is a relatively simple process for students. So in the first example, students can see how breaking apart both 48 and 23 into tens and ones leads to the set of multiplication facts $10 \times 10 = 100$, $10 \times 8 = 80$, $10 \times 3 = 30$, and $8 \times 3 = 24$.

Central to understanding the area model are not only the concepts of decomposition and distribution, but also the notion of conservation of area. Students need to recognize that the area of the entire rectangle can be broken into smaller equal parts without changing the amount of area within the rectangle itself. This is the key to understanding the area model. Note that it is okay if student models are not exactly proportional.

Student Page 10: Problems and Potential Answers

Section C: Area Models of Multiplication — Set 1

We can use what we know about breaking apart numbers to make our diagram more helpful. For example, we know that 23 = 10 + 10 + 3 and that 48 = 10 + 10 + 10 + 10 + 8. So, we can add some lines to our original rectangle to represent the problem like this.

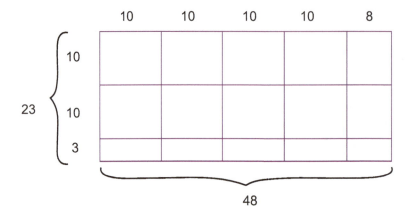

With this new drawing, we can now compute 23 × 48 by computing the total area of each of the smaller rectangles and then adding the areas together. For example, the **first square** is 10 units long on each side. To find its area, we multiply 10 × 10, so it has an area of 100

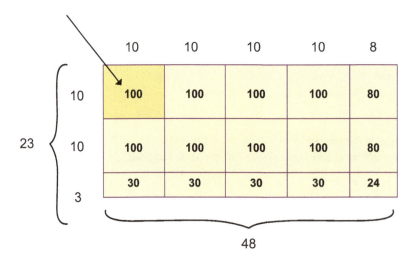

Now we can add the areas of all the rectangles together.
100 + 100 + 100 + 100 + 100 + 100 + 100 + 100 + 80 + 80 + 30 + 30 + 30 + 30 + 24 = **1104**

10   Book 4: *Multiplication and Division*

CONTINUE THE PROBLEM SOLVING

Have students turn to the example problem at the top of page 11.

MODEL MATHEMATICAL THINKING
Model the thinking so that students understand the area model at the top of page 11 by asking, *How can I use the area model to help me find the answer when I multiply 14 times 21?*

Talk Through the Thinking:
The factor 14 is on the left of the model and the factor 21 is at the top. I can break apart 14 into tens and ones; 14 is the same as 1 ten and 4 ones. I can write this at the left of the model. Then I can break apart 21 into 2 tens and 1 one, or 1 ten, another 1 ten, and 1 one. I can write this at the top of the model. Now there are lines inside the model to show how I broke apart the factors. For the top row, I begin at the left. I multiply the 1 ten from 14 and 1 ten from 21: 10 × 10. That's 100, so I write it in the correct box. Next to it is another box of 10 × 10, or 100. Right next to that I should write the product of 10 × 1, which is 10. Now I can move to the bottom row; 4 ones times 1 ten is 40, and 4 ones times another 1 ten is another 40. 4 ones times 1 one is 4. Now I can add the numbers in the boxes. I can start by grouping the tens and then grouping the ones: 100 + 100 + 40 + 40 + 10 + 4 = 294.

Have students work individually to solve the second example on page 11. As they work, circulate and monitor their recorded answers. When students finish, have them compare and discuss their work with a partner. Then have each pair share their answers in a class discussion. Refer to the **Teacher Notes: Student Page 11** for more specific ideas about this page.

As students work and report their conclusions, focus on these issues:

Facilitate Students' Thinking – You may wish to tell students that the numbers in the boxes inside the area model are partial products and that the sum of the partial products results in the answer. Continue to remind students that any 2-digit number can be broken apart into tens and ones.

Allow Processing Time – Continue to allow students ample time to understand how to break apart the factors and use the area model.

TEACHER NOTES: STUDENT PAGE 11

Teaching Strategy: Be sure to linger on these problems long enough so that students are sufficiently able to tackle the problems on the next page on their own.

Student Page 11: Problems and Potential Answers

Section C: Area Models of Multiplication Set 1

Let's do another example or two. What about 14 × 21?

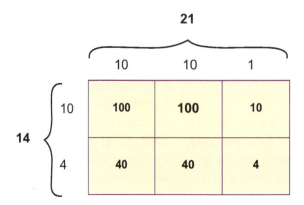

Adding the totals in each of the squares: 21 × 14 ➡ 100 + 100 + 40 + 40 + 10 + 4 = **294**

What about 34 × 18?

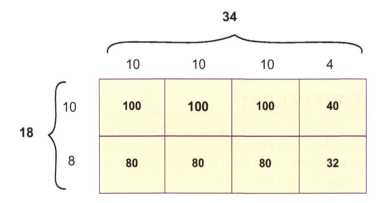

So… 18 × 34 ➡ 100 + 100 + 100 + 80 + 80 + 80 + 40 + 32 = 612

CONTINUE THE PROBLEM SOLVING

Have students work individually to investigate the problems on page 12. As they work, circulate and monitor their recorded answers. When students finish each problem, have them compare and discuss their answers with a partner. Then have each pair share their answers in a class discussion of the problem. Refer to the **Teacher Notes: Student Page 12** for more specific ideas about the examples on this page.

As students work and report their conclusions, focus on these issues:

Validate Alternate Strategies – Several students may break apart the factors in different ways to find the partial products. They may, for example, break 24 in problem 1 as 20 + 4. Have the class discuss whether these strategies lead to a correct answer.

Allow Waiting Time – When students struggle to explain their thinking, be sure to allow them ample time to organize their thoughts.

TEACHER NOTES: STUDENT PAGE 12

Page 12 is intended to give students the opportunity to create their own area models, given the numbers to be multiplied. Continue to emphasize the same ideas in these problems as you did on previous pages.

Problem 1: *Watch for:* Most students will break apart 24 as 10 + 10 + 4 and 26 as 10 + 10 + 6. *Teaching Strategy:* You might take this opportunity to contrast this strategy with a different one, that of breaking apart 24 as 20 + 4, and 26 as 20 + 6. With the latter strategy, students would need to compute these partial products: 20 × 4; 20 × 6; and 6 × 4. Comparing these two solution strategies is important so that students recognize that decomposing numbers in different ways combined with using the distributive property leads to the same final answer.

Problems 2–4: These problems provide students with additional practice in using the area model. You may wish to encourage students, particularly those who are having success with the area model, to solve the problems in different ways by using different decomposition strategies.

Student Page 12: Problems and Potential Answers

Section C: Area Models of Multiplication — Set 1

Your turn! Complete each multiplication problem using the Area Model.

1. 26 × 24   100 + 100 + 100 + 100 + 60 + 60 + 40 + 40 + 24 = 624

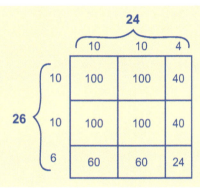

2. 17 × 42   100 + 100 + 100 + 100 + 70 + 70 + 70 + 70 + 20 + 14 = 714

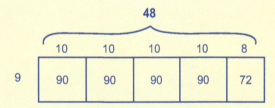

3. 9 × 48   90 + 90 + 90 + 90 + 72 = 432

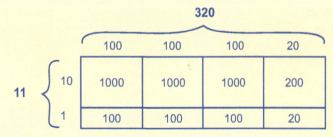

4. 11 × 320   1000 + 1000 + 1000 + 200 + 100 + 100 + 100 + 20 = 3520

		320		
	100	100	100	20
10	1000	1000	1000	200
1	100	100	100	20

(11 on the left bracketing rows 10 and 1)

12   Book 4: *Multiplication and Division*

Section D: Ratio Tables and Multiplication

SECTION D PLANNER

THE MATHEMATICS CONTENT AND GOALS

GOALS
Students will:
- Review (from Book 3) multiplicative applications of the ratio table.
- Use the ratio table to think multiplicatively.
- Use ratios and known number facts within the structure of ratio tables to complete multi-digit multiplication problems.
- Use ratios and known number facts within the structure of ratio tables in order to complete multi-digit division problems.

LANGUAGE DEVELOPMENT
Mathematical language in this section includes:

Ratio: A proportional relationship between two different numbers or quantities.
Ratio Table: A collection of equivalent ratios organized in a table.
Multiple: A number that is the product of a specific number and another number.
Row: The ratio table has two rows. In a ratio table, the top row is used for counting the number of groups in a given column and the bottom row counts the total number of objects in all the groups noted in the top row. The ratio between numbers in the top row and the corresponding values in the bottom row remains constant throughout a ratio table.
Column: Each ratio is expressed in a given column. The ratio across columns is constant.
Ratio Table Strategies: In order to use ratio tables effectively, it is crucial that students have basic understanding of commonly used computational strategies such as multiplying by 10 and doubling. Each of these key ideas is expressed below. If students are unaware of these strategies, reinforce them prior to beginning this book. Students will become comfortable with these strategies as they use them frequently throughout the text.

- *Multiplying:* It is crucial that students understand multiplication as groups of a given set. For example, 12 × 13 can be thought of as 12 groups of 13. If students understand this fundamental notion of multiplication as repeated addition, they are ready to use ratio tables.
- *Multiplying by 10:* A very common strategy with ratio tables is the process of multiplying by 10. Again, the "groups of" idea is important here. For example, 4 × 10 can be thought of as 4 groups of 10: 10, 20, 30, 40. Larger numbers work the same way: 14 × 10 means 14 groups of 10: 10, 20, 30, … 130, 140. Once students understand the idea of repeatedly adding ten, they will quickly begin to use a shortcut, simply annexing 0 to whatever number is being multiplied by 10; for example, 13 × 10 = 130.
- *Doubling:* Doubling is also an important strategy for ratio tables. For example, if 2 cases of juice contain 14 bottles, then 4 cases (double the amount) would be 2 × 14, or 28 bottles. Help students with informal methods for doubling. For example, 14 can be thought of as (10 + 4). Therefore, doubling 14 can be thought of as doubling (10 + 4), meaning that we can double the 10 (i.e., 20) and then double the 4 (i.e., 8), which is 20 + 8 = 28.

- **Halving:** Halving a given amount is also a valuable strategy. For example, if 10 boxes of apples contain 180 apples, then 5 boxes would contain 90 apples. The same informal strategy of breaking apart numbers can be used to help students divide a given quantity in half: 180 can be thought of as (100 + 80). Half of 100 is 50, and half of 80 is 40. So half of 180 is 50 + 40 = 90.
- **Adding:** Adding across the columns in a ratio table is another important strategy. For example, if 4 cartons contain 40 crayons, and 2 cartons contain 20 crayons, then taken together, the 6 cartons would contain 60, or 40 + 20 crayons.
- **Subtracting:** The same can be said for subtraction. If one carton holds 12 eggs, and 4 cartons hold 48 eggs, then three cartons would hold 48 − 12 = 36 eggs.

PACING

The projected pacing for this unit is 1–2 class periods (based on a 45 minute period).

PROBLEM SETS: OVERVIEW

The ratio table is a flexible tool that students can use to solve a variety of problems. Throughout this section, students will build on strategies developed earlier as they organize ratios in a table. Students can use intuitive strategies such as skip-counting, doubling, halving, adding on, and multiplying by 10, to help them in this section. A thorough understanding of ratio tables is important so students can later engage in topics that require proportional thinking.

Set 1 (pp. 13–14; problems 1–2)

The problems in Set 1 review the function and use of ratio tables. Students will learn that ratio tables are useful in ways other than repeated addition as they look at and use various strategies that are helpful steps in arriving at the product of two numbers. Students will explore these strategies within two multiplicative contexts that help illustrate the meaning and utility of multiplication.

Set 2 (p. 15; problem 1)

Problems 1a–1d use ratio tables to look at both multiplication and division. In the example, students see how a division problem can be expressed as a multiplication problem and how ratio tables can help illustrate both operations. The problems themselves are written as division problems. They illustrate how the same kind of proportional reasoning used in multiplication via the ratio tables can be used to solve division problems.

Set 3 (p. 16; problems 1–5)

The ratio-table puzzles in Set 3 will challenge students to use various ratio table strategies by limiting the number of steps they must take to find the solutions. Students typically enjoy these puzzles and can create puzzles of their own for their peers to solve.

CONCEPT DEVELOPMENT (PAGES 13–16)

INTRODUCE THE CONCEPT

ASSESS STUDENTS' PRIOR KNOWLEDGE
By this point in the program, students should be comfortable with applications of ratio tables. For this section, focus explicitly on the ratio table as a tool for multiplication.

Draw this ratio table on the board. Complete the table as students give correct responses.

Boxes	1	2	10	12	
Peaches	14				

Ask:
There are 14 peaches in each box of fresh peaches at an orchard. How can you use this ratio table to find how many fresh peaches there are in 12 boxes?

Listen for:
(Student understanding of the strategies needed to complete the ratio table.)
- First I can double 14 to find how many fresh peaches there are in 2 boxes. That's 28.
- Next I can multiply the number of fresh peaches in 1 box by 10 to find how many there are in 10 boxes. That's 140.
- Third I know that 12 = 10 + 2. So I can add the totals from the second and third columns to find how many fresh peaches there are in 12 boxes. 28 + 140 = 168.

MODEL MATHEMATICAL THINKING
Model the thinking for another example by asking, *Another orchard sells peaches in boxes of 16 peaches each. Orchard workers picked 352 peaches. How can I find how many boxes are needed for all the peaches they picked?*

Draw the ratio table below on the board, but fill in the cells (indicated in blue) as you talk through the thinking.

Boxes	1	2	10	20	22
Peaches	16	32	160	320	352

Talk Through the Thinking:
I can use a ratio table to find the answer. I know that there are 16 peaches in each box. So 1 box is needed for 16 peaches. If I double 16 and then double 1, I can find that 2 boxes are needed for 32 peaches. Now I can multiply both 16 and 1 by 10 to find that 10 boxes are needed for 160 peaches. If I double both of these numbers, I find that 20 boxes are needed for 320 peaches. But there are 352 peaches in all. That's a difference of 32 peaches. Two boxes hold 32 peaches. So I can add 20 + 2. So 22 boxes are needed for 352 peaches.

Ask:
Besides the fact that both problems deal with peaches and boxes, how are the two problems we did alike and different?

Listen for:
- They are alike because they can both be solved using ratio tables.
- They are alike because you can use the same strategies to find the answers.
- They are different because the first problem was a multiplication problem and the second was a division problem.

LAUNCH THE PROBLEM SOLVING

Have students work individually to solve the problem at the bottom of page 13. As they work, circulate and monitor their recorded answers. When students finish the problem, have them compare and discuss their answers with a partner. Then have each pair share their answers in a class discussion of the information and the problem on page 13. Be sure to talk through the strategies illustrated on the page. Refer to the **Teacher Notes: Student Page 13** for more specific ideas about the problems on this page.

As students work and report their conclusions, focus on these issues:
Allow Processing Time – Allow students to spend a bit of time on the ratio tables on page 13 and on the strategies used to complete them. Doing so will help students recognize how ratio tables can help them solve problems with different number types and operations.

Help Make Connections – Some students may think that ratio tables are a new tool. Remind them that they have worked with ratio tables before. You may wish to review earlier uses of ratio tables with these students.

Allow Waiting Time – When students struggle to explain their thinking, allow them at least 20 seconds to organize their thoughts and formulate their answers.

Facilitate Students' Thinking – Many students will solve ratio problems by repeated addition. Encourage them to use more sophisticated strategies, such as doubling, halving, multiplying by 3, or combining ratios.

Encourage Language Development – Be sure that students understand and can use the various ratio table strategies (e.g., doubling, halving, multiplying by 10, etc.) described above.

TEACHER NOTES: STUDENT PAGE 13

The examples on page 13 constitute a review of common strategies, such as repeated addition, doubling, and halving that are useful in completing ratio tables. The first table illustrates a repeated-addition strategy. The second table shows how a doubling strategy can significantly shorten the number of steps taken to solve the problem. The third table utilizes three strategies, multiplying by 10, halving, and adding, that students often find extremely helpful.

Teaching Strategy: Be sure to work through these strategies with your students so that they begin to see the ratio table as something more than a framework for the repeated-addition meaning of multiplication. If students do not see ratio tables as useful for more than repeated addition, they will not develop facility with them. Because ratio-table models can be used for other mathematical concepts, such as operations with fractions and decimal-fraction-percent connections, it is imperative that students come to appreciate the elegance of ratio tables as quickly as possible.

Student Page 13: Problems and Potential Answers

Section D: Ratio Tables and Multiplication and Division — Set 1

In a different book in this program, we learned how to use ratio tables to complete multiplication and division problems. In this section, we will review ratio tables as tools for multiplication.

Read this problem.

> **Luke is in charge of ordering corn seeds for the school garden. The seeds are packaged in small envelopes. Each envelope contains 14 seeds. How many seeds will he get if he orders 6 envelopes?**

Using a ratio table, we could do something like this:

Strategy 1

Envelopes	1	2	3	4	5	6
Seeds	14	28	42	56	70	84

As you can see, the ratio table helps us keep track of both the number of envelopes and the number of seeds. This ratio table illustrates the "repeated addition" method of multiplication. If we use our knowledge of multiplication and the idea of a ratio, we can be creative with the ratio table to solve the problem in different ways. For example:

Strategy 2

Envelopes	1	2	3	6
Seeds	14	28	42	84

In this solution, we saved several steps. We used the idea that if 3 envelopes contain 42 seeds, then by doubling the number of envelopes to 6, we can also double the number of seeds from 42 to 84. We can do this because we are keeping the *ratio* of envelopes to seeds the same.

Here is another strategy using a different ratio table. Can you explain this strategy?

Strategy 3

Envelopes	1	10	5	6
Seeds	14	140	70	84

Explain. Multiply the number of seeds in 1 envelope by 10. Then divide that number by two to get the number of seeds in 5 envelopes. Add the number of seeds in 1 envelope to the number of seeds in 5 envelopes to get the number of seeds in 6 envelopes.

Book 4: *Multiplication and Division*   13

CONTINUE THE PROBLEM SOLVING

Student pages 14–16 provide students with practice in solving multiplication problems through the use of ratio tables.

Have students work individually to solve the problems on page 14. As they work, circulate and monitor their recorded answers. When students finish each problem, have them compare and discuss their answers with a partner. Then have each pair share their answers in a class discussion of the problem. Refer to the **Teacher Notes: Student Page 14** for specific ideas about these problems.

As students work and report their conclusions, focus on these issues:

Help Make Connections – If students are struggling with these problems, suggest that they think about all the ratio-table strategies they learned previously. You may want to discuss some of those strategies with them.

Validate Alternate Representations – Several students may create different ratio tables for problems 2a–2b. Have them compare and discuss the ratio tables to determine whether all are valid.

Allow Waiting Time – When students struggle to explain their thinking, allow them ample time to organize their thoughts.

TEACHER NOTES: STUDENT PAGE 14

Problem 1a: The numbers selected for this problem were done so intentionally to discourage a repeated-addition approach. *Watch for:* This table compels students to use multiplication by 10 and halving strategies as the primary steps of the solution strategy. *Teaching Strategy:* Be sure students understand how these strategies are used.

This problem utilizes the strategies of doubling, multiplying by 10, and addition, and helps students develop flexibility with ratio tables. *Watch for:* First students are encouraged to double, going from 16 in 1 set to 32 in 2 sets to 320 in 20 sets. The third step is where flexibility is illustrated. For the 4th column, students must go back to the second column and double the numbers to get 64 in 4 sets. Now all the ingredients are there for a straightforward conclusion to the problem: students must add the number of pencils in 20 boxes (320) to the number of pencils in 4 boxes (64) for a total of 384 pencils in 24 boxes. It is this kind of flexibility that gives power to ratio tables. *Teaching Strategy:* Be sure to emphasize this flexibility so that students grasp the techniques and potential of ratio tables. It may be argued that this is a cumbersome process for multiplication and that there are more efficient strategies that could be used. But in using ratio tables, a significant amount of mathematical thinking is involved, and a depth of conceptual understanding must be in place.

Problems 2a–2b: These problems allow students to develop their own ratio tables. *Teaching Strategy:* Be sure to spend time having students share the different strategies they used to solve these problems. It is in the sharing of varied solution strategies that students enrich their own understanding of mathematics. *Watch for:* For these problems, look for students to use several strategies, such as multiplication by 5 and 10, or halving strategies.

Student Page 14: Problems and Potential Answers

Section D: Ratio Tables and Multiplication and Division   Set 1

1. There are 16 pencils in every box. How many pencils are in 24 boxes? (24 × 16)

   a) Complete the ratio table.

1	2	20	4	24
16	32	320	64	384

   Explain each step. Multiply the second column by 10 to get the third column. Double the second column to get the fourth column. Add the third and fourth columns to get the fifth column.

   b) Complete the ratio table.

1	10	5	16
24	240	120	384

   How is this ratio table related to the ratio table in part a?

   Explain each step. Multiply the first column by 10 to get the second column. Halve the second column to get the third column. Add the first, second, and third columns to get the fourth column.

   This ratio table computes the same product: 24 × 16. The difference is that in the first ratio table, we computed the number of pencils in 24 boxes given the ratio of 1 box to 16 pencils. The second table starts with the ratio of 1 to 24, which doesn't really fit the problem context.

2. Use a ratio table to complete each multiplication problem.

   a) 18 × 15

1	10	5	15
18	180	90	270

   b) 25 × 24

1	10	20	5	25
24	240	480	120	600

14 Book 4: *Multiplication and Division*

CONTINUE THE PROBLEM SOLVING

Work through the examples at the top of page 15 with the class. Then have students work individually to solve the problems on the page. As they work, circulate and monitor their recorded answers. When students finish each problem, have them compare and discuss their answers with a partner. Then have each pair share their answers in a class discussion of the problem. Refer to the **Teacher Notes: Student Page 15** for more specific ideas about these problems.

As students work and report their conclusions, focus on these issues:

Allow Processing Time – Allow students time to get used to thinking of ratio tables in terms of division.

Help Make Connections – When students have difficulty getting started, ask, for example, "How many groups of 15 can you make from 15 objects? (One.) How many groups of 15 can you make from 30 objects? (Two.)"

Validate Alternate Strategies – When several students use different strategies to solve the same problem, have them compare and discuss their work to determine whether all are correct.

TEACHER NOTES: STUDENT PAGE 15

Problems 1a–1d: There are many ways to solve each of these problems. What is most important as students begin is to help them think conceptually about division. Problem 1a asks students to determine how many 15s there are in 90. *Teaching Strategy:* To help students use the ratio table effectively in a division context such as this one, it is important to start with verbal representations of the problem. Students are looking for sets of 15, or how many sets of 15 there are in 90, and the ratio table can help them count these sets of 15. For example, 1 set of 15 is 15, 2 sets are 30, 10 sets are 150, etc. So the strategy is to count sets in the top row and units in the bottom row. The strategies for completing the ratio tables are all similar. The switch to divisional thinking from multiplicative thinking is the primary difference between the problems on this page and those that came before.

Student Page 15: Problems and Potential Answers

Section D: Ratio Tables and Multiplication and Division — Set 2

Because multiplication and division are related, ratio tables can be used to solve both kinds of problems. Can you use a ratio table to solve a division problem? Here is one way.

252 ÷ 12 →

1	10	20	**21**
12	120	240	**252**

So… 252 ÷ 12 = 21

Now let's use a ratio table to multiply 12 × 21.

1	10	2	12
21	210	42	252

So… 12 × 21 = 252

1. Complete each division problem.

    a) How many 15s are there in 90? __6__

1	2	4	6			
15	30	60	90			

    b) How many 20s are there in 660? __33__

1	10	20	30	3	33	
20	200	400	600	60	660	

    c) How many 16s are there in 256? __16__

1	10	5	16			
16	160	80	256			

    d) How many 18s are there in 378? __21__

1	10	20	21			
18	180	360	378			

Book 4: *Multiplication and Division* 15

CONTINUE THE PROBLEM SOLVING

Have students work individually to solve the problems on page 16. As they work, circulate and monitor their recorded answers. When students finish each problem, have them compare and discuss their solutions with a partner. Then have each pair share their answers in a class discussion of the problem. Refer to the **Teacher Notes: Student Page 16** for more specific ideas about the problems on this page.

As students work and report their conclusions, focus on these issues:

Allow Waiting Time – When students struggle to explain their thinking, allow them ample time to organize their thoughts and formulate their responses.

Allow Processing Time – Some students may need to guess and test to solve the puzzles. Allow them enough time to try out several possible solutions before writing in their final answers.

TEACHER NOTES: STUDENT PAGE 16

Problems 1–5: These puzzles are fun challenges for students. They motivate students to discover and use strategies that they may not have used in previous problems. You may wish to allow students to create their own puzzles to share with peers as an extension of this activity.

Student Page 16: Problems and Potential Answers

Section D: Ratio Tables and Multiplication and Division Set 3

Ratio Table Puzzles

The following ratio tables are puzzles. Try to solve each puzzle by filling in the empty cells in *exactly the number of columns provided*. You may need to use several strategies, such as doubling, halving, adding, multiplying, and so on.

1.

1	2	4	40
6	12	24	240

2.

3	30	15	45	48
4	40	20	60	64

3.

1	10	20	30	60
2.5	25	50	75	150

4.

5	50	25
3	30	15

5.

2	6	20	26
3	9	30	39

16 Book 4: *Multiplication and Division*

SECTION C and D ASSESSMENT (PAGE 17)

LAUNCH THE ASSESSMENT

Have students turn to the Sections C and D Assessment on page 17. An additional copy is found on page 57 of the Assessment Book. Have students work individually to solve the problems. As they work, circulate to be sure students understand what they need to do for each problem and that they are completing each part of the problem. For example, for problem 1, students need to find the product of 17 × 22 by creating both an area model and a ratio table. You may find it helpful to read the directions for all the problems before students begin, discussing the types of responses they will need to make for each problem.

Encourage students to use whatever space they need to draw their models. If the space on the page is inadequate, they should use a separate sheet of paper or the back of the page. Refer to the **Teacher Notes: Assessment Problems for Sections C and D** for more specific ideas about the problems on this page.

Evaluate Student Responses

Use the assessment rubric on page 56 of the Assessment Book (pictured on page 268 of the Teacher Edition) to evaluate student responses. The Assessment Book has some general suggestions for using the rubric that you will probably find helpful.

TEACHER NOTES: STUDENT PAGE 17

Problem 1: There are various ways to solve each part of this problem. *Watch for:* For the area model, students may draw on the commutative property and represent 22 horizontally and 17 vertically or vice versa. The result is the same, the only difference being the location of the smaller rectangles that are used to find the area. Alternatively, students who are more comfortable with the model might take advantage of using larger rectangles as illustrated below:

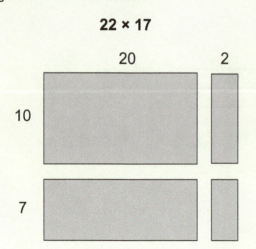

Watch for: To solve the problem using a ratio table, students may choose any number of ratio combinations. It is likely that they will use doubling and multiplying by 10 to arrive at their answers.

Problem 2: This problem asks students to think about division while using a ratio table. The process is the same, but the use of the ratio table is different. The main difference is that in the case of division, students must aim for a target number (in this case, 221) and use the relationships in the table to do so. As shown by the alternative strategy answer, they may overshoot the target, which requires them to subtract. Or as shown by the first answer, they may build to the target. The general principles and uses of strategies in the ratio tables, however, remain the same.

Student Page 17: Problems and Potential Answers

Sections C and D: Problems for Assessment

1. Show how to solve the following problem using the area model and the ratio table.

   17 × 22 (Area Model)

   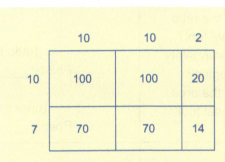

	10	10	2
10	100	100	20
7	70	70	14

   100 + 100 + 20 + 70 + 70 + 14 = 374

   17 × 22 (Ratio Table)

1	2	10	20	22		
17	34	170	340	374		

2. Use a ratio table to solve the following:

   How many 13's are in 221?

1	10	5	15	2	17		
13	130	65	195	26	221		

   Alternative strategy

1	10	5	20	2	18	17	
13	130	65	260	26	234	221	

SCORING GUIDE BOOK 4: MULTIPLICATION AND DIVISION

Sections C and D Assessment
For Use With: Student Book Page 17

PROBLEM DESCRIPTION	SCORING: WHAT TO LOOK FOR	SCORE AND COMMENTS
Problem 1 Use ratio tables and the area model to solve a multiplication problem. Level 1: Comprehension and Knowledge Level 2: Tool use	Do students: • Understand the use of the ratio table as a computational tool? • Setup the problem appropriately and use the ratio strategies? • Understand the use of the area model as a computational tool?	(ratio table) Points:_____of 2 (area model) Points:_____of 2
Problem 2 Use a ratio table to complete a division problem. Level 1: Comprehension and Knowledge Level 2: Tool use	Do students: • Understand the use of the ratio table as a computational tool? • Setup the problem appropriately and use the ratio strategies?	Points:_____of 2

TOTAL POINTS:_____ OF 6

Section E: The Lattice Method of Multiplication

SECTION E PLANNER

THE MATHEMATICS CONTENT AND GOALS

GOALS
Students will:
- Use number decomposition to develop understanding of the lattice method of multiplication.
- Develop expertise in using the lattice method of multiplication.
- Compare the traditional multiplication algorithm with the lattice method of multiplication.

LANGUAGE DEVELOPMENT
Mathematical language in this section includes:

Lattice Method: A method for multiplication in which the partial products are laid out in a lattice grid, where the diagonal columns represent place-value designations. Partial products are recorded in appropriate cells, and subsequent addition along the diagonals results in the digits of the product.

Place-Value Designations: The methods for multiplication emphasized in this section require familiarity with the following fundamental base-10 values:
- *Thousands:* Four place-value units to the left of the decimal point.
- *Hundreds:* Three place-value units to the left of the decimal point.
- *Tens:* Two place-value units to the left of the decimal point.
- *Ones:* The place-value unit immediately to the left of the decimal point.

PROBLEM SETS: OVERVIEW

The lattice method of multiplication has been used as an algorithm in various cultures for hundreds of years. While at first it looks distinctively different from the traditional column-based multiplication algorithm we typically teach in our schools, many of its smaller components are quite similar. This makes the lattice method an important tool not only for students to use to find products, but also as a way to help students develop a conceptual understanding of multiplication.

There is a rather lengthy explanation of the lattice method in this section. It is important that teachers walk students through these introductory steps so they develop both a rich understanding of this method and facility with its use. Like any alternative method, the lattice method of multiplication is a viable substitute for more traditional algorithms. While some students may eventually prefer to use different algorithms for multiplication and division, others will take to this method and make it their own. Regardless, if taught well, this method will enrich students' understanding of multiplication.

Set 1 (pp. 18–21)
The initial pages in this set of problems outline the concepts behind the lattice method and the procedure one follows when using lattice tables. After thoroughly exploring several examples, students will be ready to try to use the lattice method on their own.

Set 2 (pp. 22–24; problems 1–7)
These problems provide students with additional practice using the lattice method.

PACING
The projected pacing for this unit is 2–3 class periods (based on a 45 minute period).

CONCEPT DEVELOPMENT (PAGES 18–21)

The text on student pages 18–21 explains the lattice method of multiplication. The lattice method is a unique strategy based on number decomposition and partial products. The disadvantage of the lattice method is that once students master the steps for using it, they are able to perform calculations quickly and efficiently but may not understand exactly what it is they are doing. Therefore, it is crucial for students to spend enough time understanding this method as they become proficient at using it. This is the purpose of the three pages of diagrams and explanations. Essential to the use of the lattice method is an understanding of place value.

INTRODUCE THE CONCEPT

ASSESS STUDENTS' PRIOR KNOWLEDGE

Display and then review base-10 blocks with students. Point out that each small unit cube represents 1; that 10 unit cubes is equal to 1 rod, which represents 10; and that 10 rods is equal to 1 flat, which represents 100.

Draw these diagrams on the board, or use transparent base-10 blocks on an overhead projector.

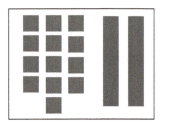
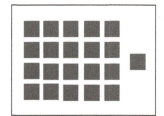
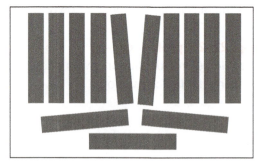

Ask:
Which number is represented by the base-10 blocks in each diagram?

Listen for:
Students' ability to regroup. For example, in the first diagram there are 13 unit cubes (13 ones) and 2 rods (2 tens, or 20), for a total of 33.
- The first diagram represents 33.
- The second diagram represents 21.
- The third diagram represents 130.

MODEL MATHEMATICAL THINKING

Model the thinking for regrouping with base-10 blocks by asking, *How can I use fewer blocks to represent the number in the second diagram?*

Talk Through the Thinking:
Let's look at this diagram. There are 21 unit cubes in all. I know that each unit cube stands for 1 one. I can put the cubes into groups of 10. Circle each group of 10 unit cubes. *I also know that each rod stands for 1 ten. So I can trade each group of 10 unit cubes for 1 rod. That will give me 2 rods, with 1 unit cube left on its own. So 2 rods plus 1 unit cube represents 2 tens and 1 one, or 21 and the same number represented by 21 unit cubes.*

Ask:
How can you trade to use fewer blocks to represent the numbers in the first and third diagrams?

Listen for:
Students should recognize that once they find 10 unit cubes, they can trade them for 1 rod. Likewise, once they find 10 rods, they can trade them for 1 flat.
- In the first diagram, I can trade 10 unit cubes for 1 rod. That will give me 3 rods and 3 unit cubes, or 3 tens and 3 ones, or 33.
- In the third diagram there are 13 rods. I can trade each group of 10 rods for 1 flat. That will give me 1 flat and 3 rods, or 1 hundred and 3 tens, or 130.

Discuss the importance of place value in our number system. Explain that students need to be especially aware of place value as they learn a new method of multiplication called the Lattice Method in the next few lessons.

TEACHER NOTES: STUDENT PAGE 18

LAUNCH THE PROBLEM SOLVING

Have students read the information on page 18. You may wish to have them discuss the information with a partner before having pairs share their thoughts in a class discussion of the page. Refer to the discussion **The Lattice Method and Decomposition** for more information.

As students progress through these pages, focus on these issues:

Encourage Language Development – Be sure to review place value through the thousands place. Encourage students to use appropriate place-value terminology, such as ones, tens, hundreds, thousands, ten thousands, etc. You may wish to use a place-value chart.

Help Make Connections – Help students see the connections between the partial products in the cells of the lattice and the partial products that have appeared in other methods of multiplication, such as in the area model and the traditional multiplication algorithm.

Facilitate Students' Thinking – Remind students to build on what they already know about partial products and decomposition of numbers as they work through lattice multiplication.

Allow Waiting Time – When students struggle to explain their thinking, allow them ample time to organize their thoughts.

The Lattice Method and Decomposition

Because there are no problems until the end of page 22, the following discussion is provided as guidance for leading students through an explanation of the lattice method.

Fundamental to the lattice method of multiplication is the recognition that multiplication can take advantage of the decomposition of numbers. Decomposition was explored thoroughly earlier in this book as students used the area model of multiplication. That a number can be expressed as the sum of smaller numbers—for example, 32 can be expressed as 30 + 2 and 43 can be expressed as 40 + 3—reflects the same principle.

The structure of the lattice method is presented on this page. This structure takes advantage of the decomposition-of-number principle mentioned above. Inform students of this fact.

Student Page 18: Problems and Potential Answers

Section E: The Lattice Method of Multiplication — Set 1

There are lots of ways to multiply two numbers. So far we have used the area model and ratio tables. You may know another method for multiplying that looks something like this:

$$\begin{array}{r} \overset{\scriptscriptstyle 1\ 2}{86} \\ \times\ 24 \\ \hline {}_1 344 \\ 1720 \\ \hline 2064 \end{array}$$

This is a perfectly fine way to multiply. But you may find it difficult to understand exactly how and why this works. A different method for multiplying is called the Lattice Method. The Lattice Method uses an important idea you discovered when you were using the area model for multiplication: <u>One large multiplication problem can be broken apart into smaller ones.</u> In the area model, you could easily see how each square was itself a smaller multiplication problem. Although the multiplication method you see above is based on the same idea, it is not as easy to <u>see</u> the smaller problems, especially after the problem has been completed. So the Lattice Method is a method that may be a bit easier to follow.

Suppose we want to multiply 32 × 43. Begin by thinking of this problem as (30 + 2) × (40 + 3). Using this understanding, we can complete several smaller calculations that will lead to the answer. To do so, we can first draw a table that corresponds to the problem:

3(0)	2	
		X
		4(0)
		3

Now what? Let's see how we can use this table to solve the multiplication problem…

18 Book 4: *Multiplication and Division*

CONTINUE THE PROBLEM SOLVING

Have students continue to read about the lattice method on page 19. You may wish to have students discuss the page with a partner before sharing their thoughts in a class discussion of the page. Refer to **The Lattice Method and Distribution** for more information.

As students discuss the information on page 19, focus on these issues:

Allow Processing Time – It will take time for students to understand how the lattice method works. Allow them enough time to grasp the information presented on the page.

Look for Misconceptions – It is especially important to be sure students understand and recognize the difference between multiplying ones and multiplying tens. For example, when multiplying 21 × 43, multiplying 2 × 3 in the lattice is really multiplying 2 tens × 3 ones, or 20 × 3. In the same way, multiplying 2 × 4 is really multiplying 2 tens × 4 tens, or 20 × 40.

TEACHER NOTES: STUDENT PAGE 19

The Lattice Method and Distribution

While again there are no problems on page 19, it is crucial for students to carefully study the steps of the method as they are described. Most important to the method is the notion of the distributive property. Remember that 5 × 15 can be thought of in the following way:

5 × 15 → 5 × (10 + 5) → (5 × 10) + (5 × 5)

A pictorial representation of this principle may be helpful for students.

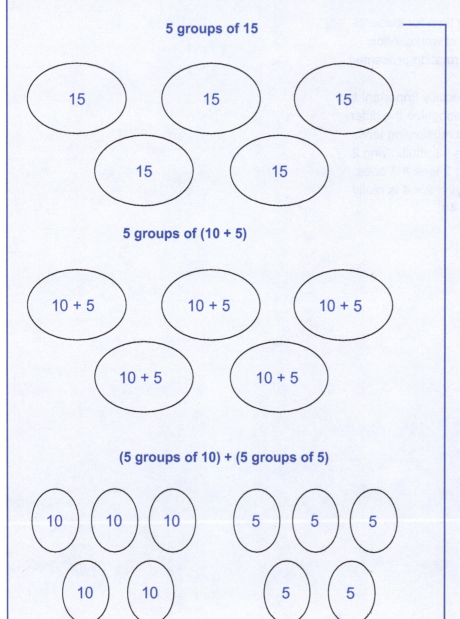

Each of these represents the same amount:
- 5 groups of 15 = 75
- 5 groups of (10 + 5) = 75
- (5 × 10) + (5 × 5) = 75

Fundamental to the lattice method is an understanding of the distributive property. What is illustrated on the student page is the way in which a larger multiplication problem can be broken down into smaller ones using the distributive property.

Be sure to pause at this example to ensure that students grasp how the cells within the lattice are divided and which multiplication products they represent.

Student Page 19: Problems and Potential Answers

Section E: The Lattice Method of Multiplication — Set 1

This table will help us keep track of what we are multiplying. Think about the area model we used earlier and the way we wrote this problem on the previous page: (30 + 2) × (40 + 3). Each of the boxes in this table will help us keep this straight.

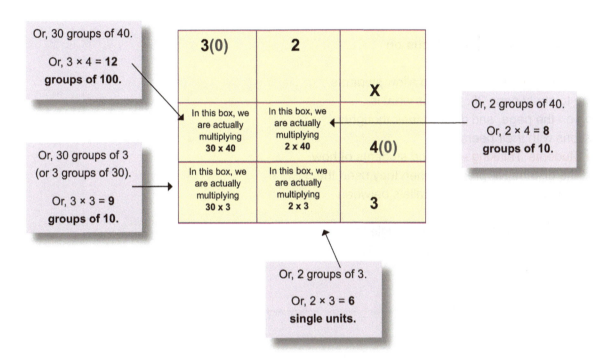

To help us keep track of what we have done, we can draw in some additional lines on our table like this.

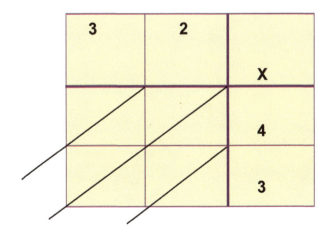

Now, let's see how this table works. Turn the page.

Book 4: *Multiplication and Division*   19

CONTINUE THE PROBLEM SOLVING

Have students read through pages 20 and 21. Some students, particularly those for whom English is a second language, will need support. You may wish to have them discuss the information on the pages with a partner. Then have pairs share their thoughts in a class discussion of the page. Refer to the discussion **The Lattice Method and the Area Model** for more information.

As students discuss the page, focus on these issues:

Allow Processing Time – Continue to allow students ample time to study page 20, process what is happening on the page, and discuss their thoughts and questions with their peers.

Facilitate Students' Thinking – Remind students of how they used the distributive property when they used the area model. Ask them to look for parallels between that method and the lattice method.

Allow Waiting Time – When students struggle to explain their thinking, allow them ample time to organize their thoughts.

TEACHER NOTES: STUDENT PAGES 20-21

The Lattice Method and the Area Model

The structure and function of the lattice method are described on this page. Before helping students work through the example, it might be helpful to return to the area model of multiplication used earlier. Recall that 32 × 43 might be represented in the following way:

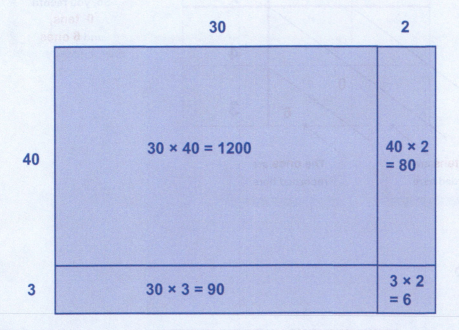

The area model is the foundation on which the lattice method is built. The rectangle used in the lattice method is divided into parts that correspond to the parts in the above model. Both methods are based on decomposition of numbers and the distributive property. Making the connection between the area model and the lattice can help students better understand the components of the lattice described on the page.
• In the first cell (upper left quadrant), we are multiplying 30 × 40 (tens times tens).
• In the second cell (upper right quadrant) we are multiplying 40 × 2 (tens times ones).
• In the third cell (lower left quadrant) we are multiplying 30 × 3 (tens times ones).
• In the fourth cell (lower right quadrant) we are multiplying 3 × 2 (ones times ones).

The lattice helps students count these groupings as described on the bottom of the page. The key to understanding the lattice is knowing which place values, ones; tens; hundreds; etc., are being counted. Just as with the traditional algorithm, there may be more than 10 in any particular place. So just as with the traditional algorithm, there may be a need to follow a step that is similar to regrouping. Be sure to allow enough time for student discussion of the information in the box at the lower right of the page because it explains this regrouping process.

Student Page 20: Problems and Potential Answers

Section E: The Lattice Method of Multiplication — Set 1

Multiply 2 × 3.

$2 \times 3 = 6$
So, you record
0 tens,
and **6** ones

The **tens** are recorded here

The **ones** are recorded here

Now multiply 2 × 40.

$2 \times 40 = 80$
So, you record
0 hundreds
and **8** tens

The **hundreds** are recorded here

The **tens** are recorded here

20   Book 4: *Multiplication and Division*

Student Page 21: Problems and Potential Answers

Section E: The Lattice Method of Multiplication Set 1

Then multiply 30 × 40 and 30 × 3.

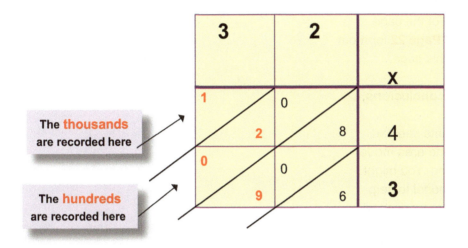

The **thousands** are recorded here

The **hundreds** are recorded here

30 × 40 = **1200**
So, you record
1 thousand
and **2 hundreds**

30 × 3 = **90**
So, you record
0 hundreds
and **9 tens**

Finally, we can count the thousands, hundreds, tens, and ones.

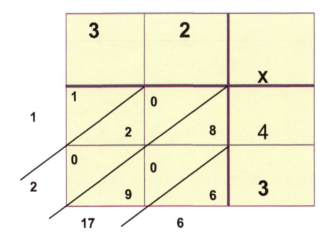

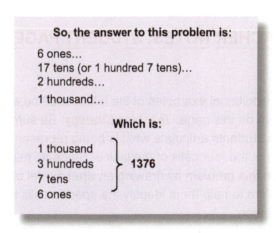

So, the answer to this problem is:

6 ones…
17 tens (or 1 hundred 7 tens)…
2 hundreds…
1 thousand…

Which is:

1 thousand
3 hundreds   } 1376
7 tens
6 ones

Book 4: *Multiplication and Division* 21

CONTINUE THE PROBLEM SOLVING

Have students work individually through the example and the problem on page 22. As they work, circulate to monitor their recorded answers. When students have finished, have them compare and discuss the example and their answers with a partner. Then have pairs share their conclusions in a class discussion of the page. Refer to the **Teacher Notes: Student Page 22** for more specific ideas about the problems on this page.

As students work and report their conclusions, focus on these issues:

Help Make Connections – Help students see and understand the connection between the area model and the lattice method for multiplication. You might suggest that they first draw an area model to help them know which place values they are working with.

Encourage Language Development – Continue to encourage students to use correct place-value terminology as they work through the problems. Doing so will serve to remind them of the place of each digit in the product.

Facilitate Students' Thinking – You may wish to remind students to use what they already know about decomposition (seeing inside numbers) and the distributive property as they work through these problems.

TEACHER NOTES: STUDENT PAGE 22

Two additional examples of the lattice method are shown on this page. *Teaching Strategy:* Be sure to have students articulate what is being represented in each of the four cells of the lattice. Students might also begin this problem by drawing an area model of the problem to help them identify the specific cells in the lattice.

Student Page 22: Problems and Potential Answers

Section E: The Lattice Method of Multiplication Set 2

Let's try another one. Hang in there. This will get easier the more you work with the tables!

Use the lattice method to compute: 13 × 22

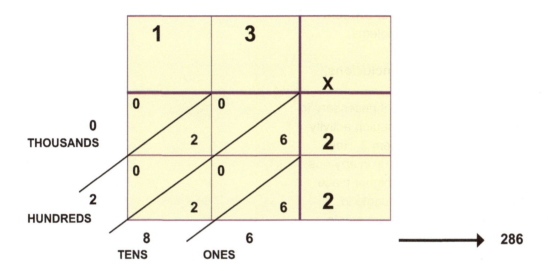

1. One more. You help fill in the boxes to solve the problem 26 × 15.

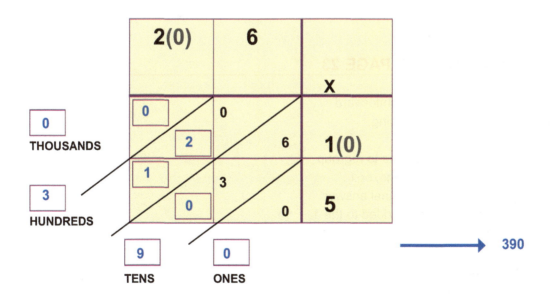

22   Book 4: *Multiplication and Division*

CONTINUE THE PROBLEM SOLVING

Have students work individually to solve the problems on page 23. As they work, you may want to circulate and monitor their work and recorded answers. When students finish each problem, have them compare and discuss their answers with a partner. Then have pairs share their answers in a class discussion of the problem. Refer to the **Teacher Notes: Student Page 23** for specific ideas about the problems.

As students work and report their conclusions, focus on these issues:

Help Make Connections – You may find it necessary to remind students to think about the regrouping activity at the beginning of this section for problem 3. Help them recall that when there is more than 9 in any one place, they need to regroup to the next higher place.

Allow Waiting Time – When students struggle to explain their thinking, be sure to allow them ample time to organize their thoughts.

Facilitate Students' Thinking – Help students understand how to use decomposition and the distributive property as an aid to using the lattice method of multiplication.

TEACHER NOTES: STUDENT PAGE 23

Problem 2: This problem is fairly straightforward because it does not require any regrouping.

Problem 3: Problem 3 requires students to regroup the tens and hundreds. There are 14 tens, or 1 hundred 4 tens. This is reflected in the final answer as an extra hundred is regrouped and added to the 1 hundred that was found by multiplying 10 × 10.

Problem 4: There is no regrouping in this problem, making it somewhat less complicated than problem 3.

Student Page 23: Problems and Potential Answers

Section E: The Lattice Method of Multiplication — Set 2

Use The Lattice Method to solve the following problems.

2. 41 × 12 = __492__

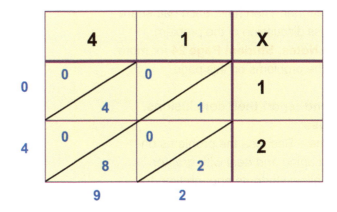

3. 13 × 19 = __247__

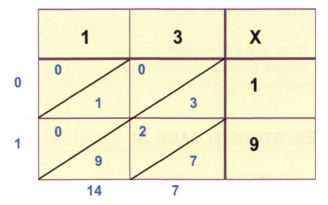

4. 52 × 22 = __1,144__

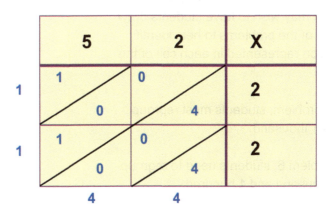

Book 4: *Multiplication and Division* 23

CONTINUE THE PROBLEM SOLVING

Have students work individually to solve the problems on page 24. As they work, you may want to circulate and monitor their recorded answers. When students finish each problem, have them compare and discuss their answers with a partner. Then have each pair share their answers in a class discussion of the problem. Refer to the **Teacher Notes: Student Page 24** for more specific ideas about the problems on this page.

As students work and report their conclusions, focus on these issues:

Allow Processing Time – Because the problems on page 24 require regrouping and deal with greater numbers, be sure to allow students enough time to complete the lattices and check their work.

Validate Representations – Some students may want to draw an area model for each problem before completing the lattice. You may wish to discuss with these students and the class how these models are related.

Allow Waiting Time – When students struggle to explain their thinking, be sure to allow them at least 20 seconds to organize their thoughts.

TEACHER NOTES: STUDENT PAGE 24

These problems provide students with additional opportunities both to practice using the Lattice Method and to use it with greater numbers. (The Lattice Method works with decimals as well.) At some point for each of these problems, students must regroup. As an extension, you may wish to have students draw area models of each of the problems to help identify the actual computation represented in each cell of the lattice.

Problem 5: In this problem, students must regroup the 10 hundreds as 1 thousand.

Problem 6: For problem 6, students need to regroup 11 hundreds as 1 thousand and 1 hundred.

Problem 7: Here students must regroup 10 tens as 1 hundred.

Student Page 24: Problems and Potential Answers

Section E: The Lattice Method of Multiplication Set 2

5. 81 × 25 = __2,025__

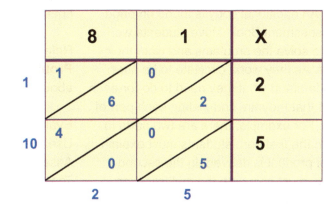

6. 123 × 42 = __5,166__

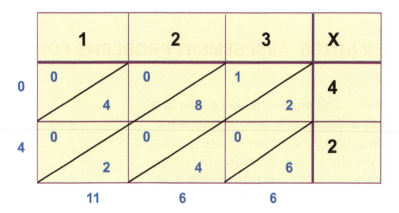

7. 242 × 31 = __7,502__

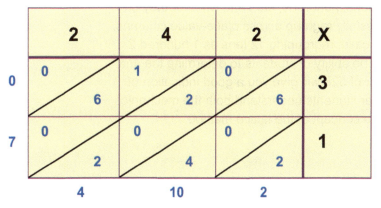

SECTION E ASSESSMENT (PAGE 25)

LAUNCH THE ASSESSMENT

Have students turn to the Section E assessment on page 25. An additional copy is found on page 59 of the Assessment Book. Have students work individually to solve the problems and write their explanations. As they work, circulate to be sure students understand what they need to do for each problem and that they are completing each part of the problem. For example, there are two parts to problem 2. In the first part, students must explain how a partial product is derived. In the second part, students must complete the multiplication in the lattice. You may find it helpful to read the directions for all the problems before students begin, discussing the types of responses they will need to make for each problem.

Encourage students to use whatever space they need to explain their thinking. If the space on the page is inadequate, they should use an additional sheet of paper or use the back of the page.

Refer to the **Teacher Notes: Assessment Problems for Section E** for more specific ideas about the problems on this page.

Evaluate Student Responses

Use the assessment rubric on page 58 of the Assessment Book (pictured on page 288 of the Teacher Edition) to evaluate student responses. The Assessment Book has some general suggestions for using the rubric that you may find helpful.

TEACHER NOTES: ASSESSMENT PROBLEMS FOR SECTION E

Problem 1: This problem is very similar to the practice problems students completed in the preceding pages. It does not require regrouping across the place-value columns, which makes it somewhat less complex than several other problems students completed.

Problem 2: Problem 2 is designed specifically to determine whether students understand both the structure of the lattice method (collecting groups of ones, tens, hundreds, etc.) and whether they can successfully regroup across place-value columns, in this case, regrouping 12 tens as 1 hundred 2 tens. The ability of students to determine the final answer of 528 will give you a good indication of whether students understand both the mechanics and the concept of the lattice method.

Student Page 25: Problems and Potential Answers

Section E: Problems for Assessment

1. Complete the following problem. Use the Lattice provided below.

    15 × 23 = __345__

    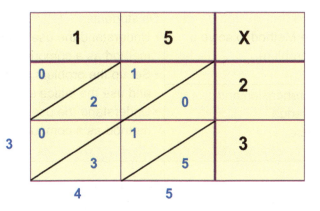

2. Examine this Lattice multiplication problem:

    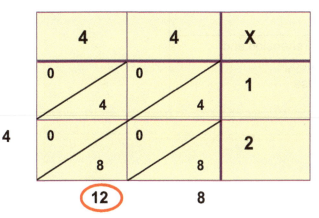

    a) Explain how the student who did the problem got the 12 and what the 12 means.

    > The 12 represents 12 groups of ten. He got it by multiplying 4 groups of ten in the upper right corner, and then 2 groups of 40 in the lower left corner. 4 groups of ten plus 2 groups of 40 is the same as 12 groups of 10.

    b) What is the final answer to this problem? __528__

Book 4: *Multiplication and Division*   25

SCORING GUIDE BOOK 4: MULTIPLICATION AND DIVISION

Section E Assessment
For Use With: Student Book Page 25

PROBLEM DESCRIPTION	SCORING: WHAT TO LOOK FOR	SCORE AND COMMENTS
Problem 1 Use the Lattice Method to solve a multiplication problem. Level 1: Comprehension and Knowledge Level 2: Tool use	Do students: • Understand the use of the lattice method as a computational tool? • Set up the problem appropriately and use the lattice strategy? • Understand the use of the lattice method as a computational tool?	Points:_____ of 3
Problem 2a–b Understand the components and processes of the Lattice Method. Level 1: Comprehension and Knowledge Level 2: Tool use	Do students: • Understand the use of the ratio table as a computational tool? • Understand place value and regrouping?	Points:_____ of 2

TOTAL POINTS:_____ OF 5

Section F: The Traditional U.S. Method of Multiplication

SECTION F PLANNER

THE MATHEMATICS CONTENT AND GOALS

GOALS

Students will:
- Explore the traditional multiplication method to understand how and why it works.

PACING

The projected pacing for this unit is 2–3 class periods (based on a 45 minute period).

PROBLEM SETS: OVERVIEW

Much of this book has been devoted to teaching methods of multiplication that are centrally connected to the traditional algorithm most often taught in schools, but seldom used or taught themselves. The intent of this section of the book is to uncover the inner workings of the traditional method. Why do we put a zero in the ones place when we compute the second partial product? Why do we regroup as we multiply? These and other questions are briefly explored in this section.

Set 1 (pp. 26–27; problems 1–2)

These problems ask students to explain each of the steps they take while multiplying using the traditional method of multiplication. This method was placed at the end of this text for a specific reason. The techniques taught earlier provide students with conceptual models to help them understand this traditional algorithm, which has essentially been stripped of any inherent characteristics or representational structures that would help students understand what they are actually doing as they use it.

CONCEPT DEVELOPMENT (PAGES 26-27)

INTRODUCE THE CONCEPT

ASSESS STUDENTS' PRIOR KNOWLEDGE

Section F in this book deals with the traditional multiplication algorithm for multiplying two 2-digit numbers. As students work through the pages, stress the connections between this algorithm and the multiplication strategies that came before it.

Write this problem on the board:

```
   32
 × 20
 ____
```

Ask:
What is the answer to this problem? How did you find the answer?

Listen for:
Students may find the answer in several ways. They may use the algorithm as written on the board or use other strategies they have learned, such as the area model, a ratio table, or the lattice method. Some students may cite the distributive property or say they found the answer mentally. You may wish to list all the strategies on the board.
• The answer is 640.

MODEL MATHEMATICAL THINKING

Model the thinking for another example. Write this problem on the board, writing the partial products and final product as well as the regrouping numbers (all in blue) as you talk through the thinking:

```
    1
   43
 × 26
 ____
  258
  860
 ____
 1,118
```

Ask:
How can we multiply if we keep the numbers in these positions?

Talk Through the Thinking:
I know that 26 is the same as 20 + 6, or 2 tens and 6 ones. I also know that 43 is the same as 40 + 3, or 4 tens and 3 ones. I notice that the ones are in the same column, and so are the tens. I can start by multiplying the ones. 6 × 3 = 18. That's 18 ones, which can be regrouped as 1 ten and 8 ones. So I'll write the 8 in the ones column. Then I'll write the 1 ten above the tens column. Now I can multiply the 4 tens by 6 ones. That's 24 tens. I have 1 more ten. That makes it 25 tens, or 2 hundreds 5 tens. I'll write the 5 tens in the tens column and start a hundreds column for the 2 ones. Now what should I do? I can multiply by the 2 tens in 26: 2 tens × 3 ones = 20 × 3, which equals 60, and is the same as 6 tens and 0 ones. So I can write the 6 in the tens column and the 0 in the ones column. Now I can multiply 2 tens × 4 tens, or 20 × 40. That's 800, or 8 hundreds. So I can write the 8 in the hundreds column. To find the final answer, I can add the product of 6 × 43; 258, and the product of 20 × 43; 860. That gives me 1,118 as a final answer.

Ask:
In the solution to problem, 258 and 860 are the partial products. Why did I add them to get the final answer?

Listen for:
Students should express understanding that this algorithm is a shortcut and uses the distributive property: 6(40 + 3) + 20(40 + 3) = [(6 × 40) + (6 × 3)] + [(20 × 40) + (20 × 3)].

LAUNCH THE PROBLEM SOLVING

Have students read through page 26 individually before discussing the page with a partner. Then have pairs share their conclusions about the information on the page with the class.

As students report their conclusions, focus on these issues:

Help Make Connections – As students discuss the steps of the algorithm, encourage them to make connections between the steps and those of the multiplication strategies they learned earlier. Have students articulate the similarities.

Facilitate Students' Thinking – Many students already use the multiplication algorithm without really understanding it. It is important to help them understand what each step of the process means.

Student Page 26: Problems and Potential Answers

Section F: The Traditional U.S. Method of Multiplication Set 1

As you have learned, there are many ways to multiply. No one method is better than another. However, you might feel more comfortable using one method than another. Whichever method you use, be sure you understand it so you can determine whether or not an answer you get is reasonable!

The most common method of multiplication used in the United States is the one you saw a few pages earlier.

$$\begin{array}{r} \overset{1\ 2}{86} \\ \times\ 24 \\ \hline 1\,344 \\ 1720 \\ \hline 2064 \end{array}$$

After using the area model and The Lattice Method, perhaps you can better understand what is happening when you use this method for multiplication. Let's take it one step at a time and begin with a slightly easier problem: **4 × 86**.

We keep track of the **2 tens** by writing the 2 above the tens column. We will add them together with the other tens we get as we continue the problem.

We multiply 4 times 86 in two steps.
Step 1:
We multiply the ones: **4 × 6**.
4 × 6 = 24, or 2 tens **4 ones**.
So, we write the **4** in the ones column.

ONES

Step 2:
We are still multiplying 4 times 86. Only, now we are multiplying the tens, **4 × 80**.
4 × 8 tens = **32 tens**.

We still have 2 extra tens from Step 1.
So, we have **34 tens**.
This is also **3 hundreds 4 tens**.

We record **4** in the tens place.
We record **3** in the hundreds place.

HUNDREDS   TENS   ONES

26   Book 4: *Multiplication and Division*

CONTINUE THE PROBLEM SOLVING

Have students work individually to solve the problems on page 27. As they work, circulate and monitor their responses. When students finish each problem, have them compare and discuss their answers with a partner. Then have pairs share their answers in a class discussion of the problem. Refer to the **Teacher Notes: Student Page 27** for more specific ideas about the problems on this page.

As students work and report their conclusions, focus on these issues:

Allow Waiting Time – When students struggle to explain their thinking, allow them ample time to organize their thoughts.

Look for Misconceptions – Some students may need to be reminded in the second example that they are multiplying tens and ones by tens and ones, not all ones.

Encourage Language Development – As students discuss the algorithm, encourage them to use proper place-value terminology as well as terms such as partial product and product.

TEACHER NOTES: STUDENT PAGE 27

Problems 1–2: These problems ask students to provide explanations of how different digits in the product and partial products are derived, similar to the explanations on pages 25–26. *Watch for:* Look for students to display understanding of the fundamental principles of multiplication developed in this book, decomposition of numbers, and the distributive property.

Student Page 27: Problems and Potential Answers

Section F: The Traditional U.S. Method of Multiplication Set 1

1. What about the following problems? Can you explain each of the steps?

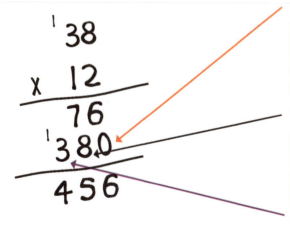

Where did the **5 ones** come from?

> 9 times 5 (ones) equals 45, or 4 (tens) and 5(ones). The 5 (ones) gets recorded. Keep track of the 4 (tens).

Where did the **2 tens** come from?

> 9 times 2(0) equals 18(0) or 18 tens. Add in the extra 4 tens to get 22 tens, or 220.

Where did the **2 hundreds** come from?

> From the 22 (tens), that is 2 (hundreds) and 2 (tens).

2. Can you explain each of these steps?

```
   ¹38
 ×  12
   76
  ¹380
  456
```

Where did the **0 ones** come from?

> 1(0) times 8 equals 8(0), or 8 tens and 0(ones).

Where did the **8 tens** come from?

> See above.

Where did the **3 hundreds** come from?

> 1(0) times 3(0) equals 3(00), or 3 hundreds.

How did you arrive at your final answer of 456?

> Adding the two sets of multiplication problems, i.e., 76 and 380, which equals 456.

Book 4: *Multiplication and Division* 27

Multiplication and Division *Teacher Edition* 293

SECTION F ASSESSMENT (PAGE 28)

LAUNCH THE ASSESSMENT

Have students turn to the Section F Assessment on page 28. An additional copy is found on page 61 of the Assessment Book. Have students work individually to solve the problems and write their answers and explanations. As they work, circulate to be sure students understand what they need to do for each problem and that they are completing each part of the problem.

You may find it helpful to read the directions for all the problems before students begin, discussing the types of responses they will need to make for each problem.

Encourage students to use whatever space they need to explain their thinking. If the space on the page is inadequate, they should use an additional sheet of paper or use the back of the page.

Refer to the **Teacher Notes: Assessment Problems for Section F** for more specific ideas about the problems on this page.

Evaluate Student Responses

Use the assessment rubric on page 60 of the Assessment Book (pictured on page 296 of the Teacher Edition) to evaluate student responses. The Assessment Book has some general suggestions for using the rubric that you may find helpful.

TEACHER NOTES: ASSESSMENT PROBLEMS FOR SECTION F

Problem 1: This problem is designed to expose a common computational error, if not a cognitive misconception about multiplication and the traditional algorithm. Students should immediately see that the second partial product should be represented as 340 and not 34. While many students will recognize the error, it is likely that some will be unable to explain why the 0 must be annexed to the 34. This is necessary because the second partial product is the result of multiplying 10 × 34 rather than 1 × 34. So Problem 1 is important in determining the depth of students' understanding.

Problem 1b: Students who answer the question in Problem 1a correctly are likely to be successful in completing Problem 1b. Once again, look for students who can use the algorithm accurately but do so without the proper conceptual understanding.

Student Page 28: Problems and Potential Answers

Section F: Problems for Assessment

1. Examine the solution strategy below.

    ```
      34
    × 12
    ----
      68
      34
    ----
     102
    ```

    a) What is the error in this solution strategy?

    Explain. There is an alignment error that is the result of a misconception about place value. The second line of the solution (34) should read 340. The problem is that the person multiplied 1 x 34 = 34, instead of recognizing that it should be 10 x 34 = 340.

    b) How would you solve the problem correctly using the traditional method?

    ```
      34
    × 12
    ----
      68
     340
    ----
     408
    ```

SCORING GUIDE BOOK 4: MULTIPLICATION AND DIVISION

Section F Assessment
For Use With: Student Book Page 28

PROBLEM DESCRIPTION	SCORING: WHAT TO LOOK FOR	SCORE AND COMMENTS
Problem 1a Demonstrate understanding of the traditional multiplication algorithm. Level 1: Comprehension and Knowledge Level 2: Tool use	Do students: • Understand the process of using the traditional multiplication algorithm? • Recognize the role of place value? • Understand the role of partial products?	Points:_____ of 1 (area model) Points:_____ of 2
Problem 1b Use the traditional model to multiply two, two-digit problems. Level 1: Comprehension and Knowledge Level 2: Tool use	Do students: • Understand the use of the traditional multiplication algorithm?	Points:_____ of 2

TOTAL POINTS:_____ OF 5

Section G: A Model for Division

SECTION G PLANNER

THE MATHEMATICS CONTENT AND GOALS

GOALS
Students will:
- Develop understanding of a model that can be used to solve division problems. The model developed in this section is similar to the traditional long division algorithm and is based on the idea of repeated subtraction of factors inherent in the problem.

LANGUAGE DEVELOPMENT
Mathematical language in this section includes the concepts and terms below. Not all of these terms are used regularly, but exposing these terms to students will help them understand the steps of the division algorithm.

Division: Division is the inverse operation of multiplication. It is the process of finding how many times a number (the divisor) is contained in another number (the dividend).

Quotient: The end result obtained when one number is divided by another.

Divisor: The number by which another number, called the dividend, is divided.

Dividend: The number that is to be divided by another number, called the divisor.

Example: If $A / B = C$, then A is the dividend, B is the divisor, and C is the quotient.

PROBLEM SETS: OVERVIEW

Much of this book has been devoted to teaching methods of multiplication that are centrally connected to the traditional algorithm most often taught in schools. In many cases, these same models can be used to solve problems that come in the form of division as well. In this set of problems, however, students will develop understanding of a division algorithm that can be used solely for the task of division.

Set 1 (pp. 29–31; problems 1–4)
These problems ask students to work with an algorithm suitable for use in contexts where division is necessary. Built on the idea that we can repeatedly subtract factors from the original number (the dividend), this model is an elaboration of the traditional division algorithm that allows students to take additional steps with factors they are comfortable with. Strategies with ratio tables, such as multiplying by 10, for example, are helpful in using this algorithm.

PACING

The projected pacing for this unit is 1–2 class periods (based on a 45 minute period).

CONCEPT DEVELOPMENT (PAGES 29-31)

INTRODUCE THE CONCEPT

ASSESS STUDENTS' PRIOR KNOWLEDGE

In this section, students will uncover a helpful strategy for dividing one number by another. Prior to learning the algorithm, however, it is important that students understand the nature of division: What contexts require an algorithm for division? Begin with the following prompt:

Consider the following two problems:
1) Each table in the cafeteria seats 10 students. Today, 6 tables were completely full. How many students ate lunch?
2) Today 60 students ate lunch in the cafeteria. There are 10 spots for students at each table. How many tables were needed for lunch today?

Ask:
What is the major difference between these two problems? How are these problems alike?

Listen for:
Listen for students to recognize the various components of the problems, and which are missing in each context. For example, in the first problem we know the two factors, but not the product (i.e., 6 tables, and 10 students per table). In the second problem we know the product (60 students) and the number of students that can sit at a table (10), but we do not know the number of tables needed for all 60 students.

MODEL MATHEMATICAL THINKING

Talk Through the Thinking:
You determined that these problems are very similar. In fact, we might even think of them as the different ways to look at the same problem. It is important to realize that multiplication and division are related. In the first problem, we multiply 10 and 6 to find that there were 60 students who ate lunch. In the second problem, we know the answer of 60 already, but we do not know how many tables we needed for all 60 students. So we divide 60 by 10 to find the number of tables needed.

In the next few pages, we are going to learn a series of steps we can always use for division even when the numbers get more complicated than the ones in the problem about the cafeteria.

LAUNCH THE PROBLEM SOLVING

Have students read and study the examples on page 29. Although there are no problems on this page, be sure to spend ample time on this page because it describes the fundamental elements of the division algorithm. Refer to the **Teacher Notes: Student Page 29** for more specific ideas about this page.

As students work and report their conclusions, focus on these issues:

Allow Waiting Time – When students struggle to explain their thinking, allow them ample time to organize their thoughts.

Look for Misconceptions – Some students may need to be reminded in the second example that they are multiplying tens and ones by tens and ones, not all ones.

Encourage Language Development – As students discuss the algorithm, encourage them to use proper place-value terminology as well as terms such as partial product and product.

Help Make Connections – As students discuss the steps of the division algorithm, encourage them to make connections between the steps and those of the multiplication strategies they learned earlier. Have students articulate the similarities. In particular, help them focus on the similarities between the strategies used in ratio tables (multiplying by ten, doubling, etc.) that will be helpful in the division algorithm.

Facilitate Students' Thinking – Some students may have already used the long division algorithm. But it is likely that they have not understood why it works. It is important to help them broaden and strengthen their understanding of what each step of this modified division algorithm means.

Student Page 29: Problems and Potential Answers

Section G: A Model for Division — Set 1

We have learned that one way to think about multiplication is in terms of "repeated addition." That is, 3 × 4 might be thought of as "three groups of four: 4 + 4 + 4 = 12."

Division is similar. In multiplication, we think, "groups of" In division, we can use the same sort of thinking. For example, consider the following problem:

$$96 \div 12$$

We might think to ourselves… How many groups of 12 are there in 96? Or… if I had 96 eggs, how many times could I fill up a carton that holds a dozen (12) eggs? Well… one group of 12 is 12… and now there are 84 eggs left. If I take out another 12 eggs, now I have filled two egg cartons, and I have 72 eggs left.

We could continue, but that would be pretty boring, especially if we had to make a lot of groups. So we need a method.

Thankfully, we already know some great tools that can help us with this task. By now you know about ratio tables and can use them with confidence. The method below uses the same kind of thinking you have used with ratio tables.

Let's take another example. How about…   224 ÷ 16

Step 1: Prepare to work the problem using the following format:

Step 2: Remember the important question: How many groups of 16 are there in 224?

Step 3: Let's begin counting groups, and keeping track of both the groups we have, and the number of items that we still have left. Follow the example below.

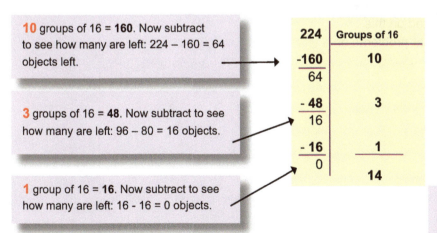

10 groups of 16 = **160**. Now subtract to see how many are left: 224 − 160 = 64 objects left.

3 groups of 16 = **48**. Now subtract to see how many are left: 96 − 80 = 16 objects.

1 group of 16 = **16**. Now subtract to see how many are left: 16 - 16 = 0 objects.

10 x 16 = 160 objects

3 x 16 = 48 objects

1 x 16 = 16 objects

In all we made **10**… then **3**… then **1** (10 + 3 + 1) = **14 groups** So… 224 divided by 16 is… 14!

Book 4: *Multiplication and Division*

TEACHER NOTES: STUDENT PAGE 29

There are no problems on this page. However, the fundamental concepts underlying the division algorithm presented in this section are outlined. Be sure to emphasize the relationship between multiplication and division, noting in particular the language that will help students develop conceptual understanding of the operations. *Teaching Strategy:* Specifically, help students use the language of "groups of" as they set up the problems. In multiplication, we might say, "How many would we have if we collected 3 groups of 4 objects?" In division, the same idea is used, but in this case, we know the result rather than both of the factors. So we might say, "I know I have 100 objects. How many groups of 20 can I form from 100 objects?" If students can make sense of the concepts inherent in this language, they are likely to understand both division itself and the procedures of the algorithm.

You should note the similarities between the method presented in this book and the traditional division algorithm often taught in the U.S. Common to many algorithms, our traditional division algorithm attempts to be as efficient as possible. Similar to the rationale of the ratio table presented throughout this series, this division algorithm is less concerned about efficiency, and more concerned about understanding.

Given this rationale, you might help your students understand division in terms of repeated subtraction, much like we think of multiplication as repeated addition. If I want to know how many groups of 20 I can form from 500 objects, I might begin by thinking about how many groups of 20 I could form from 100 objects: 5 groups of 20. Using the proportional reasoning common to ratio table applications, we could then reason that if we have accounted for 5 groups of 20 in the first 100 objects, then we have another 400 objects to distribute in groups of 20. If there are 5 groups in 100, then there would be 20 groups in 400. So in all, there are 25 groups of 20 in 500.

CONTINUE THE PROBLEM SOLVING

Have students read and study the examples on page 30. Be sure to spend ample time on this page, which continues to develop the fundamental elements of the division algorithm. Refer to the **Teacher Notes: Student Page 30** for more specific ideas about the problems on this page.

TEACHER NOTES: STUDENT PAGE 30

There are no problems on this page. Continue to lead students through the examples presented on this page, preparing them to complete similar problems on their own.

Student Page 30: Problems and Potential Answers

Section G: A Model for Division — Set 1

Let's try another example: 432 ÷ 18

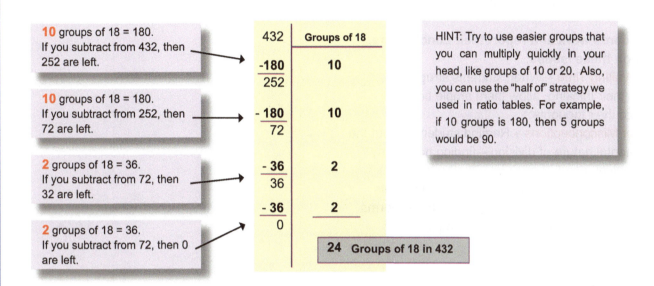

You can be as creative as you want in making groups – just like you are when you use a ratio table – using easy numbers that you can calculate in your head. One more example: 5124 ÷ 42 = ? Here are two ways you might find the quotient.

5124	Groups of 42
−1680	40
3444	
− 3360	80
84	
− 84	2
0	
	122

5124	Groups of 42
−4200	100
924	
− 840	20
84	
− 84	2
0	
	122

122 groups of 42 in 5124

30 Book 4: *Multiplication and Division*

CONTINUE THE PROBLEM SOLVING

The problems on page 31 give students ample opportunity to practice this new algorithm. Refer to the **Teacher Notes: Student Page 31** for more specific ideas about the problems on this page.

As students work and report their conclusions, focus on these issues:

Allow Waiting Time – When students struggle to explain their thinking, allow them ample time to organize their thoughts.

Look for Misconceptions – Remind students about the fundamental nature of division – finding how many times a given number goes into another number.

Encourage Language Development – As students discuss the algorithm, encourage them to use terms such as quotient, divisor, dividend, and groups.

TEACHER NOTES: STUDENT PAGE 31

Problem 1: In this problem students are likely to begin by grouping by 10; 10 groups of 9 is 90, leaving a remainder of 45. Students may recognize the multiplication fact 5 × 9 = 45 immediately, while others may attempt some additional trial and error. A likely strategy in this case would be to take half of 10 (5 groups) and then half of 90 (45) to solve the problem.

Problem 2: Look for students to begin with a grouping that is comfortable for them, for example, 100 groups of 3 is equal to 300. Of course, there are more efficient choices (such as 400 groups of 3), but do not rush students to what may seem to be more sophisticated selections. Rather, allow students to continue to complete the repeated subtraction as they become familiar with the process and meaning of this algorithm.

Problem 3: This is another practice problem. Encourage the use of intuitive strategies.

Problem 4: This problem has a remainder. Encourage students to continue thinking in terms of groups of numbers. At the end of this problem, students are faced with the question: "How many groups of 16 can I make from 9 objects?" Students should realize that this is not possible and may simply indicate that there were a total of 16 groups, with 9 objects left over.

Student Page 31: Problems and Potential Answers

Section G: A Model for Division — Set 1

Sometimes you will end up with a few leftover objects, but not enough to make another whole group. We call these leftover objects **the remainder**. Check out the following example that has a remainder.

284 ÷ 18 = ???

284	Groups of 18
−180	10
104	
− 90	5
14	

Now, since there are only 14 objects left, we do not have enough to make an additional group of 18. So, we are left with an answer of **15 groups with a remainder of 14 (15 remainder 14)**

You try these.

1. 135 ÷ 9

135	Groups of 9
−90	10
45	
− 45	5
0	
	15 groups

2. 1308 ÷ 3

1308	Groups of 3
−300	100
1008	
− 300	100
708	
− 300	100
408	
− 300	100
108	
− 30	10
78	
− 30	10
48	
− 30	10
18	
− 18	6
0	
	436 groups

3. 299 ÷ 13

299	Groups of 13
−130	10
169	
− 130	10
39	
− 39	3
0	
	23 groups

4. 265 ÷ 16

265	Groups of 16
−160	10
105	
− 80	5
25	
− 16	1
9	16 groups with a remainder of 9

Book 4: *Multiplication and Division*

SECTION G ASSESSMENT (PAGE 32)

LAUNCH THE ASSESSMENT

Have students turn to the Section G Assessment on page 32. An additional copy is found on page 63 of the Assessment Book. Have students work individually to solve the problems and write their answers and explanations. As they work, circulate to be sure students understand what they need to do for each problem and that they are completing each part of the problem. For example, You may find it helpful to read the directions for all the problems before students begin, discussing the types of responses they need to make for each problem.

Encourage students to use whatever space they need to explain their thinking. If the space on the page is inadequate, they should use an additional sheet of paper or use the back of the page. Refer to the **Teacher Notes: Assessment**

Problems for Section G for more specific ideas about the problems on this page.

Evaluate Student Responses

Use the assessment rubric on page 62 of the Assessment Book (pictured on page 306 of the Teacher Edition) to evaluate student responses. The Assessment Book has some general suggestions for using the rubric that you may find helpful.

TEACHER NOTES: ASSESSMENT PROBLEMS FOR SECTION G

Problems 1–2: Check for student understanding of this division method.

Student Page 32: Problems and Potential Answers

Section G: Problems for Assessment

1. Solve the following problem: 930 ÷ 30

   31

2. Imagine that you work at a candy factory, and your job is to put chocolate candies into containers so they can be mailed to stores. Each container holds 15 chocolate candies.

   a) On Monday, you were given 240 chocolates to put into containers. How many containers did you need? _____

   16

   b) On Tuesday, you were given 495 candies. How many containers did you need? _____

   33

Book 4: *Multiplication and Division*

SCORING GUIDE BOOK 4: MULTIPLICATION AND DIVISION

Section G Assessment
For Use With: Student Book Page 32

PROBLEM DESCRIPTION	SCORING: WHAT TO LOOK FOR	SCORE AND COMMENTS
Problem 1 Use division algorithm to divide 930 by 30. Level 2: Tool Use Level 4: Evaluation	Do students: • Understand the concept of division? • Understand the steps of the division algorithm? • Correctly apply the division algorithm?	Points:_____ of 3
Problem 2a–b Understand and solve division problem context. Level 2: Tool Use Level 3: Connection and Application	Do students: • Understand the context of the division problem? • Apply the division procedure appropriately?	Points:_____ of 6

TOTAL POINTS:_____ OF 9

End-of-Book Assessment (Pages 33–35)

LAUNCH THE ASSESSMENT

These problems are intended not only to serve as assessment items for the whole book, but also as a way for students to further assimilate ideas and conceptual explanations associated with each of the methods for multiplication and division presented in this book.

Have students turn to page 33 of the End-of-Book Assessment. An additional copy is found on page 66 of the Assessment Book. Have students work individually to solve the problems and write their answers and explanations. As they work, circulate to be sure students understand what they need to do for each problem and that they are completing each part of the problem. For example, students must show how they would solve the multiplication problem using three different methods. You may find it helpful to read the directions to all the problems before students begin, discussing the types of responses they will need to make for each problem.

Encourage students to use whatever space they need to explain their thinking. If the space on the page is inadequate, they should use an additional sheet of paper or use the back of the page.

Refer to the **Teacher Notes: End-of-Book Assessment, Page 33** for more specific ideas about the problems on this page.

Evaluate Student Responses

Use the assessment rubric on page 64 of the Assessment Book (pictured on page 313 of the Teacher Edition) to evaluate student responses. The Assessment Book has some general suggestions for using the rubric that you may find helpful.

TEACHER NOTES: END-OF-BOOK ASSSESSMENT, STUDENT PAGE 33

Problem 1: There are a great many strategies students can use, so their strategies will vary.

Problems 2–3: This problem requires students to solve one multiplication problem in several ways. Be sure to encourage students to spend time answering Problem 3 because it will provide you with a window into their thinking as well as into their understanding of multiplication.

Multiplication and Division *Teacher Edition*

Student Page 33: Problems and Potential Answers

End-of-Book Assessment

1. What are some strategies you can use with the multiplication table to help you remember the multiplication facts?

   Answers will vary.

2. Solve the following multiplication problem in three different ways: 13 × 42

   Method 1

   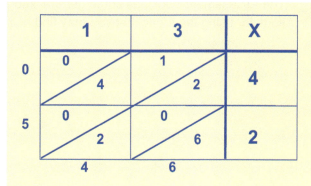

   546

   Method 2

1	10	20	40	2	42
13	130	260	520	26	546

   Method 3

   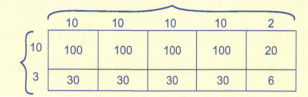

   100 + 100 + 100 + 100 + 30 + 30 + 30 + 30 + 20 + 6 = 546

3. Which method do you prefer? Why do you prefer it?

   Answers will vary.

CONTINUE THE ASSESSMENT

Continue the assessment by having students turn to page 34. An additional copy is found on page 67 of the Assessment Book. Have students work individually to solve the problems and write their explanations. As they work, circulate to be sure students understand what they need to do for each problem and that they are completing each part of the problem. For example, problem 4 has three parts: explaining the meaning and derivation of the digits in a cell of a lattice, explaining how one of the partial products is derived; and explaining the strengths and weaknesses of the lattice method of multiplication. You may find it helpful to read the directions for all the problems before students begin, discussing the types of responses they will need to make for each problem.

Encourage students to use whatever space they need to explain their thinking. If the space on the page is inadequate, they should use an additional sheet of paper or use the back of the page.

Refer to the **Teacher Notes: End-of Book Assessment, Page 34** for more specific ideas about the problems on this page.

Evaluate Student Responses

Use the assessment rubric on page 65 of the Assessment Book (pictured on page 314 of the Teacher Edition) to evaluate student responses. The Assessment book has some general suggestions for using the rubric that you might find helpful.

TEACHER NOTES: END-OF-BOOK ASSESSMENT, STUDENT PAGE 34

Problem 4: *Watch for:* Students should express their understanding of the Lattice Method by being able to describe the contents of each of the highlighted cells. Part C will give you an indication of the dispositions of students with regard to this method of multiplication.

Multiplication and Division *Teacher Edition*

Student Page 34: Problems and Potential Answers

End-of-Book Assessment

4. Here is a problem done with The Lattice Method.

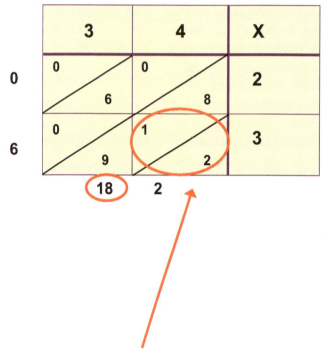

a) Explain what has happened in this cell. Where did the 1 and the 2 come from? What do the 1 and 2 represent?

> 4 times 3 equals 12, or 1 (ten) and 2 (ones).

b) What does the 18 represent? Where did it come from?

> It represents 18 (tens) and it came from finding the sum of the 9, 1, and 8 from the tens section.

c) What are the strengths of using the lattice method for multiplication? Weaknesses?

> Responses will vary.

34 Book 4: *Multiplication and Division*

CONTINUE THE ASSESSMENT

Continue the assessment by having students turn to page 35. An additional copy is found on page 68 of the Assessment Book. Have students work individually to solve the problems and write their explanations. As they work, circulate to be sure students understand what they need to do for each problem and that they are completing each part of the problem. For example, for problem 5 students must not only draw an area model for the multiplication, but also show how the parts of the model combine to reach a product. You may find it helpful to read the directions for all the problems before students begin, discussing the types of responses they need to make for each problem.

Encourage students to use whatever space they need to explain their thinking. If the space on the page is inadequate, they should use an additional sheet of paper or use the back of the page. Refer to the **Teacher Notes: End-of Book Assessment Problems, Page 35** for more specific ideas about the problems on this page.

Evaluate Student Responses

Use the assessment rubric on page 65 of the Assessment Book (pictured on page 314 of the Teacher Edition) to evaluate student responses. The Assessment book has some general suggestions for using the rubric that you might find helpful.

TEACHER NOTES: END-OF-BOOK ASSESSMENT, STUDENT PAGE 35

Problem 5: Check for student understanding of the area model of multiplication. Be aware that some students might break apart the factors into larger parts, such as 44 = 20 + 20 + 4.

Problem 6: Check for student understanding of the ratio table as a method for multiplication.

Problem 7: Check for student understanding of the division algorithm developed in Section G.

Student Page 35: Problems and Potential Answers

End-of-Book Assessment

5. Solve the following problem using an area model: 36 × 44

	10	10	10	10	4
10	100	100	100	100	40
10	100	100	100	100	40
10	100	100	100	100	40
6	60	60	60	60	24

   (36 on the left side bracketing the rows)

   = (100 + 100 + 100 + 100 + 100 + 100 + 100 + 100 + 100 + 100 + 100 + 100) + (60 + 60 + 60 + 60) + (40 + 40 + 40) + 24
   = 1200 + 240 + 120 + 24
   = 1584

6. Solve the following problem using a ratio table: 21 × 31

1	10	20	30	31
21	210	420	630	651

   21 × 31 = 651

7. Solve this division problem: 308 ÷ 14

1	10	20	2	22
14	140	280	28	308

   308 ÷ 14 = 22

Book 4: *Multiplication and Division*

SCORING GUIDE BOOK 4: MULTIPLICATION AND DIVISION

End-of-Book Assessment
For Use With: Student Book Page 33

PROBLEM DESCRIPTION	SCORING: WHAT TO LOOK FOR	SCORE AND COMMENTS
Problem 1 Describe strategies to recall multiplication facts. Level 1: Comprehension and Knowledge Level 3: Connection and Application	Do students: • Know the times tables? • Articulate strategies for recalling multiplication facts?	Points: _____ of 2
Problem 2 Solve a multiplication problem in three different ways. Level 1: Comprehension and Knowledge Level 2: Tool use	Do students: • Understand various multiplication strategies (ratio table, area model, Lattice Method, traditional method)? • Correctly implement strategies?	(method #1) Points: _____ of 2 (method #2) Points: _____ of 2 (method #3) Points: _____ of 2
Problem 3 Statement of preference for multiplication strategies. Level 4: Synthesis and Evaluation	Do students: • Articulate their strategy preference and rationale?	Points: _____ of 4

STUDENT PAGE 33. TOTAL POINTS _____ OF 12

Multiplication and Division *Teacher Edition*

SCORING GUIDE BOOK 4: MULTIPLICATION AND DIVISION

End-of-Book Assessment
For Use With: Student Book Pages 34–35

PROBLEM DESCRIPTION	SCORING: WHAT TO LOOK FOR	SCORE AND COMMENTS
Problem 4a–c Statement of preference for multiplication strategies. Level 4: Synthesis and Evaluation	Do students: • Understand the Lattice Method? • Articulate a conceptual understanding of the method?	(part a) Points: ___ of 2 (part b) Points: ___ of 2 (part c) Points: ___ of 2
Problem 5–6 Solve problems using area model and ratio table. Level 2: Tool Use	Do students: • Understand the area model? • Appropriately implement the strategy? • Understand the ratio table? • Appropriately implement the strategy?	(#5) Points: ___ of 2 (#6) Points: ___ of 2
Problem 7 Solve division problem using division algorithm. Level 2: Tool Use	Do students: • Have a conceptual understanding of division? • Understand the division procedure?	Points: ___ of 2

STUDENT PAGE 34–35, TOTAL POINTS _____ OF 12